Istria

WHAT'S NEW | WHAT'S ON | WHAT'S BEST

www.timeout.com/istria

Contents

Don't Miss

Itineraries

Istria by Area

Essentials

Published by Time Out Guides Ltd
Universal House
251 Tottenham Court Road
London W1T 7AB
Tel: + 44 (0)20 7813 3000
Fax: + 44 (0)20 7813 6001
Email: guides@timeout.com
www.timeout.com

Managing Director Peter Fiennes
Editorial Director Ruth Jarvis
Business Manager Dan Allen
Editorial Manager Holly Pick
Assistant Management Accountant Ija Krasnikova

Time Out Guides is a wholly owned subsidiary of Time Out Group Ltd.

© **Time Out Group Ltd**
Chairman Tony Elliott
Chief Executive Officer David King
Group Financial Director Paul Rakkar
Group General Manager/Director Nichola Coulthard
Time Out Communications Ltd MD David Pepper
Time Out International Ltd MD Cathy Runciman
Time Out Magazine Ltd Publisher/Managing Director Mark Elliott
Production Director Mark Lamond
Group IT Director Simon Chappell
Marketing & Circulation Director Catherine Demajo

Time Out Croatia
Directors David Plant, Vanda Vučićević

Time Out and the Time Out logo are trademarks of Time Out Group Ltd.

This edition first published in Great Britain in 2010 by Ebury Publishing
A Random House Group Company
Company information can be found on www.randomhouse.co.uk
Random House UK Limited Reg. No. 954009
10 9 8 7 6 5 4 3 2 1

Distributed in the US by Publishers Group West
Distributed in Canada by Publishers Group Canada

For further distribution details, see www.timeout.com

ISBN: 978-1-84670-178-8

A CIP catalogue record for this book is available from the British Library.

Printed and bound in Germany by Appl.

The Random House Group Limited supports The Forest Stewardship Council (FSC), the leading
international forest certification organisation. All our titles that are printed on Greenpeace
approved FSC certified paper carry the FSC logo. Our paper procurement policy can be found
at www.rbooks.co.uk/environment.

Time Out carbon-offsets all its flights with Trees for Cities (www.treesforcities.org).

Istria Shortlist

The **Time Out Istria Shortlist** is one of a new series of guides that draws on Time Out's background as a magazine publisher to keep you current with what's going on in town. As well as Istria's key sights and the best of its eating, drinking and leisure options, the guide picks out the most exciting venues to have recently opened and gives a full calendar of annual events. It also includes features on the important news, trends and openings, all compiled by locally based editors and writers. Whether you're visiting for the first time, or you're a regular, you'll find the Time Out Istria Shortlist contains all you need to know, in a portable and easy-to-use format.

The guide divides Istria into four areas, each of which contains listings for Sights & Museums, Eating & Drinking, Shopping, Nightlife and Arts & Leisure, with maps pinpointing all their locations. At the front of the book are chapters rounding up these scenes country-wide, and giving a shortlist of our top recommendations overall. We include itineraries for days out, plus essentials such as transport information and hotels.

Our listings give phone numbers as dialled within Croatia. The international code for Croatia is 385. To call from outside the country, follow this with the number given, dropping the initial '0'. Some listed numbers (usually 091 or 098) are mobiles, and have been indicated as such.

We have noted price categories by using one to four **K** signs (**K-KKKK**), representing budget, moderate, expensive and luxury. Major credit cards are accepted unless otherwise stated. We also indicated when a venue is NEW.

All our listings are double checked, but places do sometimes close or change their hours or prices, so it's a good idea to call a venue before visiting. While every effort has been made to ensure accuracy, the publishers cannot accept responsibility for any errors that this guide may contain.

Venues are marked on the maps using symbols numbered according to their order within the chapter and colour-coded according to the type of venue they represent:

❶ Sights & Museums
❶ Eating & Drinking
❶ Shopping
❶ Nightlife
❶ Arts & Leisure

Map key	
Major sight or landmark	
Railway station	
Park	
College/hospital	
Ruins area	
Neighbourhood	NIMFEJ
Main road	
Pedestrian street	
Steps	
Church	✚
Airport	✈

Time Out **Istria** Shortlist

EDITORIAL
Editor Peterjon Cresswell
Main contributor Alex Crevar
Researcher Vesna Pazin
Proofreader Kieron Corless

DESIGN
Art Director, Croatia Igor Spanjevic

Art Director Scott Moore
Art Editor Pinelope Kourmouzoglou
Senior Designer Henry Elphick
Graphic Designers Kei Ishimaru, Nicola Wilson
Advertising Designer Jodi Sher

Picture Editor Jael Marschner
Deputy Picture Editor Lynn Chambers
Picture Researcher Gemma Walters
Picture Desk Assistant Ben Rowe
Picture Librarian Christina Theisen

ADVERTISING
Commercial Director Mark Phillips
International Advertising Manager
 Kasimir Berger
International Sales Executive Charlie Sokol

MARKETING
**Sales & Marketing Director, North America
 & Latin America** Lisa Levinson
Senior Publishing Brand Manager
 Luthfa Begum
Art Director Anthony Huggins
Marketing Intern Alana Benton

PRODUCTION
Production Manager Brendan McKeown
Production Controller Damian Bennett

CONTRIBUTORS
This guide was researched and written by Alex Crevar. Very special thanks to Tomislav Popovic, Ozren Grbavčić, Daniela Fanjkutić and all at the Istria Tourist Board, Pionirska 1, 52440 Poreč, Croatia (www.istra.hr). The editor would very much like to thank Alison and Rajko for all previous work; and Pinelope Kourmouzoglou.

PHOTOGRAPHY
All photography by Vanda Vučićević, except: pp2 (top left, bottom right), 12, 14, 22, 26, 35, 44, 92, 105, 121, 139 (top, bottom right) Rajko Radovanović; pp3 (bottom left), 10, 37, 47, 52, 55, 66, 71, 72, 96, 119 (top), 125, 127, 136, 142 Dave Jepson; pp50, 51, 87, 117, 131, 135, 145, 146, 147 Eni Nurkollari; pp46, 49, 78, 85, 94, 98, 100, 104, 124, 162, 172 Fumie Suzuki; pp2 (bottom left), 7, 8 Mario Romulić; pp38, 61, 139 (bottom left), 175 Carly Calhoun; pp2 (top right), 91, 110 Matthew Field; pp3 (bottom right), 70 Damir Fabijanovic; pp179 Željko Bobanović Bobo; pp159, 160, 166 Maistra Hotels; pp3 (top right), 168 Kempinski Hotel; pp24, 57 Monvi Center; pp28 Motovun Film Festival; p32 Pula Film Festival; p48 Pula Aquarium; p88 Casino Mulino; p89 Konoba Buščina; p93 Jimmy Woo Club Lounge; pp103, 164 Valsabbion; pp118, 119 (bottom) Brijuni Tourist Board; p163 Stancija Meneghetti; p170 Hotel Palazzo; p171 Hotel Nautika; p176 Hotel Kaštel; p180 Valamar Hotel. Cover: Port of Rovinj, Istria. Credit: Photolibrary.com.

MAPS
Maps by JS Graphics (john@jsgraphics.co.uk)

About **Time Out**

Founded in 1968, Time Out has expanded from humble London beginnings into the leading resource for those wanting to know what's happening in the world's greatest cities. As well as our influential what's-on weeklies in London, New York and Chicago, we publish nearly 30 other listings magazines in cities as varied as Beijing and Mumbai. The magazines established Time Out's trademark style: sharp writing, informed reviewing and bang up-to-date inside knowledge of every scene.

 Time Out made the natural leap into travel guides in the 1980s with the City Guide series, which now extends to over 50 destinations around the world. Written and researched by expert local writers and generously illustrated with original photography, the full-size guides cover a larger area than our Shortlist guides and include many more venue reviews, along with additional background features and a full set of maps.

 Throughout this rapid growth, the company has remained proudly independent, still owned by Tony Elliott four decades after he started Time Out London as a single fold-out sheet of A5 paper. This independence extends to the editorial content of all our publications, this Shortlist included. No establishment has been featured because it has advertised, and no payment has influenced any of our reviews. And, for our critics, there's definitely no such thing as a free lunch: all restaurants and bars are visited and reviewed anonymously, and Time Out always picks up the bill.
For more about the company, see www.timeout.com.

Don't Miss

Pula Amphitheatre p98

Sights & Museums

Visitors to Istria soon learn that heritage attractions are not hived off into the traditional format that other holiday destinations follow. Monuments, not museums, are the magnets for the towns that dot the coast and teeter on hilltop precipices. With influences right back to Roman times, key tourist hubs on the peninsula feel like open-air museums in themselves. And with typical Croatian nonchalance, the treasures here can be touched, walked on and captured on film – some even work as cafés and other businesses.

Pula and the South

For those visiting the southern tip, the top sights of interest focus heavily on antiquities, which cram Istria's only real city, Pula. Chief among these monumental venues, most of which form a circle around a hilltop fortress in the middle of Old Town ('Pietas Iulia' to the Romans), is the Amphitheatre (p98), referred to locally as the Arena. A walk inside still fills the ear with the phantom shouts of 20,000 spectators cheering gladiators against lions. The city continues to hold major events here such as the Pula Film Festival and big-name concerts. In the centre, the Roman Forum (p100) still acts as the main square; alongside, the Temple of Augustus (p100) was reconstructed after a direct bomb hit during World War II. The city centre also features the Hercules & Twin Gates (p100) and the magnificent Triumphal Arch of the Sergi (p100), which is said to have inspired the Arc de Triomphe.

Being a city, Pula has a more extensive choice of museums than elsewhere in the peninsula. The Archaeological Museum of Istria (p98) between the Hercules & Twin Gates by the Italian minority building houses a fair display of ancient artefacts and is continually growing as more pieces are found. Atop the hill in the centre of town, the Venetian Castle & Historical Museum of Istria (p101) has a real maritime element; its setting is a spot to unwind and enjoy the view.

Of note and north of the city in Vodnjan, the Church of St Blaise (p117) and its sacral art collection houses the so-called Vodnjan mummies: a collection of body parts from six saints, which draws thousands yearly. The Brijuni Islands (p117) north-west of Pula are another big tourist draw. Famously Tito's playground, where he hosted diplomats and movie stars, today Brijuni houses Tito's exotic animal assemblage, a 1,600-year-old olive tree and Roman ruins from the second century BC.

West Coast

The visit-worthy sights lining Istria's western shore are ecclesiastical in nature. Rovinj, the peninsula's most heralded tourism destination, is dominated by the Cathedral of St Euphemia (p56), built in Venetian Baroque at the beginning of the 18th century. The town's welcoming Balbi's Arch (p54) ushers you into the Old Town under the famous book-holding Venetian lion. Two museums of consequence in town are the Rovinj Heritage Museum (p58), which resides in a bright-red Baroque palace and displays archaeological findings, Renaissance paintings and Croatian contemporary works; and Batana House (p56), which focuses on Rovinj's traditional

SHORTLIST

Best museums
- Batana House, Rovinj (p56)
- Gallerion Naval Museum, Novigrad (p80)
- Museum Lapidarium, Novigrad (p82)

Best Roman sights
- Pula Amphitheatre (p98)
- Triumphal Arch of the Sergi, Pula (p100)

Best Byzantine sights
- Euphrasian Basilica, Poreč (p71)

Best Baroque
- Cathedral of St Euphemia, Rovinj (p56)
- Istrian Assembly Hall, Poreč (p72)

Most diverse collections
- Labin Museum (p151)
- Rovinj Heritage Museum (p58)

Best for kids
- Aquarium Poreč (p71)
- Rovinj Aquarium (p58)

Best church art
- Church of St Blaise Sacral Art Collection, Vodnjan (p117)
- Parish Church of St Bernard, Funtana (p67)
- St Mary of the Rocks Church, Beram (p145)

Best Venetian sights
- Balbi's Arch, Rovinj (p54)
- Cathedral of St Euphemia, Rovinj (p56)
- Venetian Castle & Historical Museum of Istria, Pula (p101)

Best belltower views
- St Jerome Church, Vižinada (p136)

DON'T MISS

batana-style boat: an unusual vehicle for familiarising yourself with local culture. Moving up the coast, the Dušan Djamonja Sculpture Park (p67) between Vrsar and Funtana sits on ten hectares and contains more than 50 years of the great sculptor's work.

Poreč is the location of Istria's must-see sight: the sixth-century Euphrasian Basilica (p71), and its neighbouring Bishop's Palace. The main attractions within are the well-preserved gold-gilt and mother-of-pearl mosaics. A walk along the Roman thoroughfare of Decumanus, still the main street today, follows a path littered with relics: from Roman temple ruins to 15th-century Gothic villas.

Further along the shore, in Novigrad, the Museum Lapidarium (p82) is the key cultural sight, sheltering Roman finds in a modern building (a rarity on the Croatian coast) that effortlessly blends with the old fishing town. In line with the fishing tradition is the Gallerion Naval Museum (p80). The main focus here is the Austro-Hungarian Navy from 1815 to the end of World War I, when Istria and its ports were no longer under Habsburg control. North of Novigrad, in the settlement of Savudrija, two boat-related sights are super photo-ops: the Savudrija Lighthouse (p89) – the oldest one active in the Adriatic – and the traditional boat cranes (p87), which suspend skiffs with a system of pulleys and poles.

Inland Istria

Here the medieval hilltop villages are sights in themselves, providing free-of-charge medieval squares, frescoes and panoramas from stone fortifications. Motovun is the classic example. A walk around the old walls and through the 13th-century gate, with vistas of

Euphrasian Basilica, Poreč p71

It's time to truly indulge yourself in Poreč and Rabac

Our resorts offer comfortable accommodation in hotels, apartments, villas and camp sites (including naturist camps). Crystal clear water, clean beaches, swimming pools, sports and animation programmes for children and adults, unforgettable Istrian cuisine and much more to enable you to relax and unwind.

Information and reservations:
Poreč **T** + 385 52 465 100 **F** + 385 52 451 440
Rabac **T** + 385 52 465 200 **F** + 385 52 872 561

Take a look at our special offers at
www.valamar.com

Istria
Green Mediterranean.

CRO A TIA

VALAMAR
HOTELS & RESORTS

Labin Museum p151

the Mirna valley and Motovun forest below, gives visitors a handle on Motovun's role in history in one easy morning's stroll.

North-east of Motovun, the prototypical town-as-museum is Hum (p132). The so-called smallest town in the world has a layout that hasn't changed much over the last 1,000 years. Its neighbours, Roč (p131) and Draguć (p132), also share this lost-in-time theme and make for fine afternoon jaunts.

The western half of the interior is offers a variety of tourist venues. Chief among them is the town of Grožnjan (p136). One of the most beautiful in Istria, it combines an easy-going grace with dozens of galleries – Grožnjan is known as the Town of Artists. The municipal Fonticus City Gallery (p137) is part gallery, part museum, with a display of historical crests and coats of arms. To the south and west, the Baredine Cave (p137) is a well-run attraction with tours of five-chamber site. Due east, Pazin (p142) contains the 1,000-year-old Pazin Castle (p143), housing its Town & Ethnographic museums (p143). The castle alone, built in 983, is worth the visit. In nearby Beram, St Mary of the Rocks Church (p144) contains the famous fresco 'Dance of the Dead'.

East Coast

Smaller in size and population, the East Coast has fewer sights. Labin Museum (p151) has ancient finds but visitors most remember the reconstruction of a mineshaft. In Dubrova, a sculpture park is the product of the Mediterranean Sculpture Symposium (p151), assembled every summer to create new works. The quirkiest sight is Raša (p152), a town built by Mussolini to house miners. Its Church of St Barbara (p151) is shaped like an overturned mine cart, and its campanile resembles a miner's lamp.

Eating & Drinking

Gastronomy is a way of life in Istria. The peninsula teems with marvellous wineries and olive oil producers. There are black and white truffles in summer and winter, and seasonal specialities such as wild asparagus in spring. Quality food can be found in every town, village or outpost. The ingredients are typically fresh but some restaurants do a better job of sourcing and cooking that day's menu than others.

When possible, we have done our best to ferret out places that make local produce a priority. Not all venues go to great lengths to advertise the fact. Istria is blessed with fine ingredients – it is not always safe to simply write off a business because it looks touristy. Even restaurants with tacked-up pictures of their food often have a

decent selection of interesting wines and truffles to accoutre dishes. Our recommendations generally prioritise food quality over atmosphere.

Although good food can be found anywhere (and in every price range), there are, naturally, establishments that put the whole package together – ingredients, expertise, service and setting – in ways that make you realise that Croatia, and in particular Istria, is no longer a culinary backwater. Top-end restaurateurs understand that certain guests are willing to pay for such an experience and if you fall into this category, you should expect to be charged accordingly. Reservations at such places are a must.

On the coast, expect to find top-quality fish, shellfish, octopus and squid cooked in myriad ways. The specific varieties will vary with location. Though small, the peninsula does place importance on local produce.

Inland restaurants are generally meat-oriented. Though you'll occasionally find seafood at spots in the rolling hills of the interior, you're more likely to come across menus listing pasta, steaks, veal, lamb and, of course, truffles on everything from eggs to ice-cream.

Some terms to be familiar with include *konoba* (tavern); *manestra* (vegetable soup); *fuži* (pasta twists); *pršut* (prosciutto); *boškarin* (Istrian ox), and *rakija* (grappa). There's a full menu vocabulary at the back of this book.

Coastal quality

From coast to coast, there is a head-spinning number of first-class restaurants in which to sample the Adriatic's offering. And first-class doesn't mean costly. There are fine spots to grab delicious meals without paying through the nose. Still, fresh white fish (300kn per kg) and lobster (500kn per kg) do come with a premium price tag. The types of fish you can expect to find are sea bass, monkfish, john dory and scorpion fish. In the north-west, sole is common.

In Pula, you'd be hard-pressed to eat better than at Valsabbion (p107), where atmosphere, seafood and cuisine combine to make a memorable, if pricey, experience. Further south, in Banjole, Batelina (p111) is the big hitter. Owned by a fisherman, here the catch is guaranteed fresh and determines the evening's menu. North of Pula, Fažana specialises in sardines, prepared in many styles; every spot on its harbour follows suit.

In Rovinj, look out for Blu (p58), where you can take a dip before

SHORTLIST

Best new
- Caffè Bar Divino, Novigrad (p82)
- Pepenero, Novigrad (p84)

Best luxury blow-outs
- San Rocco, Brtonigla (p91)
- Valsabbion, Pula (p107)

Best themed bars
- Caffè Uliks, Pula (p102)
- Yesterday, Poreč (p77)

Best wine bars
- Parentino Bar, Poreč (p76)
- Sorso Wine Bar, Pula (p107)

Best for seafood
- Batelina, Banjole (p111)
- Fjord, Limski kanal (p70)
- Restaurant Sidro, Novigrad (p85)

Best party bars
- Barracuda Beach Bar, Medulin (p111)
- Buba, Vrsar (p67)

Best Istrian
- Konoba Morgan, Buje (p90)
- Vodnjanka, Vodnjan (p121)

Best for families
- Al Porto, Vrsar (p67)
- Istarska konoba, Vrsar (p68)
- Konoba Porer, Premantura (p114)

Best music bars
- Kamene Priče, Bale (p120)
- Lapidarij, Poreč (p75)

Best locations
- Blu, Rovinj (p58)
- La Puntulina, Rovinj (p62)
- Viking, Limski kanal (p70)

Best cheapie
- Konoba Kantinon, Rovinj (p60)

settling down to sea bass or scallops with truffles; also recommended are Monte (p62) and the restaurant at the Hotel Monte Mulini (p171). Before moving too far north up the coast make sure to stop at the Limski kanal for a meal at Fjord (p70), a restaurant that takes advantage of the canal's abundance of mussels and oysters.

Due to the shallow depth of the sea around Novigrad, sole is a speciality. Restaurant Sidro (p85) on the harbour has been preparing it for four decades. The newest restaurant in town is Pepenero (p84), with dishes such as home-made ravioli stuffed with sea bass.

Inland for truffles

Istria equals truffles. You'll have a hard time finding a place of note in the interior without them popping

White truffles, Zigante p129

up on the menu, often in the most unexpected of places: liqueurs, biscuits, honey and even ice-cream. The pungent treasure is unearthed mostly from Buzet to the Motovun in ten varieties, six black and four white. Business is cut-throat, with some types going for thousands of euros per kilo. Keep an eye out for restaurants with the '*tartufo vero*' sign, which means they've met Istria's high standards for handling and serving the fungus.

Truffles are not the only delicacy in the interior. Wild game, wild asparagus, lamb and mushrooms are paired with home-made pastas, for instance. And though decent olive oil can be found all over, it is inland where the highest quality varieties are produced.

Prices inland are usually quite reasonable because the *konobas* and restaurants aren't as highbrow as their coast-side cousins.

In Buzet, Stara oštarija (p134), combines fine views with flavourful meals, in which truffles figure heavily even in dishes such as trout. Nearby, Restaurant Vrh (p134) and Konoba Zlatni Breg (p133) have chefs who insist on home-made ingredients. Both establishments display certificates allowing them to serve *boškarin*, an organic beef from the Istrian ox.

North of Motovun, Livade has a clutch of eateries that specialise in local dishes that lean heavily on truffles, most famously Zigante (p129). You'll pay for its fame but the food is outstanding.

In the north-west reaches of the interior Marino (p138) sits on the edge of the gastro enclave of Momjan. Slow food and Muškat wine are the orders of the day here. Outside Brtonigla, Konoba Morgan (p90) serves rabbit, pheasant, wild boar, venison and quail, and complements them with truffles and top wines.

At Vodnjan, Vodnjanka (p121) dishes out home-made meals: it's worthy of a visit even if you're not planning to do anything else here.

Drink up

Wine is generally the drink of choice in Istria, and for very good reason. There are scores of top-notch wineries across the peninsula and even a government-produced wine-road map (p40) leading you to the different vineyards.

As well as cellars, Istria has so many cocktail lounges, beach bars and cafés that you wonder how they all stay in business. The best are thriving, offering imaginative drink choices and fostering an enjoyable atmosphere. Bars are particularly prevalent in the coastal tourist zone. They operate like pubs and serve a variety of hard liquors, table wine by the glass, local Favorit (and/or Slovene Laško or Union) beer on draught, and usually cocktails. Expect to pay 15kn-20kn for a half-litre of domestic beer and 40kn-60kn for cocktails. Inland establishments are more relaxed, less expensive and more about kicking back with friends. A fine example is the Caffè Bar Montona Gallery (p126) in Motovun. Its patio tables by the town walls overlook surrounding forests. *Biska*, a mistletoe grappa, is a typical popular tipple here. A place to watch the sunset is Caffè Bar Vero (p138) in hilltop Grožnjan. As elsewhere, the table wine is served as a *gemišt* (spritzer with sparkling water).

For all that, the coolest places to imbibe are on the coast, where the number of bars and drinkers keen to fill them have found an equilibrium. The Pula scene is fragmented but for big sunglasses and gossip, head for the bars lining Flanatička. In Rovinj, look for chilled drinking stations with great views over the water in the lower part of town, on Sv Križa. In Poreč, start at the Riva promenade of Obala maršala Tita and you can't go wrong. The town's Roman forum, Marafor, can also be counted on for drinking action.

Batelina, Banjole p111

Shopping

More and more authentic Istrian shops are starting to pop up. The Istrian 'handmade' movement mainly operates among southern communities – Pula, Medulin, Premantura and Fažana – to promote homespun souvenirs and uses as its informal slogan 'Say no to blue dolphins', referring to the kitschy foreign-produced plastic dolphins that come complete with the word 'Croatia' stamped on for good measure. Its members travel the most popular destinations around the peninsula in the high season, to set up stalls (in Pula's Roman Forum, for instance) to display their wares – glass products, ceramics, jewellery, olive-wood bobbles, stone motifs and lavender, giving tourists a real value-added souvenir to pack, while keeping the profits local.

Liquid assets

Wine and olive oil are the standout items to stow away in your case when you leave. For more on where to shop and who to buy from, see our wine and olive oil itinerary (p38). Because Istria is so vinocentric, the line between gift and wine shop can be blurred. The best wine selections are found at Piassa Granda (p62) in Rovinj and Vinoteque Epvlon (p78) in Poreč. Always make reservations at any vineyard or olive oil producer's venue you are planning to visit.

The other peninsular liquid of choice is *rakija*, a cross between grappa and brandy. There are as many different types as there are herbs and fruits with which to infuse them. There is also honey *rakija* called *medenica*, delectable

Sheriff & Cherry, Rovinj p65

and dangerous. Honey producer Svetozar Janković in Livade (Livade 9, 052 664 143) is also responsible for a noteworthy *medenica*. For herb *rakija*, or *travarica*, head for the distillery of Miro Petohleb near Buzet (Stjepana konzula 6, 052 662 750). *Biska* is made from mistletoe, ideally in the area around Hum; Imela Shop (p134) sells the finest brand, as well as varieties such as ones made with truffles.

Snaffle a truffle

Truffles are a whole industry. Truffle-infused products include jarred truffles, pâté, honey, biscuits, olive oil, sausages and cheese, to name but a few. Zigante in Livade (p129) is Istria's most famous truffle restaurant and the brand holds a virtual monopoly on the retail end as well. You'll see branches all over Istria – Buje, Buzet, Grožnjan, Motovun and Pula – but the mother ship is in Livade (Livade 7, 052 664 030). The other

DON'T MISS

Loggia, Oprtalj p141

brand of real consequence is Karlić (p143). A visit to its ranch near Buzet may include a truffle hunt.

Market value

You might wonder where all the locals are when you go out to eat. The answer is simple: they cook at home and do their shopping at the produce market. Nearly every town or village of any size has one. Most are located right in the centre and offer a cheaper version of the same ingredients that Istria's better restaurants use to make your meals out memorable.

Pula's grand produce market (p108) is off the main promenade; rows of colourful, naturally organic vegetables and fruits cover the tabletops. The fish and meat markets are filled with butchers and fishmongers selling lamb, pork, veal, squid, sardines, salmon, octopus and shellfish. The Rovinj open-air market (p64) is also worth a browse and is a good place to grab a cheap snack or ingredients for the evening meal. A one-stop shop, this is also the spot to buy lavender, oil and lots of kitsch.

Stores and boutiques

Istria is not a place for high-street shopping. The clothes shop most worthy of note is Rovinj's Sheriff & Cherry (p65), which stocks the kind of urban gear you'd find in London or Barcelona – plus pieces by a select few Croatian designers. Rovinj (and Poreč) also specialise in galleries with worthwhile artworks. Don't be afraid to ask where something was made before buying it. Motovun is rich in original crafts. Etnobutiga Ča (p129) is a stand-out with gifts as varied as hand-woven baskets, sculptures and liqueurs. Look out also for Sanifor (p158) in Labin, on the east coast – it packs a lot into a beautifully designed store and stocks only fine hand-made objects, from soaps to Clai wine.

For art, Gallery Potočnjak (p77) is where many works by the eponymous artist spill from numerous rooms and a yard by the Basilica. For galleries, ateliers and artists all in one place, Rovinj's Grisia (p65) acts as a gallery and sells first-class pieces and top-notch junk with equal enthusiasm.

Monvi Center, Rovinj p65

Nightlife

Istria is no Ibiza. Although it is attracting more visitors, the peninsula still heads for bed after the regular bars close around 2am. The lack of past-midnight fun is more prounounced inland, even with its longer tourist season. All the same, there is a noticeable upswing of late-night happenings around Pula and on the west coast, where revelry is stepping up to meet the burgeoning demand.

With new clubs finding their feet, more established venues are offering international DJs, all-nighters and themed parties. The idea that Istria is just a place to sip wine, eat truffles and be in bed by midnight is changing, albeit slowly. Whether that fits in with Istria's plans to encourage tourism of quality rather than quantity remains to be seen.

For the most part, being at a club here means partying until four or five in the morning, with a couple of venues open 24 hours. Most have no cover charge. The recent national no-smoking rule in certain public buildings has made the air inside tolerarable and outdoor venues more popular. Crowds run the gamut from the teenage to the late middle-aged.

South strutting

As Istria's only city, Pula has an assortment of all-night spots. Clubs are scattered across the city and outlying districts. The standard and stand-by is Uljanik (p109), in operation since 1965. One long-time Uljanik patron described it as a *cipelarka* ('shin-kicking') good time. The place has a rockers' vibe with cheap drinks and a grungy interior, but DJs play everything to multiple-age crowds in multiple rooms and a courtyard.

The Zen Club (p109) has an older feel. It only operates at weekends, when the music tends to favour R&B and house. If good old local Slavic beats are what you crave, Zen's down-the-street neighbour Stella (p109) can provide domestic rhythms but only in winter when it caters to locals. For something more alternative, Karlo Rojc (p110) has a varied DJ agenda.

Aruba (p109), at the edge of the city centre, plays an assortment of music over its two-floor enterprise and has salsa nights on Thursdays. In nearby Verudela, Ambrela (p108) is a newly renovated club on a terrace spilling out on to a stone beach. The DJs play it all here to a crowd that gathers under the stars in the sea breeze. South of town in the resort community of Medulin, Summer Club Dali (p115) stays open until 5am in season and caters to the tourist crowd.

The west is the best

For clubbing, the west coast from Rovinj to Umag is the place to be, with the party spots around Poreč leading the dance brigade. These are real nightclubs that keep real nightclub hours, bring in heavy-hitting DJs, and have risqué theme nights that change every evening. Not quite Ibiza, they at least bring balance to Istria's overall package.

For late-night carousing, there's only one place to go in Rovinj: the Monvi Center (p65). Inside this open-until-5am complex are bars, discos, restaurants and global DJs filling a summer programme. Just north, the 24-hour Dionys Beach Bar (p69) in Vrsar employs go-go girls to dance between the olive trees in front of the sea.

SHORTLIST

Best newcomers
- Ambrela, Pula (p108)
- Jimmy Woo Club Lounge, Umag (p93)

Best for big-name DJs
- Byblos, Poreč (p79)

Best beachside nightspots
- Casanova Beach Club, Vrsar (p69)
- Dionys Beach Bar, Vrsar (p69)
- Waikiki Sunset, Novigrad (p86)

Best themed venue
- Caffè Bar Vampire (p147)

Best kitsch nightspot
- Aruba Club, Pula (p109)
- Club 190, Buzet (p135)

Best all-in-one venues
- E&D, Pula (p109)
- Monvi Center, Rovinj (p65)

Best post-party chill-out
- Paradiso Beach Bar, Poreč (p79)

Best outrageous night out
- Plava Club, Poreč (p79)
- Zen Club, Pula (p109)

Best glitzy destination
- Saint & Sinner, Poreč (p79)

Best for live acts
- Bamboo, Umag (p91)
- Kamene Priče, Bale (p120)
- Uljanik, Pula (p109)
- Villa Club, Poreč (p79)

Best barstaffs
- Daylight Cocktail Bar, Umag (p93)
- Waikiki Sunset, Novigrad (p86)

Hedonistic? Maybe, but it's nothing compared to the Plava Club (p79) disco in Poreč, where full-nudity lesbian shows and pole dancing are part of a typical night's entertainment. Opened in 2007, Byblos (p79) in Zelena Laguna outside of Poreč, can be thanked for the upsurge in the coastal nightlife scene. It's a huge space with top DJs – note the admission charge. Apart from Rovinj's Monvi, Byblos is probably the only establishment in the peninsula that can attract names such as David Guetta, Deep Dish and Roger Sanchez.

Up the coast, Umag is gradually losing its Poreč Lite tag. Beach bars and discos supply the annual, late-July, tennis-tournament spike in tourism but they also keep visitors rollicking through summer. Near the tennis centre, Jimmy Woo Club Lounge (p93) opened in 2008. There's talk of an MTV party contract. More established, the Daylight Cocktail Bar (p93) offers solid music, a stellar waterside setting, and some of the best cocktails in Istria. Also expect go-go dancers and theme nights from Chinese to Mexican.

Odd spots inland

Inland Istria is quiet but there are a few places worthy of mention if for no other reason than to congratulate them as torchbearers.

Buzet has one spot: Club 190 (p135), which pumps R&B all evening inside a kitsch interior that has a flat-screen fireplace and a VIP lounge. Down the hill and heading west along the Mirna, the Old River Grill (p135) has DJs spinning from a wooden deck in the open evening air. On the menu are cocktails and truffles. Further afield, the Caffè Bar Vampire (p147), south of Pazin in Kringa, is a goon-filled good time based on the 17th-century legend of a local vampire who had his own nightlife gig ravaging women and sampling villagers' blood. While the Vampire is technically a bar, there are weekend DJs and the place stays open late for locals with nowhere else to go.

If you're here in late July, don't forget that the Motovun Film Festival (p35) features five nights of DJs spinning in this medieval hilltop town, while visitors drink pretty much continuously.

Karlo Rojc, Pula p110

CROATIA

MOUNTAIN BIKING
IN THE MORNING.

CARMEN
IN THE EVENING.

Only in Istria.

Istria
Green Mediterranean.

www.istra.hr
Info & Booking Center Istria:
☏ +385 52 85 8448

Motovun Film Festival p35

Arts & Leisure

Istria's extraordinarily varied arts scene manifests itself in an equally diverse number of festivals, many of them open-air and free of charge. Two major film festivals, festivals of jazz, of accordions, of non-verbal theatre, symposia of sculpture, annual happenings of street art – festivals are the prism through which Istria's cultural scene is perceived. Meanwhile, it seems that every other business on the peninsula, if not a restaurant, is a gallery of some sort.

Leisure opportunities abound in a landscape that is as beautiful as any in Croatia. The rolling hills of the lush interior make for perfect hiking and bike riding while the coast provides the playground for water-related endeavours. Spectator sports, though, are limited – Istria has no major

football side to speak of, or sports arena, come to that. Those hoping to catch a game will have to hop over to nearby Rijeka, and the famous Kantrida stadium.

Events and celebrations

Istria's most established arts event is the Pula Film Festival (p35). Over half a century old, it started as a way to showcase the Yugoslavian film industry. Today there is a bevy of international flicks and, best of all, Pula's Roman amphitheatre becomes an open-air cinema. Throughout the summer, this atmospheric setting also serves as the stage for big-name acts from the world of popular music – Elton John was a recent visitor. Staying in Pula but moving underground, Karlo Rojc (p110) is a former

Habsburg barracks converted into an arts and community centre housing 100 NGOs, a stream of theatre productions and DJed raves. North of Pula, in Bale, the Last Minute Open jazz festival (p116) pulls in 120 players from around the globe and attracts some 5,000 fans yearly – and all sponsor-free.

Other cultural events involve arts disciplines the visitor wouldn't expect to be on the agenda – DJs at the Motovun Film Festival (p35) for example. Over in Poreč, it doesn't get any quirkier or more eclectic than the Street Art Festival (www.poup.hr), when musicians, jugglers and breakdancers take centre stage. The main criteria for getting yourself on the bill: you need to be able keep a crowd's interest. In Vrsar in July, lovers of erotica show up for the Casanova Fest (p35). In the town's old beachside quarry, titillating flicks are shown and topless DJs are embraced by dancers.

Across the peninsula in Labin, the Labin Art Republic (p150) is a two-month series of events including music, arts and impromptu street performance. In Svetvinčenat, between Rovinj and Labin, the Dance and Non-verbal Theatre Festival (p35) is now into its second decade. The title says it all but what's not mentioned is the drama of watching modern interpretive dancers convert the 16th-century Grimani Castle into a theatre of the surreal. The Roč Accordion Festival (p33) is dedicated to the five-tone version of the instrument and brings together an all-ages gaggle of music lovers in this tiny medieval village.

In August, Grisia in Rovinj hosts an all-day-and-night art exhibition open to any artist who wants to set up shop on the cobbled street. This is a great way to take in every imaginable local form of creativity.

SHORTLIST

Best for alternative arts
- Karlo Rojc, Pula (p110)

Best for diving
- Diving Centre Shark, Medulin (p116)
- Premantura Windsurfing (p116)

Best for kids
- Aquarium Pula (p109)
- Barba Tone, Barban (p158)
- Boškarin farm, Višnjan (p141)

Best photo galleries
- Batana Photo Art Gallery, Rovinj (p65)

Best venues for local art
- Galleria Adris, Rovinj (p65)
- Gallery Rigo, Novigrad (p86)

Best art thoroughfare
- Grisia, Rovinj (p65)

Best open-air stages
- Kamene Priče, Bale (p120)
- Poreč Theatre (p79)
- Pula Amphitheatre (p98)

Best multi-sports venues
- Premantura Windsurfing (p116)
- Sports Centre Montraker, Vrsar (p69)

Best for sculpture
- Aleksandar Rukovina Memorial Gallery, Brtonigla (p93)
- Mediterranean Sculpture Symposium, Dubrova (p151)

Best theatre arenas
- Istrian Assembly Hall, Poreč (p72)
- Karlo Rojc, Pula (p110)
- Poreč Theatre (p79)

Grisia, Rovinj p65

Visual arts

The many forms of art on offer around Istria can be viewed in every kind of setting. Rovinj has civically sponsored photo art exhibitions, free-of-charge private collections and the gallery hub of Grisia (p65). Equally well-provided is Grožnjan (p136) with its 26 galleries crammed into a compact medieval hilltop space.

On the east coast, Labin has galleries stocking everything from paintings to pottery. Art Gallery Valenta (p158) focuses on five Croatian artists with different styles and prices. Summer's Labin Art Republic is perhaps Istria's most significant event in the visual arts calendar.

In the north, Novigrad's Gallery Rigo (p86) is one of Istria's most important independent venues, housing contemporary art, modern works, photography and a permanent display of Byzantine fragments. In nearby Brtonigla, the Aleksandar Rukovina Memorial Gallery (p93) is dedicated to the famed sculptor and displays his works in bronze, stone and wood.

Outdoor activities

Set in the rolling hills at the foot of the Alps, Istria's landscape lends itself well to many activities. For starters, it is criss-crossed with scores of bike trails (p45) that cover thousands of kilometres. Hiking paths are also abundant. The more demanding ones can be found in the undulating, east-coast countryside near Labin, which sits in the shadow of Učka mountain, and further north on the Slovenian border in the Ćićarija mountains. There, Raspadalica (p135) can arrange guided hiking, paragliding and climbing.

Between Labin and Pula, near Barban, Ranch Barba Tone (p158) runs horseback tours including a ride ending in the sea. As for watersports, the main one is diving, with dozens of reefs and wrecks. A windsurfing culture thrives around Pula. The Diving Centre Shark (p116) in Medulin, goes to 30 sites of varying difficulty; nearby Premantura Windsurfing (p116) uses several spots on the coast to take advantage of the winds that swirl about Istria's southern tip.

Calendar

Pula Film Festival p34

Unlike the rest of Croatia with its two-month tourist season, Istria prides itself on a year-round docket of events. These run the thematic gamut. There is, a heavy gastro presence, with festivals celebrating wine, sausage, olive oil and cheese – among others – giving a sense of what peninsula residents find important and when. Music is also often a focus or an accompaniment. As Catholics, locals rank religious feasts and saints' days high on the list of reasons to celebrate. Equally, history, especially Roman, will get citizens sharing the local inebriant.

January

Mid Jan **Antonija**
Rovinjsko Selo, Rovinj
www.istria-rovinj.com
A wine and olive oil exhibition held in this tiny community just east of Rovinj. Open to the public, Antonija combines gastronomic treats with diverse musical performances, local folkloric activities and crafts.

Late Jan **Sausage Festival**
Dom kulture, Marušići
www.istria-buje.com
Since 1993, sausage-makers have travelled to this village in north-east Istria near Buje to see who makes the best variety. Huge sausage omelettes are then made for festival patrons.

Late Jan **Night of the Museums**
Various locations
www.croatia.hr
On the last Friday in January, museums across Croatia open free of charge from 6pm to 1am. Among them in the peninsula are Umag Town Museum and the Archaeological Museum of Istria in Pula.

February

Mid Feb **Buzet Carnival**
Trg Fontana, Buzet
www.istria-buzet.com
Buzet's Sunday parade is a swirl of masks and wagons from surrounding villages. On the Tuesday, the evil *pust* is burned to cast away all bad deeds.

Mid Feb **Honey Days**
Spomen Dom, Pazin
www.istria-central.com
This focuses on the long-standing family tradition of honey-making in Istria. Tastings are arranged.

March

Mid Mar **Oleum Olivarum**
Dom kulture, Krasica (Buje)
www.istria-buje-buie.com
This event near Buje is dedicated to olives and olive oil and holds tastings, lectures, exhibitions and awards.

Late Mar **Istrakon**
Spomen Dom, Pazin
www.istrakon.hr
Beginning on a Friday and lasting 48 hours, Istrakon is a 'Sci-Fi journey' devoted to offbeat sciences. There are creative-writing workshops, fashion shows and themed parties.

April

Easter Monday
Wines of Central Istria
Various locations, Grašišće
www.istria-central.com
This wine event gives visitors the chance to peruse the different labels.

Apr/May **Istrian Asparagus Days**
Various locations
www.istra.hr
Collected in spring, asparagus is on nearly every Istrian menu – this loose, multi-venued event celebrates the fact.

Mid Apr **Olive Oil Exhibition**
Community Centre, Vodnjan
www.istria-vodnjan.com
Vodnjan's quality of oil is legendary. This event promotes various types, hosts tastings and awards prizes.

Late Apr **Voga Teleferika Boat Race**
Rabac
www.istria-rabac.com
This boat race off Rabac on the eastern coast is accompanied by free drinks, anchovies and serious all-night dancing, plus a giant post-race tug-of-war, sales, exchange and donations.

Late Apr **BOOKtiga**
Trg Marafor, Poreč
www.istria-porec.com
This three-day book fair is held in the ancient Roman square of Marafor, with sales, exchange and donations.

Late Apr-early May
Vin Istra
Zatika Sports Arena, Poreč
www.vinistra.com
The top event for wine and other gastro products in Istria, this is a can't-miss for the food trade.

Late Apr **Kamenjak Marathon**
Cape Kamenjak
www.istra.hr
At Istria's southern tip, runners compete for the Junior Marathon and Mini Marathon over a course of coves and beaches from Kamenjak to Kolomarica.

May

Early May **International Walking Day**
Pazin
www.istria-central.com
Every year a new trail is hiked by weekenders (10km) and experienced trekkers (15km). The trails take four hours. The event ends at Dušani, 2km from Pazin.

Early May **Floral Carpet**
Parish Church of St Bernard, Funtana
www.istria-funtana.com
This event is devoted to scattering flowers in Funtana's parish church, making floral carpets and figures as a tribute. Held the first Sunday in May.

Mid May **Accordion Festival**
Roč
www.istria-buzet.com
Exponents of the *trieština* five-tone accordion gather to play, drink and make merry. The festival attracts musicians from across Central Europe.

Film fests

The two biggest dates in Istria's crowded calendar don't concern food or music, but film.

No one could argue that **Pula** has the best location for film screenings. Crowds sit under the stars in the historic Roman Amphitheatre watching movies. The festival was initiated in 1953 as a showcase for the then Yugoslav film industry. Patronised by Tito and celebrity guests, this was an event of national significance. After 1991 it fell into decline, shrinking to state-sponsored offerings with little global impact. Local independent filmmakers set up their own alternative in Motovun. These days Pula is being revived as a presenter and promoter of Croatian cinema. Showings also take place at Pula Castle (Kaštel) for the first week. Pula still stages the equivalent of Croatia's Oscars.

Motovun, meanwhile, is a cross between Sundance and Glastonbury. For five days this medieval town is transformed into a party-mad hub, with open-air screenings in the main square. Established in 1999 to promote independent film, this modest event has burgeoned – today it is almost too big. With a resident population of a few hundred, Motovun's annual inundation of 50,000-plus has it bursting at the seams. But then again, that's all part of the fun.

The festival presents some 80 documentaries, features and shorts competing for the top prize of the Propeller of Motovun. Filmings are followed by live music and DJs until late. Accommodation is always at a premium – many festivalgoers just sleep in their cars.

Late May **Wine Day**
Various locations
www.istria-gourmet.com
On the last Sunday in May, wine cellars open their doors between 10am and 6pm. This is one of the best ways – and one of the best days – to tour Istria tasting the many varieties.

June

Mid June **Hum election**
City loggia, Hum
www.istria-buzet.com
On the second Sunday in June the smallest town in the world, Hum, selects a new governor of its 20 citizens. See democracy in action and sample the famous Hum mistletoe grappa.

Mid June **Pula Superiorum**
Various locations, Pula
www.pulasuperiorum.com
Pula's streets, museums, Forum and Amphitheatre are used as the city goes back to its Roman roots. The fest features costumes, juggling, arts and crafts, gladiator games and parades.

Mid June **Dvigrad Festival**
Ancient ruins, Dvigrad
www.istria-kanfanar.com
This event brings this old walled community to life with music and dance.

21-22 June **Astrofest**
Tican observatory, Višnjan
www.istria-visnjan.com
Astronomers, winemakers and musicians come together for all-night dancing and star-gazing around a bonfire.

Late June **Croatian Summer Salsa Festival**
Various locations, Rovinj
www.crosalsafestival.com
Workshops, classes and lectures by day, dance parties by night.

Late June **Jules Verne Days**
Various locations, Pazin
www.istria-central.com
Pazin pays tribute to its appearance in the novel 'Mathis Sandorf' with Verne-inspired events around the city.

Accordion Festival, Roč p33

Late June **Goat Festival**
Grimani Castle, Svetvinčenat
www.istria-svetvincenat.com
On the Day of St John the Baptist, goats
from all over Istria vie to be the best.

Late June **Hang-gliding
championship**
Raspadalica, Ćićarija (Buzet)
www.istra.hr
Flyers use the ring of mountains and
rocky plateaus around Buzet.

June-Sept **Grožnjan Music
Summer**
Various locations, Grožnjan
www.istra.hr
Music of all types every night in this
beautiful hilltop town of artists.

July

Early July **Casanova Fest**
Various venues, Vrsar
www.casanovafest.com
The main focus is on the open-air films
and topless DJ parties at the Montraker
quarry. Cas would have approved.

Mid July **Novigrad Music Nights**
Veliki trg, Novigrad
www.istria-novigrad.com

Fairly big names – most recently the
Temptations and ex-Stones guitarist
Mick Taylor – play in the main square.

Mid July **Malvasia Festival**
Glavni trg, Brtonigla
www.istria-brtonigla.com
Wine promotion, talks and tastings.

Late July **Pula Film Festival**
Amphitheatre & Kaštel, Pula
www.pulafilmfestival.hr
See box p34.

Late July **Dance & Non-verbal
Theatre Festival**
Various locations, Svetvinčenat
www.svetvincenatfestival.com
Dance as storytelling is the idea behind
this event. Performances take place in
a medieval castle among other venues.

Late July-early Aug **Croatia Open**
Stella Maris Tennis Centre, Umag
www.croatiaopen.hr
Istria's main sports event, played by
the sea, with gala dinners and parties.

Late July **Motovun Film Festival**
Various locations, Motovun
www.motovunfilmfestival.com
See box p34.

August

Early Aug **Sepomaia Viva**
Various locations, Umag
www.istria-umag.com
Roman-themed fest in full costume.

Early Aug **Grisia Festival**
Grisia, Rovinj
www.istria-rovinj.com
A one-day exhibition on Rovinj's street
of galleries – walls are covered in art.

Mid Aug **Sweet Istria**
Main square, Vižinada
www.istria-vizinada.com
Around the well in the piazza on the
Feast of the Assumption, Istria's pastry
chefs present *pandešpanja*, *fritule*,
kroštule, *povetica* and other delights.

Late Aug **Trka na prstenac**
Barban
www.istria-barban.com
Held in 1696, revived in 1976, this is a
jolly costumed joust with old weapons.

Aug-Sept **Mediterranean
Sculptors' Symposium**
Dubrova, Labin
www.istria-rabac.com
As well as a way for sculptors to learn
and network, this event builds on the
sculpture park just outside Labin.

September

Early Sept **Porečkci delfin**
Poreč
www.poreckidelfin.com
Swimmers can use anything they need
to stay afloat in this swim marathon:
rafts, floaties or fins.

Mid Sept **Subotina**
Trg Fontana, Buzet
www.istria-buzet.com
Buzet's big truffle omelette fest, known
across Croatia. 2010 means 2010 eggs.

Late Sept **Grape Festival**
Various locations, Buje
www.istria-buje-buie.com
This opens the harvest with a donkey
race, grape-mashing and music shows.

Sept-Nov **Truffle Days**
Various locations
www.istria-gourmet.com
Tuberfests take place across Istria;
Buzet's and Livade's of special note.

October

Early Oct **Downhill Gračišće**
Various locations, Gračišće
www.istria-central.com
Extreme cycling on dirt roads.

Mid Oct **Labinjonski armonikaši**
RKUD Rudar Hall, Raša
www.istria-rabac.com
Accordion fest; lashings of folklore.

Late Oct **New Wine Festival**
Grimani Castle, Svetvinčenat
www.istria-svetvincenat.com
New wines in a historic setting.

Late Oct **Review of Grappa**
Church Square, Hum
www.istria-buzet.com
Rakija producers and aficionados gather
to sample clear, fruity spirits.

November

Early Nov **Children's Festival**
Sports Hall, Vrsar
www.istria-vrsar.com
Kids' talent show for St Martin's.

Early Nov **Glijvarijada**
Trg sv Zenona, Brtonigla
www.istria-brtonigla.com
Mushrooms are the focus of this event
near Buje: lectures, meals and music.

11 Nov **Martinja**
Various locations
www.istria.hr
For St Martin's, new wines are sampled
all over Istria.

December

From mid Dec **Christmas fairs**
Brtonigla & Pula
www.istra.hr
Yuletide craft fairs set up around Istria,
particularly in Pula and Brtonigla.

Itineraries

Wine & Olive Oil Routes

During the middle of the last decade, as Croatia was finding its bearings after the war that broke up Yugoslavia, Istria was already making some executive decisions about its future. The main one was simple albeit easier said than done: take the products the peninsula excels at producing, and refine them. Though the philosophy covers many products from truffles to *pršut* ham, the keys to it were olive oil and wine.

Vines and wines

Istria's new generation of vintners, whose families may have been producing wine for generations, have been undertaking five-year courses of specialist study. The local *konobas* remain picturesque but are being equipped with the latest technology. The general standard of production has improved beyond all recognition.

Many of the scores of producers across the peninsula compete in the annual Vin Istra fair, dedicated to supporting, educating and promoting Istrian wine producers.

The cultivation, production and, above all, consumption of wine is fundamental to Istrian culture. Whiling away a summer afternoon in a cool *konoba* sampling your host's wines direct from the barrel is a time-honoured tradition – and the best way to try it for yourself is to explore the Istrian Wine Roads. The Istrian Tourist Board produces a map listing 80 wine producers throughout the region. A car is essential, as the guide will take you to tiny, inland villages via winding country roads. The routes are signposted but a detailed road map is recommended.

Istrian vineyards

facilities. These range from humble *konoba* taverns to full-blown cellars. **Kabola**, in Kremenje, hosts a wine-making museum and slow-food events. Other top producers are Arman, Benvenuti, Damjanić Coronica, Kozlović, Matošević, Piquentum, Poletti and Sirotić. Of note is the vineyard of **Giogio Clai**, whose strong organic wines will instantly have you reaching for your wallet. An increasing number are also providing accommodation – **Matijašić** in Pekasi is a good example. Cross-refer venues on the Wine Road map with the Istrian Tourist Board's *Agrotourism* publication, both available from local tourist information offices or at www.istra.hr.

Oil fields

Istrian olive oil is some of the most expensive in the world. It's also some of the best. Because of its relatively high price, little of the oil is currently exported, so you really need to be here to experience it. Under the Romans, Istria was

For clarification, the phrases 'Wine Road' (and 'Olive Oil Road') are misnomers. You won't find the wines and oils down one specific road but dotted all over Istria. The highest concentration of quality production is in the north. While driving, you will see signs pointing to a producer who makes his house or cellar available for tasting and buying (often he will make both wine and oil). As a matter of protocol, it is best to call before visiting to make sure there is someone home before stopping by.

Malvasia, a white, is Istria's most famous wine. Teran, a red, follows close behind. You'll find Merlots, Chardonnays, Pinot Grigios and Cabernet Sauvignons, along with sparkling wines. Because Istria has two distinct soil types, there is a marked difference between wines produced in the coastal areas, such as Poreč, where the red soil enriches the wine structure, and those from the lighter soil of the hinterland, which tends to give a more delicate bouquet.

Most of the producers marked on the Wine Road map have tasting

Kozlović wine cellar

ITINERARIES

Winemakers

Umag/Novigrad

1 **Moreno Degrassi**/Savudrija 052 759 844/ www.degrassi.hr
2 **Moreno Coronica**/Umag 052 730 196
3 **Vina Kraljević-Cuj**/Marija Na Krasu 052 732 121
4 **Kabola-Marino Markezić**/Momjan 052 779 047 www.konoba-marino-kremenje.hr
5 **Armando & Franko Kozlović**/Momjan 052 779 177/ www.kozlovic.hr
6 **Armando & Rino Prelac**/Momjan 052 779 003
7 **Libero Sinković**/Momjan 052 779 032
8 **Veralda-Luciano Visintin**/Brtonigla 052 774 111/ www.veralda.hr
9 **Istravino-Podrum** Brtonigla 052 774 717
10 **Ravalico**/Brtonigla 052 774 152
11 **Vina Cattunar**/Brtonigla 052 774 722/ www.vina-cattunar.hr
12 **Giorgio Clai-Bijele Zemlje**/Krasica 091 577 6364
13 **Ibm-Vina**/Novigrad 098 976 8005
14 **Vinaria Novigrad** 052 726 060
15 **Leonardo Palčić**/Novigrad 052 735 354
16 **Davor & Boris Skrli**/Novigrad 052 735 269
17 **Nerino Visintin**/Brtonigla 052 774 417
18 **Bruno Fernetic**/Brtonigla 052 774 207
19 **Irineo Čelega**/Buje 091 511 5157
20 **Andrea Bassanese**/Buje 098 164 7665
21 **Andelo Brajko**/Momjan 052 779 077
22 **Vina Činić-Gambaletto**/Krasica 052 776 293/ www.gambaletto.com
23 **Antonio Cecco**/Brtonigla 052 774 132

Poreč & area

24 **Mladen Rozanić**/Nova Vas 052 421 367/ www.roxanich.com
25 **Agrolaguna**/Poreč 052 432 111/ www.agrolaguna.hr
26 **Vina Damjanić**/Poreč 052 444 553/ www.damjanic-vina.hr
27 **Valter Legović**/Kaštelir-Labinci 052 455 401
28 **Vina Cossetto**/Kaštelir-Labinci 052 455 204
29 **Elvio Kokolo**/Tar 091 506 6238
30 **Obitelj Radoš**/Kaštelir-Labinci 052 455 246

Vrsar & area

31 **Ivica Matošević**/Sv Lovrec 098 367 339/ www.matosevic.com

Central Istria

32 **Vina Zigante**/Grožnjan 052 776 320/ www.vina-zigante.hr
33 **Marko Dešković**/Grožnjan 052 776 315
34 **Elido Pilato**/Vižinada 052 446 281
35 **Marijan Arman**/Vižinada 052 446 229/ www.arman.hr
36 **Franc Arman**/Vižinada 052 446 226/ www.franc-arman.com
37 **Vina Rossi**/Vižinada 052 446 230
38 **OPG Gerzinić**/Vižinada 052 446 285
39 **Vina Radovan**/Višnjan 052 462 166
40 **Vina Polet** www.vina-poletti.com
41 **Mario Peršurić**/Višnjan 052 460 272
42 **Djordano Peršurić**/Višnjan 052 460 362
43 **Vina Matić**/Višnjan 052 449 382

44 **Vina Benvenuti**/Motovun 098 421 189/ www.benvenutivina.com
45 **Vinarija Matijašić**/Zamaski Dol 052 682 126
46 **Ranko Andelini**/Pazin 052 622 599
47 **Vina Visintin**/Pazin 052 621 146
48 **Dimitri Brečević-Piquentum**/Buzet 091 527 5976
49 **Dorjan Jakac**/Buzet 052 662 924
50 **Damir Širotić**/Buzet 052 663 027
51 **Dario Širotić**/Buzet 052 667 194
52 **Adriano Černeka**/Buzet 052 667 185
53 **Edo Pincin**/Završje 052 776 212
54 **Roberto Pulin**/Višnjan 052 449 156
55 **Guido Bernobić**/Višnjan 052 449 132
56 **Aldo Bernobić**/Višnjan 052 449 119
57 **Valter Zikovic**/Višnjan 052 449 336
58 **Andjelo Brčić**/Nova Vas 052 421 104
59 **Vina Vičinim**/Višnjan 052 651 883
60 **Josip Tidić**/Baderna 052 462 074
61 **Miro Petohleb**/Buzet 052 662 750
62 **Sergio Vivoda**/Buzet 052 662 913
63 **Ivan Jermaniš**/Buzet 052 667 141
64 **Diego Nežić**/Buzet 052 662 293
65 **Edvin Petohleb**/Buzet 091 507 9973
66 **Anton Grbac**/Buzet 052 667 130
67 **Franko Grbac**/Buzet 091 532 5120
68 **Zdravko Černeka**/Buzet 098 577 295
69 **Denis Markežić**/Buzet 052 669 158
70 **Adriano Putinja**/Grasisce 052 687 023
71 **Josip Bazon**/Gračišče 091 738 1458
72 **Renato Krulčić**/Pazin 091 738 1458
73 **Podrum Motovun Krančić** 052 616 616
74 **Obitelj Paljuh**/Karojba 052 422 211
75 **Vina Tomaz**/Motovun 052 681 997
76 **Vina Tikel**/Karojba 052 683 404

Rovinj & Bale

77 **Miroslav Pliso-Sv Meneghetti**, Bale 091 455 3221/www.meneghetti.info
78 **Davor Vivoda**/Rovinj 052 813 816
79 **Rino Šuran**/Rovinj 052 815 647
80 **Damir Dobravac**/Rovinj 052 813 006
81 **Igor Zužić**/Rovinj 052 848 502
82 **Zeljko Lanca**/Rovinj 052 821 009
83 **Mladen Matošević**/Rovinj 052 821 011
84 **Mirko Popović**/Rovinj 098 946 6508
85 **Giansandro Rudan**/Rovinj 052 815 719
86 **Silvano Trošt**/Rovinj 098 255 786

Pula & area

87 **Dario Marceta**/Valbandon 098 219 308
88 **Giacometti-Moscarda**/Vodnjan 052 511 237
89 **Demian-Dejan Milic**/Marcana 098 903 4330
90 **Josip Siljan**/Marcana 052 553 155
91 **Vina Trapan**/Pula 098 244 457/www.trapan.hr
92 **Podrum Vodnjan** 052 511 334
93 **Franko Macan**/Vodnjan 052 51160
94 **Sergio Bile-Biljni**/Barban 052 503 313

Labin & Rabac

95 **Goran Bačać**/Pićan 052 869 105
96 **Florian Radičanin**/Sv Nedelja 052 865 688
97 **Vina Zatka**/Krsan 052 867 424
98 **Vina Ružić**/Pićan 052 885 333
99 **Sinisa Sergo**/Pićan 052 850 653
100 **Doriano Licul**/Raša 052 875 063
101 **Romeo Licul**/Sv Nedelja 052 865 401

Wine Routes

SLOVENIA

CROATIA

Jelovice

Savudrija
1

Plovanija
3
20
19
Kaštel
4 5 6 7
Momjan
21

Petrovija
2

B9
Buje
22
8
33 53
Gružnjan
9 17 18
32
Brtonigla
10
11 12 23
21

69 49
Zrenj
62
Oprtalj
Livade
73
45
Motovun
44

Buzet
61 63
48
Sovinjak 64 65
Roč
Vrh
Prodani
50
67 66
Paladini
52 51
Hum
Draguć
68

15 16
13 14
Novigrad

Kaštelir-Labinci
29
Vabriga
Tar
28
40
Nova Vas
54
57 59
58
24
25
48
26
B9
31

35 36
37
Vižinada
34 55 56
Ferenci 76
Karojba
74

Beram
Pazin
47
46
Tinjan
70 71
Gračišće
72
64
95
Kršan
Brestova
66

Poreč

Funtana

Vrsar
Limski kanal

82 83
84
85
Rovinj
78 79
81 80

86

Bale

77
B9
21

Kringa

Žminj

Kanfanar

Svetvinčenat

Barban
Raša

94
66
Divšići

92 93
Vodnjan
88

Marčana
89 90

Labin
Rabac

99
96
101

100
Trget

Gulf of
Venice

Fažana
17
87
Brijuni Islands

Pula

91
Banjole
Premantura
Kamenjak
C. Promontore

Ližnjan
Medulin

0   10 km
0   5 miles

© Copyright Time Out Group 2010

Time Out Shortlist | Istria **41**

Olive Oil Producers

Umag/Novigrad

1 **Agrofin**/Savudrija 052 759 281/ www.agrofin.hr
2 **Leoni-Kraljević, Cuj**/Umag 098 219 277
3 **Alozije Pavlović**/Savudrija 052 737 097
4 **Uljara Pilar-Stella Maris**/Umag 052 751 395
5 **Al Torcio**/Novigrad 052 758 093/www.altorcio.hr
6 **Uljara Babić**/Novigrad 098 335 460
7 **Sv Roko**/Brtonigla 091 142 0738
8 **Agro Millo-Valter Smilović**/Buje 052 774 256
9 **Flavio Kmet**/Umag 052 463 786
10 **Enio Zubin**/Umag 052 732 158
11 **Olive Charm**/Umag 052 743 593/
12 **Branko Čeko**/Umag 052 751 801
13 **OPG Buršić**/Brtonigla 052 774 102
14 **Vina Cattunar**/Brtonigla 052 774 370/
15 **F&F Ravalico**/Brtonigla 098 219 045
16 **Renato Spitz**/Karigador 052 735 192
17 **San Rocco-Obitelj Fernetich**/Brtonigla 052 725 000/www.san-rocco.hr
18 **Veralda**/Brtonigla 052 774 111/www.veralda.hr
19 **Nerino Visintin**/Brtonigla 052 774 417
20 **Franco Basiaco**/Buje 052 772 189
21 **Marijan Cossetto**/Buje 052 776 184
22 **Ciai-Bijele Zemlje**/Buje 091 577 6364
23 **Nino Činić**/Buje 052 776 164
24 **Ulja Činić-Gambaletto**/Buje 052 776 293
25 **Remiggio Benvegnu**/Buje 052 776 189
26 **Romano Radešić**/Buje 052 776 275
27 **Bruno & Mario Radešić**/Buje 052 776 181
28 **Kabola-Marino Markežić**/Momjan 052 779 047/www.konoba-marino-kremenje.hr
29 **Franko Kozlović**/Momjan 052 779 177/
30 **Ivan Perossa**/Momjan 052 779 160
31 **Andjelo Brajko**/Momjan 052 779 077
32 **Robert Vuković**/Umag 091 520 4003
33 **Elvino Miletić**/Umag 052 751 402
34 **Armando Degrassi**/Umag 052 752 358
35 **Vedran Sinožić**/Novigrad 091 754 4161
36 **Aldo Zubin**/Novigrad 052 757 179
37 **Antonio Cecco**/Brtonigla 052 774 254
38 **Franko Fernetić**/Brtonigla 052 730 224
39 **Maurizio Scrignar**/Brtonigla 052 774 284
40 **Tulio Paoletić**/Brtonigla 052 774 345
41 **Obitelj Pregara**/Buje 052 774 465
42 **Bruno Vardabasso**/Buje 052 773 643
43 **Oriano Benvegnu**/Buje 052 776 379
44 **Roberto Goran Gardoš**/Buje 091 533 8926
45 **Silvino Radešić**/Buje 052 776 176
46 **Obitelj Valentić**/Buje 052 772 316

Poreč & area

48 **Agrolaguna Poreč** 052 432 111
48 **Obrad Kocijancic**/Kaštelir 052 455 109
49 **Farm Pino**/Baderna 052 462 341
50 **Obitelj Zužić**/Tar 052 443 141
51 **Paolo Mahne**/Kaštelir-Labinci 052 431 996
52 **MIH**/Poreč 052 432 224/www.mih.hr
53 **Uljara Torac**/Poreč 052 460 020
54 **Stipe Ogresta**/Poreč 052 431 926
55 **Andjelo Brčić**/Nova Vas 052 421 104

Vrsar & area

56 **Mario Vošten**/Sv Lovrec 052 448 403
57 **Zoran Mićetić**/Vrsar 052 441 328

Rovinj & area

58 **Meneghetti**/Bale 052 528 815/
59 **Uljara Grubić**/Bale 052 824 284

60 **Vedran Lupić**/Bale 098 369 917
61 **Uljara Novi Torac**/Rovinj 052 816 308
62 **Damir Dobravac**/Rovinj 052 813 006
63 **Zeljko Lanča**/Rovinj 052 821 009
64 **Dario Malusa**/Rovinj 052 817 138
65 **Mladen Matošević**/Rovinj 052 821 011
66 **Klaudio Pokrajac**/Rovinj 052 848 447
67 **Mirko Popović**/Rovinj 098 946 6508
68 **Giansandro Rudan**/Rovinj 052 815 719
69 **Anton Šturman**/Rovinj 099 598 7503
70 **Klaudio Šturman**/Rovinj 052 848 506
71 **Rino Šuran**/Rovinj 099 528 9960

Pula & area

72 **Brist Olive-Uljara San Lorenzo**/Linzjan 052 535 112/www.brist-olive.hr
73 **Antonio Pastrovicchio-Tonin**/Vodjnan 052 511 599
74 **Agroprodukt Uljara Vodjnan** 052 511 334
75 **Lorenzo & Livio Belci**/Vodjnan 052 511 035
76 **Maurizio Biasiol**/Vodnjan 052 511 644
77 **Sandi Chiavalon**/Vodnjan 052 511 906/
78 **Sergio Delton**/Vodnjan 052 511 518
79 **Livio Biasiol**/Vodnjan 052 511 356
80 **Aldo Cetina**/Vodnjan 052 573 168
81 **Giacometti-Moscarda**/Vodnjan 052 511 237
82 **Gianfranko Macan**/Vodnjan 052 511 606
83 **Lucio Toffetti**/Vodnjan 052 511 808
84 **Zeljko Mirković-Fiore**/Vodnjan 052 579 380
85 **Olea BB**/Rabac 052 872 724/www.oleabb.hr
86 **Perić-Ostojić**/Medulin 052 576 664/
87 **Obitelj Balija**/Fažana 052 521 565
88 **Dario Marčeta**/Pula 052 520 795
89 **OPG Crnobori Mario**/Pula 098 900 4446
90 **Mario Peršić**/Pula 052 505 882
91 **Mario Šimunović**/Galižana 052 511 248
92 **Ante Šučić**/Vodnjan 052 512 133
93 **Uljara Olea D'Oro**/Pula 052 534 646
94 **Baicco Andrej Djuric**/Galižana 052 512 473
95 **Odino Fioranti**/Vodnjan 052 511 040
96 **Livio Miljavić**/Vodnjan 052 511 403
97 **Livio Cossara**/Vodnjan 098 206 203
98 **OPG Matic-Terra Caviada Virgulan**/Pula 052 300 200/www.milan1967.hr

Central Istria

99 **Torkop-Sergio Černeka**/Buzet 052 663 058
100 **Djino Antonac**/Grožnjan 052 664 287
101 **Obitelj Cernaz**/Grožnjan 052 776 122
102 **Obitelj Pucer**/Grožnjan 052 776 116
103 **Viviano Antolović**/Grožnjan 052 776 107
104 **Obitelj Dešković**/Grožnjan 052 776 315
105 **Milan Vizintin**/Grožnjan 052 664 297
106 **Marija Šeme Baričević**/Grožnjan 052 776 128
107 **Klaudio Ipša**/Oprtalj 052 664 010
108 **Casa Maršić**/Oprtalj 052 664 202
109 **Giancarlo Zigante**/Oprtalj 052 777 409
110 **OPG Geržinić**/Vižinada 052 446 285
111 **Rossi**/Vižinada 052 446 230
112 **Robert Fatorić**/Vižinada 052 446 062
113 **Franko Vranić**/Vižinada 052 446 422
114 **Peter Poletti**/Višnjan 052 449 251
115 **Sanjin Sirotić**/Buzet 052 663 030
116 **Damir Sirotić**/Buzet 052 663 027
117 **Adriano Černeka**/Buzet 052 667 185
118 **Miljenko Prodan**/Buzet 052 665 057
119 **Lucio Bernobich**/Višnjan 052 449 160
120 **Dorjan Jakac**/Buzet 052 662 481
121 **Vlado Jerman**/Buzet 052 663 087
122 **Sandra Oklen**/Vižinada 052 446 101
123 **Miro Petohleb**/Buzet 052 662 750

Olive Oil Routes

a thriving centre for top-quality production. Because of its northerly latitude, olives ripen later and produce very few acids. They are far superior to those of Dalmatia for this reason. Although the crop yields only a relatively small amount of oil, the quality is the very finest. It is said that only olive oil from Istria – Terra Magica to the Romans – was allowed to grace the tables of the Caesars, and it was exported all over the Empire.

After the Romans left, the olive-oil trade largely disappeared and the fruit was harvested for local consumption only. After World War II cheap sunflower oil from Slavonia swamped the domestic market and family olive groves were mostly abandoned.

The resurgence of world-class production here is young and vibrant. Only in the last decade has there been a systematic approach in place and results are outstanding. In 2005 there were two Croatian producers listed in the Italian bible of olive oil, *L'extravergine*; in 2006 there were ten; and a year later, 24, 20 of those from Istria. The aim is to have one million olive trees planted in Istria before Croatia joins the EU, slated for 2012.

Oils can be smooth or piquant or both in a single mouthful. They are wonderful for cooking and slathering on fish. When trying quality oil you'll receive a small amount in a clear plastic cup. Cover the top with one hand and the bottom with the other to heat it up. Take a deep sniff to inhale the aroma. Then taste – try not to cough or risk looking like a rookie.

The Olive Oil map lists centres sited mainly around Buje and Oprtalj. There is a second, smaller cluster, further south, around Vodnjan, where the Romans based their production. You'll need a car – the map will lead you to tiny villages and hamlets, many set in spectacular landscapes.

Most producers have tasting rooms and a few types to try. Names include **Sergio Černeka**, **Stancija Meneghetti** and **Ipša**, set on a hill on the way to Oprtalj. In 1998, with only three trees left under cultivation, Klaudio Ipša (052 664 010, 098 219 538) reinstated 300 years of family tradition. Today he has 1,000 trees, and needs another 4,000 fully grown ones to compete in the UK market. He was also the first producer here to categorise his oil in the same way as wines.

Olives

Istria by Bike

Travelling along Istria's many biking trails is an ideal way to get an up close and personal view of the peninsula. Trails here shine a special light on its villages and character. You'll also get a sense of the area's history, which saw a succession of controlling groups starting with tribal Histrian clans, which submitted to the Romans in the third century BC. There are reminders of the different rulers and their prevailing architecture at every turn of the handlebars.

The pedalling is a mixed bag. There are asphalt-only routes, where cyclists are comfortable atop the skinny wheels of their road or touring bikes. The 93.5-kilometre (58-mile) Montanara Trail climb-a-thon from **Umag** (p87), which loops northern Istria, is a fine example of such a route. For the most part, plan on a mountain-bike-demanding combination of asphalt and macadam in varying ratios depending on preference. In total,

2,600 kilometres (1,615 miles) of trails stretch across Istria in every direction. For a complete list, see www.istria-bike.com. It makes recommendations for bikers' hotels, hire companies, sights to visit on the way and solid dining venues.

If you are a mountain biker or experienced road cyclist who prefers to enjoy their landscapes through wraparound lenses rather than a car's windshield, the first thing you'll notice here are the rolling hills and the seemingly endless possibilities for being on two wheels. If you're not a seasoned rider, you'll love the chance to spin around **Rovinj** (p54), for instance, at human speed while soaking in culture. You'll see the constant stream of fellow bikers hugging paved roadside shoulders or gliding along macadam byways. And if you are gastronome with a need to grind gears, you'll have the chance to earn that post-ride bowl of pasta smothered in truffles at trail's end.

The most numerous trails are found in the undulating terrain of the interior. One combining both grit and gourmet is the **Truffle's Trail**, which is about 60 per cent tarmac riding (40 per cent asphalt) and begins and ends in **Buzet** (p131). Starting at the foot of the **Ćićarija Mountains** (p131), the route covers nearly 35 kilometres (22 miles) and takes three hours to complete. The elevation gain is 870 metres (2,850 feet). Buzet, known to the Romans as Piquentum, was the seat of Venetian government in Istria; its architecture, including two town gates and a Baroque well, serve as reminders. Equally importantly for today's riders, it is also the City of Truffles. From here you'll head south and begin an almost immediate steep climb, and then skirt below the hilltop village of **Vrh** (p134). At this point the trail dives and soars until it again starts to head north following the **Mirna river**. At the two-thirds mark and after a descent, the path makes what has to be considered one the best planned ride stop-offs in Istria: the Yugo-era thermal spas of **Istarske Toplice** (p130).

The **Bella Vista** trail, which begins and ends in **Labin** (p150), is filled with what its title suggests: magnificent panoramas of Kvarner Bay and a continuous string of photo-ops. This easy-going to moderate trail is three-quarters asphalt so there's less need to worry about loose stones when readying the camera. The route travels 33 kilometres (20 miles) and should take roughly two hours to complete. The loop leaves the Old Town main square of this art-filled city and first heads inland, down the tiny, mini-peninsula in which Labin sits at its most northernly point. The route stays at between 300 and 500 metres (985-1,640 feet) in altitude until it reaches the

Poreč p71

Skitača mountain hut. About one kilometre away is a spring called the 'Tears of St Lucia', which, according to legend, can help those with bad vision. From here, you'll be bombing it downhill until **Ravni beach**. Take a swim and enjoy the rest – you'll need it for the steady 14-kilometre (nine-mile) climb along the eastern seaside rim of the trail back to Labin.

For culture, the **St Euphemia trail**, which rolls through Rovinj, is an ideal choice. A medieval town that was an island until 1763, when the channel separating it from the mainland was filled, Rovinj is Istria's main tourist attraction, with scores of galleries, fine restaurants and a posh atmosphere. St Euphemia refers to the grand church atop the hill guarding the city. The ride takes in Rovinj's sights with a majestic view of the town and the Adriatic beyond.

The circular route starts just south of Rovinj at the campsite in **Polari**, a coastal resort. A straightforward 27-kilometre (17-mile) ride with negligible altitude change, it spends the majority of its

Mirna river

time on asphalt. The jaunt takes about two hours and passes a good handful of medieval churches while travelling north and inland before heading south and back to the coast. It also comes within a stone's throw of the **Limski kanal** (p70), best known for its oysters.

Up the coast, the **Trail of Captain Morgan** and **Casanova** are two rides that straddle the Limski kanal and provide a quirky microscope on Istrian history. As the story goes, pirate Captain Morgan hid his treasure and himself near the canal while on the run. This moderate biking route, of equal parts path and road, starts just south of Rovinj and makes a 61-kilometre loop around the canal's head, through the town that bears the pirate's name – **Mrgani**, where his treasure is reportedly buried – before travelling south again through the beautiful cobbled town of **Bale** (p116).

On the north side of the canal, the Casanova trail is a quick, easy 22-kilometre (14-mile) ramble which begins and ends in **Vrsar** (p66), where the famous lover visited on two occasions in the 10th century for wine and women. The route follows much of the length of the Limski kanal, moving east from the mouth. More than 75 per cent tarmac, it is a roll through the country and relatively flat, so the trip should only take 90 minutes.

One of the longest and most challenging trails is the **Motovun East** ride, completely asphalt and cycle-friendly. At 72 kilometres (45 miles) it should take about four hours, but be warned that this route gains a total of nearly 1,500 metres (5,000 feet) en route. The circular ride starts with a heavy climb to the perfectly preserved Old Town of **Motovun** (p124), which stands over the truffle-filled forest and Mirna river below. This view attests to the town's former status as Istria's communications hub. Past the **Butoniga Lake**, the road rushes by the medieval settlement of **Draguć** (p132) and down to Istria's administrative centre of **Pazin** (p142) and its castle built in 983. From here it is mostly a descent back to the car park at the bottom of Motovun.

ITINERARIES

Aquarium, Pula p109

Istria for Kids

Istria has no theme parks and few sandy beaches with rides, stalls and arcades. Its tourist offering is somewhat highbrow – vineyards, gastronomic meccas and medieval churches. Alongside, however, there are a couple of obvious ways to keep the kids entertained, one coastal and one land-based.

Rail trail

The **Parenzana trail** follows the route of the railway that once connected Poreč and Trieste. The narrow-gauge line was constructed in 1902 and then dismantled in 1935. In 2002, plans were made to convert the derelict rail into a path. It now uses 61 kilometres (38 miles) of track bed; it leads over bridges and through old stone tunnels and links the territories of **Vižinada** (p136), **Motovun** (p124), **Oprtalj** (p136), **Grožnjan** (p136), and north-west through Buje (p87) and

Savudrija (p87), to the Slovene border. Along the way there is an elevation of 600 metres (1,970 feet); the trail is nearly all tarmac.

Today known as 'The Route of Health and Friendship', the trail can either be hiked or biked, ideal options for families. If need be, you could follow it in the car, a pity given all there is to see when moving at human speed between each of the villages along the way. If you break the trail into easily digestible hiking segments (say ten kilometres, six miles, per day, or 20 for serious hikers), the entire trek would take three days to a week. Groups can end each stage of trekking with a stay at different historic village each night.

One itinerary would start in Savudrija, on the north-western coast. Home to the oldest lighthouse in the Adriatic, this town is Croatia's westernmost point. From here, there's roughly

a ten-kilometre (six-mile) hike
to Buje, with its distinct two-bell
tower skyline and vineyard-covered
panorama, with negligible elevation
gain. The next stage is only six
kilometres (3.5 miles) but makes
up for it in climb. The reward: the
gallery-filled town of Grožnjan,
where kids can play in the streets
and squares of the magnificently
preserved medieval centre and
parents can sip wine and browse
the shops.

Day three's stage is the longest,
though it is virtually all downhill.
From Grožnjan to Oprtalj is 13
kilometres (eight miles). In Oprtalj
there are more than a dozen
churches to investigate, including
St Mary's with its renowned
frescoes. The next stage, a 12-
kilometre (7.5-mile) walk, makes
a big descent to the truffle-famous
town of Livade before climbing
again to one of the highlights:
Motovun. This storied settlement,
known for its film festival and
majestic views across the Motovun
Forest and Mirna river, is just
the spot to buy the makings for
tomorrow's lunch and rest up
for the final stage. Though only
12 kilometres (7.5 miles), this can
be a taxing climb. Its terminus
is Vižinada, whose town square
features a well built in 1722.
Several churches, most notably the
beautifully frescoed St Barnabas,
and the nearby Oklen lavender
fields, also await.

Fishy fun

When travelling along the coast,
taking the kids to an aquarium
provides a fun break from the
beach and it can be an educational
reminder that the sea is not only a
place to play. Just being near the
shore, you'll spot some fish darting
around in the Adriatic, but even
with a mask, snorkel and fins,

Novigrad p80

Poreč p71

you won't get the close-up view of marine life that an aquarium offers. But don't expect to see splashy Sea World-style displays of dancing whales and trained dolphins. The government has a policy of keeping the dolphins in the sea.

There are four aquariums along the south and west coasts of the Istrian peninsula. The **Pula Aquarium** (p109), the largest, was opened in 2002 and is set inside the Verudela Fort. There are 30 exhibits including a touch pool: an open-topped basin where visitors can pet the scary shark-shaped dogfish. There's also a turtle, crabs and sundry sea creatures. A tunnel through the back of the fortress leads to a freshwater pond containing fish native to Croatia's lakes and rivers. Other exhibits include fishermen's nets and traps, and underwater photography. The Pula Aquarium is also the home of the Marine Turtle Rescue Centre.

One of Istria's oldest aquariums is found along the west coast in Rovinj and based at the Rudjer Bošković Institute's Centre for Maritime Research. The **Rovinj Aquarium** (p58), founded in 1891, is in a stone building on the outskirts of Old Town; a decent collection of residents include a fearsome octopus, scorpion fish and lobsters. Further north, the **Poreč Aquarium** (p71) is in the heart of the old area of the city so fits in with other sightseeing expeditions. A modern venue, it contains 25 tanks displaying fish, flora and fauna from the Adriatic. Many artefacts have been donated by local fishermen.

The **Umag Aquarium** (1.svibnja, 052 721 041; summer daily 9am-11pm; admission 40kn and 25kn) in the north-western tip of Istria, is owned by the same company that runs the aquarium in Poreč and is quite similar. Opened in 2005 and set in a shopping centre near the Old Town, it contains 25 tanks, including one open-topped pool, all featuring species from the Adriatic.

Hum

Istria by Area

Poreč p71

West Coast

The west, specifically the coast, is the most stereotypically tourist-friendly of the regions in Istria. Starting in the south with **Rovinj** and stretching all the way up to **Savudrija**, Croatia's westernmost point, beach-focused resorts, sightseeing landmarks, seafood restaurants, party spots and family-based activities characterise the area. Though more tourist-oriented than the other regions, the towns and still retain, in large part, their character, with fishing skiffs and cafés crowding their harbours.

Rovinj is Istria's gem. The peninsular town, once an island, has a posh feel, with galleries scattered among the many bistros. Rovinj is also the only town in Croatia, capital Zagreb excepted, with any kind of gay scene.

Up coast, travellers can visit the **Limski kanal** and its fjord-sheltered wealth of oysters before making their way to the pleasant towns of **Funtana** and **Vrsar**, which Casanova visited on two occasions. **Poreč** sits in the middle of the region and holds the peninsula's calling-card attraction: the UNESCO-protected, mosaic-laden **Euphrasian Basilica**.

Moving north, the town of **Novigrad**, often overlooked by its more famous cousins down the coast, is a relaxing spot that retains a fisherman's heart and has a slew of solid eateries to prove the point. **Umag** is most famous for its annual pro tennis tournament, but is gradually attracting nightlife-seekers all summer. Savudrija hangs out on a point in the sea, making it a perfect place for the Adriatic's oldest active lighthouse built in 1818. Further inland, visitors can take a break from the beach and sun in the towns of **Buje** and **Brtonigla**, which rest in the heart of gourmet country.

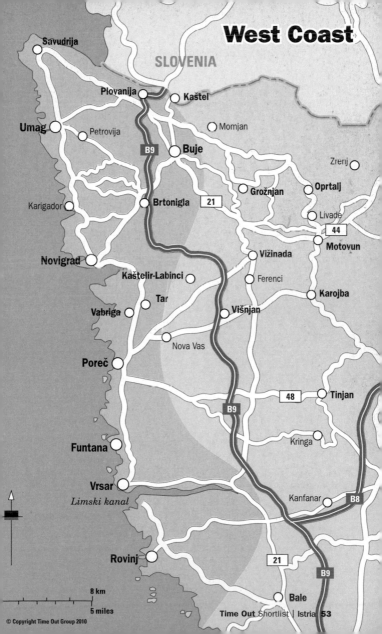

West Coast

SLOVENIA

Savudrija

Plovanija · Kaštel

Umag · Petrovija · Momjan

B9 · Buje

Zrenj

Karigador · Brtonigla · 21 · Grožnjan · Oprtalj

Livade

44

Novigrad · Kaštelir-Labinci · Vižinada · Motovun

Ferenci

Tar · Karojba

Vabriga · Višnjan

Nova Vas

Poreč

48 · Tinjan

B9

Kringa

Funtana

Vrsar · Kanfanar · B8

Limski kanal

Rovinj · 21

B9

8 km

5 miles · Bale

© Copyright Time Out Group 2010

Rovinj

Rovinj is Istria's showpiece; the peninsula's answer to Dalmatia's Dubrovnik, with far fewer crowds and a more realistic view of itself. It maintains a meticulously cared-for old quarter and extensive tourist amenities without feeling fake or overdone. The natural setting is stunning. Its harbour was nicknamed 'the cradle of the sea' by ancient mariners because the archipelago of islands, stretching from here to Vrsar, ensured calm, untroubled waters. The man-made structures in the Old Town are also attractive: tightly clustered old houses, painted in cheery Venetian reds and Habsburg pastels, all connected by cobbled streets barely wider than a footpath.

These attractions, combined with shaded, rocky beaches, have been bringing in groups of tourists since 1845, when a steamship line from Trieste stopped here. And yet tourism has not overwhelmed Rovinj or closed the local fishing trade, which still brings fresh catches to its excellent restaurants. Traditions are celebrated, hence the newly opened multimedia museum dedicated to the local batana fishing boat, **Batana House**. Rather than overdevelop, Rovinj has sought to retain its old charm, a charm for which tourists pay a premium. This is one of Croatia's nicer, and pricier, resort towns.

Before World War II, Rovinj was Italian, and the large Italian community, including many restaurateurs, encourages an emphasis on fine dining and good living. Many venues are dotted around the car-free Old Town, its shape defined by the hill created in 1763 when Habsburg engineers attached Rovinj island to the rest of Croatia, turning it into a peninsula. An easy stroll up the spiralling road to the top affords views of surreal beauty.

Sights & museums

Balbi's Arch

Trg maršala Tita. **Map** p55 B4 ❶
This 17th-century arch is the main entrance to Old Town, built on the site of the old town gate in 1678. The result, named after then mayor Daniel Balbi, is the grandeur still evident today:

Rovinj market

Rovinj

Rovinj

200 m
200 yds

© Copyright Time Out Group 2010

A **B** **C**

OBALA PALIH BORACA

PECINE

DIETRO LA GOTTA

Rovinj Aquarium **6**

3

BRAÆ LORENZETTO

Franciscan Monastery **5**

MARCA CARBINA

VLADIMIRA SVALBE

BREGOVITA

VLADIMIRA SVALBE

GIUSEPPE GARIBALDI

DRIOVIER

TREVI

AUGUSTO

ESMONDA DE AMICISA

PONTERA

4

Cathedral of St Euphemia **3** ✚ **12**

GRISIA

CASALE

SVALBA

GRISIA

34

PIETRO IVE

16

VLADIMIR GORTANA

14

18

35

CARERA

GIUSEPPA MAZZINA

40

32

GRISIA

25

GARZOTTO

9

7

29

1

OBALA ALDA RISMONDA

23

MONTALBANO

15

CADERA

GIUSEPPE CARDUCCHIA

21 **36**

TREVISOL

22

28

31

2

33

30

8

19

26

4

MATTEA BENUSSIA

27

SVETOGA KRIZA

24

13

38

RICCARDO DAPSTRA

N. QUARANTOTTO

5

OBALA VLADIMIRA NAZORA

OBALA ALDA NEGRI

17

1 Sights & museums
1 Eating & drinking
1 Shopping
1 Nightlife
1 Arts & leisure

3

10

37 **39**

a beautiful welcome of white stone blocks supporting the characteristic Venetian lion holding an open book, a reference to a time of peace. Opening out on to the main square of Trg maršala Tita, with its clock tower, fountain, pier, blue waters and fishing skiffs, this is a meeting point and place to begin any walking tour of Rovinj's small squares and cobbled streets. The Old Town was proclaimed a monument of culture in 1963.

Batana House

Obala P Budičina 2 (052 812 593, www.batana.org). **Open** *June-Sept* 10am-1pm, 7-10pm Tue-Sun. *Oct-Dec, Mar-May* 10am-1pm, 3-5pm Tue-Sun. Closed Jan, Feb. No credit cards. **Map** p55 B5 ❷

This has to be the Med's first multi media museum dedicated to a fishing boat. The craft in question is the *batana*, the traditional wooden vessel of the Rovinj region. Still very much in use today, the *batana* is a living symbol of Rovinj culture. This modern museum features film, music and interactive exhibits, plus guides in traditional costumes, and workshops where you can try your hand at making fishing nets or demijohns.

Cathedral of St Euphemia

Petra Stankoviča (052 815 615). **Open** 10am-6.30pm daily. **Admission** free. **Map** p55 A4 ❸

This Venetian Baroque structure was built between 1725 and 1736 to house the remains of Euphemia, a virgin martyr, who was fed to the lions by the Roman Emperor Diocletian in around 304. Legend has it that Euphemia's massive stone coffin disappeared from Constantinople, floating ashore in Rovinj in 800, thus providing a fishing town with a catch from heaven and a patron saint at the same time. St Euphemia's tomb and relics can be seen inside the cathedral; panoramic vistas stretch all the way from this hilltop vantage point.

Church of the Holy Trinity

Trg na Lokvi. **Map** p55 C5 ❹

The heptagonal, 13th-century church, today a gallery, combines Romanesque and Gothic influences. It is the among the town's oldest and best preserved buildings. Under its double-tiered, domed, terracotta roof is a transenna with the images of Mary, St John the Baptist, St Peter and St John the Evangelist. This architectural find sits, in all places, at Rovinj bus station.

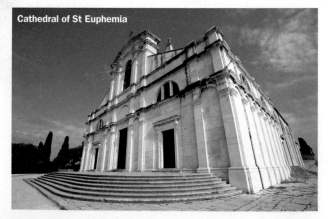

Cathedral of St Euphemia

One nightspot fits all

Rovinj's one-stop **Monvi Center** makes it easy to find the party. Essentially what it does is to gather all the best places to drink and dance, and put them in a single place. The concept simplifies matters considerably for party-minded visitors and locals alike. For Rovinj's city officials, Monvi corrals and consolidates the rough-housing away from the otherwise family-centric tourist hub in town.

The large complex contains a pizzeria, and Mexican-themed and fast-food restaurants. There's a games room. Most importantly, it has multiple discos and bars that are jammed all year long. There's a bar dedicated to Croatian pop and folk music called the In-Balkan Bar. Another, Summer Bar Mangus, is devoted to rock. La Playa is the cocktail lounge. Presidente is a dance club with go-go girls. Club Temple's dance floor has a 1,500-person capacity.

A key site within the centre is the open-air Amfiteatar, which hosts concerts, contains a pool bar and has become a major destination for touring bands or DJs. On summer nights its club can see some serious talent on the decks and on the dancefloor. It can also get expensive by nightlife standards in this part of the world. Last year Monvi hosted John Digweed to the tune of 180kn a head, although generally admission prices stick to the 70kn-80kn range.

The collection of bars can feel a bit shopping-mallish, but as the evening wears on, there's a sense of security in knowing there are about a half a dozen places to slip away to for a drink and a chat. The club is south of town, near the big resort hotels but far enough away for everything to go on all night.

The Monvi is well established but its key venues might need to raise their game to compete with the recently introduced superclub Byblos in nearby Poreč, and with its superior sound system. This is a fickle game, after all.

Franciscan Monastery

De Amicis 36. **Map** p55 C4 **⑤**
Completed in 1710, this monastery is dedicated to St Francis of Assisi. Its library holds 12,000 books dating back to the 16th century. There is also a museum, which shines a light on traditional arts and crafts, including the 'Reliquary of the Holy Cross and the Torture Pole' from the 18th century. Classical music events take place within the Baroque building.

Rovinj Aquarium

Giordana Paliage 5 (052 804 712).
Open *Apr-Nov* 9am-9pm daily.
Admission 20kn. **Map** p55 C3 **⑥**
Opened in 1891 as an adjunct to Berlin's Aquarium, this modest venue is set in the villa housing the Maritime Institute of the Rudjer Bošković Institute. Here, in the dark interior, you can see the creatures you might later find on your dinner plate: *hobotnica*, *jastog* and *škrpina*; octopus, lobster and scorpion fish, all kept in clean tanks.

Rovinj Heritage Museum

Trg maršala Tita 11 (052 816 720, www.muzej-rovinj.com). **Open** *Summer* 9am-3pm, 7-10pm Tue-Fri; 9am-2pm, 7-10pm Sat, Sun. *Winter* 9am-3pm Tue-Sat. **Admission** 15kn. **Map** p55 B4 **⑦**
Opened in 1954, this museum in a red Baroque palace contains something for everyone. The permanent collection includes Roman finds, Renaissance paintings, 1,500 Croatian contemporary art pieces and a maritime exhibition. Only a percentage of the holdings are displayed. Organisers find room elsewhere for monthly events that cover the art spectrum.

Eating & drinking

Amorfa

Obala Alda Rismondo 23 (052 816 663). **Open** 11am-midnight daily.
KKK. **Restaurant**. **Map** p55 C5 **⑧**
The harbourside Amorfa is one of the pricier places in town, but slick service

and impressive decor (indoor goldfish pond, nicely appointed terrace) help make the meal an event. Dishes include hearty portions of excellently prepared seafood standards, along with specialities like salted sea bass.

Balbi Restaurant

Veli trg 2 (052 817 200). **Open** *Apr-Oct* 11am-11pm daily. **Restaurant**.
K. No credit cards. **Map** p55 B5 **⑨**
A solid place to eat with locals' prices in a quaint piazza through the arch on the Old Town side of the main square, Balbi serves up dishes including fish soup, octopus salad and pork chops with fries, all at rock-bottom prices. Sea bass with potatoes comes in at 75kn. The small dining room has a busy vibe; most choose the big, covered terrace.

Blu

Val de Lesso 9 (052 811 265). **Open** *Summer* 10am-11pm daily. **KKK**.
Restaurant. **Map** p55 C3 **⑩**
Blu has a great location, best enjoyed over a leisurely lunch. Starter, swim, main, swim, dessert, swim. Peruse the menu over a Malvazija wine and home-made, pizza-style focaccia bread with rosemary, sea salt and award-winning olive oil produced nearby. Food is fish-and seafood-based and ranges from a simple seafood spaghetti through to scallops with truffles and polenta, or sea bass with caviar and saffron. Simple roast fish with potatoes is the ideal dish to be shared among a table of four. The chocolate soufflé is scrumptious. Prices are lower than you'd imagine considering the quality and view over the sea to Rovinj's Old Town. Inside, evening dining is more formal, around an old Roman garden.

Caffè Bar Copacabana

Obala Pina Budičina 1 (091 205 0034 mobile). **Open** *Apr-Oct* 7am-2am daily.
No credit cards. **Café**. **Map** p55 B5 **⑪**
On the waterfront by the fishermen's boats, Copacabana serves sandwiches, *pršut* ham, cheese, kebabs, salads, ice-

cream, coffee and decadent desserts such as banana splits with little umbrellas. It also serves beer and the harder stuff under a giant corner-engulfing terrace that shelters different comers for different reasons: tourists drawn in by the shade; families drawn by complaint-silencing *gelato*; and folks after a quick budget-minded bite.

Caffè Bar XL
Sv Križa (no phone). **Open** *Summer* 10am-2am daily. No credit cards.
Café. Map p55 A4 ⑫
Possibly the one spot you should seek out for a drink, coffee or otherwise, in Rovinj. It is all about location. Sitting by the Cathedral atop the Old Town, it has fine views of the sea and the sunset. Wicker chairs and wooden tables overlook a field, then the view dives straight to the water. XL serves Favorit on tap, house wines, cocktails and fruit juices such as mango or guava.

Caffè Cinema
Trg Brodogradili (no phone). **Open** *Winter* 7am-midnight Mon-Thur, Sun; 7am-1am Sat. *Summer* 7am-2am daily. No credit cards. **Café.** Map p55 C5 ⑬
A fashionable terrace adds a touch of class to this busy corner of the harbour, drawing a sizeable, mixed crowd. The spacious, dramatic, black-and-white interior is dedicated to great films, with classic stills and a life-sized Alfred Hitchcock doing his cameo in the bathroom mirror. Behind the long bar is an oversized clock and, generally, a smiling face serving drinks. Music ranges from pop to electronic to hip hop.

Calisona
Trg na mostu 4 (052 815 313). **Open** *Feb-Dec* 8am-midnight daily.
KK. Fish restaurant. Map p55 B4 ⑭
Just beyond Balbi's Arch you'll find a small square and a large covered terrace where diners tuck into sophisticated seafood. Along with Istrian standards like fettuccine with truffles, lobster with tagliatelle and succulent

fresh grilled fish, there are creative offerings such as squid stuffed with scampi and sole in chardonnay. The alternatives for carnivores include steak and a grill platter for two.

Enoteca Al Gastaldo
Iza Kasarne 14 (052 814 109/099 555 2244 mobile). **Open** 11am-3pm, 6pm-midnight daily. No credit cards. **KKK. Restaurant.** Map p55 B5 ⑮
Sitting on a quiet little corner, Enoteca serves fine seafood amid a cosy clutter of antiques and paintings, around an Istrian-style fireplace used for cooking. This family-run restaurant is not the cheapest, but it's perfect for that special meal with that special someone. Fresh shellfish, sole and lobster are dressed in superior sauces. Specialities include meat dishes baked in a clay oven. In summer, a terrace is set out for alfresco, if not sea-view, dining.

Giannino
Augusto Ferri 38 (052 813 402). **Open** *Summer* 11am-3pm, 6-11pm Tue-Sun, 6-11pm Mon. *Winter* 11am-3pm, 6-11pm Tue-Sun. **KKK. Restaurant.** Map p55 B4 ⑯
This popular spot by the Old Town draws repeat customers. Giannino specialises in Istrian-fused Italian cuisine. The menu features fresh catches from Rovinj's fishermen; the sauces and the pastas have a distinctly Italianate influence. Istrian touches include rigatoni with lobster.

Havana Club
Obala Alda Negria (no phone). **Open** *Apr-Oct* 9am-2am daily. No credit cards. **Bar.** Map p55 C5 ⑰
On the water down from the bus station, Havana is a peaceful shaded oasis with bamboo chairs and sun umbrellas framed by rum bottles. The brick patio, with an Easter Island head at the entrance, looks out to the marina. Palms stand in giant stone vases. Here you can order 'natural drinks': mango, melon, passion fruit and pineapple.

Beach escapes

Miles of beaches and indented shore in Rovinj's general area, starting south around the port of Veštar and north to the Limski kanal, provide an escape from the tourist grind. The best sites are away from the Old Town, but hardly a trek.

In town there is a small, busy beach area by the **Hotel Rovinj**, currently closed for a refurb. For the pine-forested beaches at the edge of town, take sandals to wade on the jagged shore. The lack of sand means the sea is incredibly clear, ideal for snorkelling or diving.

Sv Katarina Island and **Sv Andrea** or **Crveni ('Red') Island**, offer beach fun a hop by taxi boat from Rovinj's main harbour.

Head south of town, past the marina and the Hotel Park, to the area south of Monte Mulini – Lone Bay – and the wooded peninsula of **Zlatni Rt** (Golden Cape) for some of the best sunbathing. The walk along the water is just over a kilometre from town. There is a cluster of resorts around here, but it's all uphill, so the beaches are mostly undisturbed nature.

If you keep going south, there are quiet stretches to find your own private boulder to sun on. Some three kilometres (two miles) south of town you'll find two nudist beaches, **Polari Bay** and the adjacent **Cape Eve**. The 13 small islands around here have thick forests lined by rocky beach, with a remote feel.

For details of beaches and sea getaways, see www.rovinj.info.

Alternatively, savour the Alabama Slammer of Southern Comfort, vodka, amaretto, grenadine and orange juice.

Kavana Al Ponto

Monsena (052 805 500). **Open** 7am-midnight daily. No credit cards. **Café**. **Map** p55 B4 ⑱

By a line of cafés near the main square, Al Ponto has a posh little sweet-shop interior, marble floors and wooden tables on private-ish nook landings. Amid an old-fashioned brass bar with black-and-white photos of Rovinj and little tidbits of history in English, families enjoy sugary treats such as ice-cream, milkshakes, iced coffee, baklava and tiramisu. The menu also offers domestic beer and wine.

Konoba Kantinon

Obala Aldo Rismondo (052 816 075). **Open** *Apr-Nov* 11am-3pm, 6pm-midnight daily. **KK**. **Restaurant**. **Map** p55 C5 ⑲

An old-fashioned cantina on the waterfront, Kantinon has much the same interior as it did when fishermen drank here and lamented long days of work. There's a giant wine barrel in the centre and ox yokes on the walls. A large colour photo of Rovinj hangs behind the bar, where you can fill bottles of wine, merlot and malvasia, for 65kn a litre. The staff have an old-school, get-it-yourself charm. Give in to it and order from the barrel-shaped menus: grilled shrimp and sea bass are among the choices.

Konoba Lampo

Sv Križa 22 (052 811 186). **Open** *Mar-Dec* 11am-midnight daily. **KK**. **Restaurant**. **Map** p55 A5 ⑳

Disregard the photos of the food and the sign reading 'Fish-Meat'. The place is touristy, no doubt, but the choices are good and the prices are reasonable. And you simply can't beat the view. On a steep little two-tiered overhang with bamboo and canvas sunshades, you'll eat mussels, shrimp, salads and pastas

Rovinj

while staring down at the water and away from the more touristy spots along the harbour.

La Puntulina

Sv Križa 38 (052 813 186). **Open** noon-3pm, 6pm-midnight daily. *Cocktail bar* 6pm-2am daily. KKK. No credit cards. **Restaurant/bar**. **Map** p55 A5 ㉑

Perched on a drop above the sea, this spot adds a gourmet Italian touch to local cuisine. La Puntulina starts with the same fresh ingredients sold around town, but its dishes stand out by virtue of creative sauces and a careful mix of flavours. The fish fillet Puntulina, with a delicately spiced tomato sauce, the scallops in brandy, and the local squid in polenta provide exciting ways to enjoy fresh seafood. Get the table by the window and afterwards go down to the cocktail bar, with a stunning secluded terrace by the sea.

Mali Raj

Trevisol 48 (052 816 242). **Open** *mid Apr-Oct* 10am-3pm, 6pm-midnight daily. KK. No credit cards. **Restaurant**. **Map** p55 A5 ㉒

Another good local place that gets overlooked for the mediocre ones on the harbour, Mali Raj ('Little Heaven'), is below the Cathedral but strangely off the tourist conveyor belt. Owned by the Lesdedaj family, the bistro has all the basics: seafood spaghetti; tagliatelle with truffles; and black risotto. Diners sit on a pleasant terrace covered in grapevines just off a stone passage.

Monte

Montalbano 75 (052 830 203). **Open** *Apr-mid Oct* noon-2.30pm, 6.30-10.30pm daily. KK. **Restaurant**. **Map** p55 A4 ㉓

Standing like an apparition just below the Cathedral of St Euphemia, Monte offers fine dining with an informal, funky feel. This is fusion with Istria at its heart. The ingredients from Rovinj market are given new life thanks to

owners Tjitske and Danijel Djekić, who recommend the five-course, three-hour degustation menu with an array of delicate creations, a choice of suckling pig or lamb and wines (they have more than 100) to suit each dish.

Monte Carlo Caffè Bar

Sv Križa 21 (no phone). **Open** *Apr-Nov* 8am-1am daily. No credit cards. **Café**. **Map** p55 A5 ㉔

It's dark inside Monte Carlo, where exposed stone meets a hodgepodge of antiques scattered about the place. Pseudo-classic murals are thrown in, with carnival masks, random lamps and paintings. But who cares? The seaside terrace across the car-free street tapers down to a ledge on the water, ideal for après-beach. This is the budget version of the pricier places along a street of galleries and chi-chi cafés.

Piassa Granda

Veli trg 1 (052 811 374/098 824 322 mobile). **Open** *Summer* 10am-1am daily. *Winter* 10am-11pm daily. **Wine bar**. **Map** p55 B4 ㉕

Ex-lawyer Helena Trošt moved from Zagreb to Rovinj to open this wine bar, shop and café. Set in Veli trg, the main square when Rovinj was an island, Piassa Granda has the interior of a serious wine haunt. Under wooden beams with ceiling fans, the shelves are filled with 150 labels, 130 of them Istrian. All can be sampled on site, most by the glass, or taken home. Clai, Poletti and top varieties can be found; a fifth of them are offered by the bottle. Sandwiches, truffle biscuits, truffle *rakija*, top-end olive oil and salads are also sold, plus rarer beer brews such as Chimay Blue and Rochefort 8.

Trattoria Dream

Joakima Rakovca 18 (052 830 613). **Open** 11.30am-11.30pm daily. KKK. **Restaurant**. **Map** p55 C5 ㉖

On a bustling Old Town side street just in from the harbour, TD tries hard, and mostly succeeds. The food is good and

Blu p58

the service friendly, but prices aren't cheap, especially for wine. The charming interior has a working fireplace and skylight. Seafood includes salted sea bass, salmon, tuna and frogfish.

Valentino

Sv Križa 28 (052 830 683). **Open** *Winter* noon-midnight daily. *Summer* 6pm-2am daily. No credit cards. **Bar**. Map p55 A5 ㉗

Grab a hold of the rope railing and walk gingerly down the marble steps just off Sv Križa and into this pricey cocktail bar, set at the end of the harbour. It has fabulous outdoor seating on a terrace just over the sea. Get off the tourist path, lose the crowds and commune with nature, your cocktail and your companion.

Veli Jože

Sv Križa 1 (052 816 337). **Open** 11am-midnight daily. **KKK. Restaurant**. Map p55 B5 ㉘

Istrian-style dishes comprise the menu at this quaint spot near the harbour with a high-ceilinged interior crammed with antiques and sea-going kitsch. There is seating for 40 on a pavement terrace. Specialities include shellfish lasagne, crab with truffles, cod in white wine and baked lamb with potatoes.

Viecia Batana

Trg maršala Tita 8 (091 539 9172 mobile). **Open** 7am-1am daily. No credit cards. **Café**. Map p55 B4 ㉙

Something of a landmark, Viecia Batana is popular with locals for breakfast or an early-evening drink. The terrace has a sunny southern exposure facing the busy harbourside square by the Hotel Adriatic and the sea beyond. Neighbouring bars share the view, but they're never quite as full. Your coffee may take a minute longer, but it will arrive with a smile.

Zanzibar

Obala Pina Budičina (052 813 206). **Open** 9am-1am daily. No credit cards. **Bar**. Map p55 B5 ㉚

Big, loungey wicker chairs with bright red cushions surround low drinking tables on the terrace of this oriental-themed cocktail bar near a busy section of the harbour. At happy hour, tables fill with people keen to gawp at other people or the gorgeous sunsets over the sea. There's a covered patio behind see-through orange tapestries, where you can sprawl on cushioned divans. Inside, the DJs encourage you to hang around for the rest of the night, an enjoyable if pricey proposition in the case of some cocktails.

Shopping

Art Antique

Vrata pod Židom 4 (052 812 004).
Open *May-Oct* 10am-2pm, 6-11pm
daily. **Map** p55 B5 ③①

The name of this shop, on a little side-street just off the harbour promenade, reflects what's inside. Offering a mix of old oddities and knick-knacks, it's a good way to avoid the Croatian souvenir clichés and learn a little about the antiques collected on this side of Europe. As well as paintings, old photographs, furniture, parasols and hats, there are driftwood sculptures made by the owner and jewellery from local designers. Prices range from three to 3,500 euros for the French candelabras.

Atelier Devescovi

Grisia 13 (098 928 6711 mobile).
Open *Apr-Nov* 10.30am-11.30pm daily.
No credit cards. **Map** p55 B4 ③②

The setting couldn't be better: Rovinj's gallery promenade leading up to the Cathedral, in a lovely late Renaissance palace from the 17th century, with a wrought-iron balcony. Here 33-year-old artist Dean Devescovi sells paintings that combine draughtsmanship and abstract influences. The subjects are generally insects or jazzmen; jazz also plays in the stone space with amphorae randomly scattered. The paintings are acrylic on canvas with artistic splatterings, and range from 50 to 1,200 euros.

Atelier Sottomuro

Vrata pod Židom 2 (091 732 9164 mobile, www.ateliersottomuro.com).
Open *May-Nov* 10am-2pm, 7-10.30pm daily. **Map** p55 B5 ③③

This gallery is a super little find for someone looking for reasonably priced, interesting art made right in town. The artist is Jan Ejsymontt, who grew up in England and hung a shingle at the base of the Porta di Sottomuro, one of the original seven city gates, five years ago. Her paintings are generally acrylics, some with shards of stone and tiles incorporated, giving the pieces a three-dimensional quality. Inside the small, all-white interior, Jan ('Yan') also makes jewellery from stones, silver and interesting tidbits she finds during her travels. She'll arrange for the export of larger pieces. Prices in the shop range from 45 to 500 euros.

Rovinj market

Trg Valdibora. **Open** 7am-4pm daily.
No credit cards. **Map** p55 B4 ③④

Valdibora hosts a hectic open-air market selling the day's catch and local produce. The array of fresh seafood is reason enough to go self-catering.

Sheriff & Cherry p65

Browsing is great fun and there are plenty of items you can take with you: home-made grappa, wine and lavender oil. By 1pm, many fresh-food vendors go, leaving souvenir shops to hawk knick-knacks made from shells, Croatian-flag beach towels, paintings, postcards and sundry non-essentials.

Sheriff & Cherry

Karera 6 (052 842 310, www.sheriff andcherry.com). **Open** *Summer* 9am-9pm Mon-Sat; 9am-2pm Sun. *Winter* 10am-4pm Mon-Fri; 10am-2pm Sat, Sun. **Map** p55 B4 ③

A minimalist white space with imaginative maritime touches displays a range of delectable goodies from Jordi Labanda, Juan Antonio López and other urban stylists. Modish sportswear is a strong suit. The brainchild of Rovinj-born Mauro Massarotto, fashion consultant in Barcelona, S & C has proved a great success, expanding into Zagreb and Dubrovnik.

The Sixth Sense

Sv Križa 39 (052 812 525/099 704 2931 mobile). **Open** 11am-2pm, 6pm-midnight daily. **Map** p55 A5 ③

Part gallery, part atelier, part art education and part slow-food experience, the Sixth Sense pulls together assorted artistic forces in a little shop on Rovinj's southwest edge. Nominally it is the atelier of Nataša Fiala, who paints on the basement floor with the sound of the sea splashing against the walls. Her work is for sale along with pieces by other photographers and sculptors. The space also works as an improv eaterie, with decent scran, fine coffee and quality wine.

Nightlife

Monvi Center

Luja Adamovića, Monvi (052 545 117, www.monvicenter.com). **Open** *Summer* 11am-5am daily. *Winter* according to event. **Map** p55 C5 ③
See box p57.

Arts & leisure

Batana Photo Art Gallery

Trg brodogradilišta 2 (no phone). **Open** *Summer* 9am-noon, 7-10pm Mon-Fri, Sun; 9am-noon Sat. *Winter* according to event. **Admission** free. **Map** p55 C5 ③

A perfect place for photography, this white-walled, marble-floored gallery has monthly shows that run the gamut from astronauts to post-war. Funded by the Italian community and the tourist office, it's a central and accessible place to see top work at good prices. Curator Marijana is savvy and speaks English. Openings may have the photographer and/or subjects on hand.

Galleria Adris

Obala Vladimira Nazora 1 (052 801 312, www.adris.hr). **Open** *Apr & Nov* 5-9pm daily. *May & Sept* 6-8pm daily. *June-Aug* 7-11pm daily. **Admission** free. **Map** p55 C5 ③

Run by the Adris investment group, this private gallery has shows every two months, the openings violin and bubbly affairs. Paintings, and sometimes sculpture, are set over two floors against a backdrop of the marina, seen through giant floor-to-ceiling windows. Big money has created a stunning place to enjoy Croatian-only works.

Grisia

Map p55 A5 ④

This stone-paved thoroughfare leading up to the Cathedral is the best place to find Rovinj's noted galleries, plus ateliers and shops selling crafts and amateur seascapes. In summer, most spill on to the pavement. On the second Sunday in August, amid music and wine, there's a one day, open-air art exhibition, when any artist can set up shop here. On display, and covering every inch of available wall space, is everything from handbags, jewellery, fine art and painted plates to snow globes. A discerning patron can leave with a few good deals or serious kitsch.

Vrsar

Vrsar & Funtana

Vrsar has a different feel to its
larger neighbours. The natural
landscape is more in evidence.
It's more genteel. Like Istria in
miniature, this medieval hilltop
town, with its 12th-century
Romanesque bishop's palace,
sits above a natural harbour at the
mouth of the Limski kanal, with its
own mini-archipelago of islands.

Casanova fell in love with the
place – its Venetian-style
architecture lining narrow streets,
its wine and its women – and he
wrote about it in his copious
memoirs. Legend has it that he
spread enough disease on his first
visit here to make the local doctor
rich. Not surprisingly, the doctor
invited him back. He accepted.

Vrsar was the site of the first
all-nudist colony in Europe and,
in its historical heyday, the seat of
the Poreč bishopric. A more recent
feature of note is **Montraker**,
an abandoned stone quarry on
the main beach near the promenade
where the town's social action takes
place. Already known for its
sculpture summer schools, this
stunning setting framed by nature
stages an ongoing beach party and
the Casanova 'Love & Erotic' fest
inaugurated in 2008.

Two kilometres up the coast
is the lesser-known village of
Funtana, which gets its name
from a freshwater spring on its
northern edge. It comprises a string
of bays and inlets that stretches
from Zelena Laguna to Valkanela.
The centre, on the road from Poreč
to Vrsar, is awash with drive-by
offerings. Significant stops include
a 200-berth marina, a string of 30
restaurants, three campsites (one
naturist) and the **Resort Funtana**.

Sights & museums

Basilica of St Mary of the Sea

Obala maršala Tita, Vrsar (no phone).
On the harbour between the Montraker
quarry and the seaside promenade, St
Mary's is a Romanesque church first
built in the eighth century. Over the
next 400 years the structure was mod-
ified, and what you see today is a 12th-
century incarnation. The three-nave
church hosted Pope Alexander III
when he celebrated Mass here in 1177.

Dušan Džamonja Sculpture Park

Valkanela 5, Vrsar (052 445 260, www.dusan-dzamonja.com). **Open** *Mar-Oct* 9am-8pm Tue-Sun. *Nov-Feb* 9am 5pm Tue-Sun. **Admission** free.

On the road north to Poreč, between Vrsar and Funtana, the Sculpture Park is a ten-hectare, outdoor display of Džamonja's works over a rolling grass field. The pieces are abstract and made of marble, aluminium, granite and cement. Džamonja earned his reputation in the 1960s for his original use of shapes and materials. His work has appeared at the Tate Modern and the Museum of Modern Art in New York.

Parish Church of St Bernard & Borisi Castle

Trg sv Bernarda, Funtana (no phone). The church, originally one nave and built in 1621, bears the coat of arms of the Borisi family, former town patrons. Inside are multiple oil paintings of Mary and child, one from the 17th century, among the most valuable pieces of artwork in town. Nearby is Borisi Castle, dating back to 1610.

St Martin Church

Gradska Vrata 9, Vrsar (no phone). **Open** *Bell tower* 10am-noon, 5-7pm daily. **Admission** *Church* free. *Bell tower* 10kn.

Though beautiful, there's nothing that really sets this relatively young (1804), three-nave church apart beyond its position in the main square, near the 12th-century Bishop's Palace known as Kaštel. Its bell tower, built in 1991, provides wonderful views of Vrsar's archipelago and, on clear days, Venice to the west and the Alps to the north.

Eating & drinking

Al Porto

Obala maršala Tita 33, Vrsar (052 441 001). **Open** 6am-1am daily. No credit cards. **Café**.

Al Porto offers 48 types of ice-cream (plus six diabetic choices) and a mind-boggling array of sundaes, complete with paper umbrellas and lashings of whipped cream. Its terrace on the quayside is where the fishing boats moor, a prime location for 'Fishermen's Fests', and the main reason it opens so early. In bad weather, don't be surprised to see it filled with card-playing sea salts.

Buba

Dalmatinska 8, Vrsar (no phone). **Open** *July, Aug* 7am-2am daily. *Sept-June* 7am-midnight daily. No credit cards. **Bar**.

Buba is Croatian for 'bug' – there's half a VW Beetle suspended over the entrance. You'll find more inside, along with Hajduk Split football shirts and, weirdly, ancient terracotta amphorae. There are also square leather chairs and a big screen over the fireplace for football. This local hangout is buzzing even out of season; on summer weekends there's also a DJ in residence.

Café L'Angelique

Orlandova 47, Vrsar (098 570 352 mobile). **Open** *Apr-Nov* 8am-1am daily. No credit cards. **Café**.

The best spot for coffee in town, L'Angelique opened in 2007. The beans, organic Arabica, are imported direct from farms in Bolivia, the Galapagos and Ethiopia, and you can taste the difference. Inside has a French feel: a swirl of marble; a glass case with home-made cakes; and little abstract paintings. The café sports two terraces, one by the front door, the other behind the bell tower. Owner Tomislav Maslać's mean cocktails complement tap beers and wines.

Fančita

Dalmatinska 38, Vrsar (052 441 019). **Open** *May-Oct* noon-11pm daily. No credit cards. **Pizzeria**.

Vrsar has plenty of pizzerias, but this was voted one of the top five in Istria. The main dining area is the large, roofed terrace, which makes up for its lack of sea views with rustic knick-knacks. Inside, the traditional wood-fired oven is the main draw. This is a relaxed, family-run restaurant, with plenty of traditional Istrian dishes and a good local wine list.

Istarska konoba

Koštar 11, Vrsar (052 444 599). **Open** *Summer* noon-11pm daily. *Winter* 4-11pm Mon, Tue, Thur, Fri; noon-11pm Sat, Sun. No credit cards. **KK**. **Restaurant**.

This claims to be the first *konoba* (tavern) in Istria. A family restaurant, here the owners make their own sausages and pair them with potatoes and sauerkraut. They also dish up traditional favourites like goulash, grilled meats, fish, pasta with truffles, home-made *pršut* ham and sheeps' cheese.

Konoba Bare

Kamenarija 4, Funtana (052 445 193). **Open** 5-11pm Mon, Tue, Thur; noon-11pm Fri, Sun. **KK**. **Restaurant**.

This rustic spot with stone walls and a wooden-beamed ceiling strikes a balance between down-home and something more formal. The menu features goulash, fish soup, sole with truffles and veal. Wine is a strong suit. Top whites such as Matoševič Malvasia are on the docket as well as a fine selection of local Terans.

Marinero

Obala maršala Tita 9, Vrsar (052 441 797). **Open** *July, Aug* 7am-2am daily. *Sept-June* 7am-midnight daily. No credit cards. **Bar**.

This atmospheric bar gives a new meaning to the term 'watering-hole'. Set in an old cisterna, its vaulted ceilings and stone columns are offset with funky wall murals and nautical paraphernalia. Cocktails are the big thing. House special Marinero combines white rum, Curaçao and Red Bull; beer mixes include a Moscow Mule of lager and lime with vodka, and a Dream of Beer of white rum, lager and champagne. It's also a decent place to take in the morning papers and grab breakfast of croissants and coffee.

Nives

Obala maršala Tita 23, Vrsar (052 442 325). **Open** *July, Aug* 7am-2am daily. *Sept-June* 7am-midnight daily. No credit cards. **Bar**.

Although this building is Yugo concrete naff and the venue small, Nives is Vrsar's focal bar in summer. It's also an internet café and contains the only pool table in town. Much of the action takes place outside on the harbourfront and the large grass area nearby.

Srdela

Saline, Vrsar (098 440 590 mobile). **Open** *Apr-Oct* 11am-11pm daily. No credit cards. **K**. **Fish restaurant**.

By the green market, behind the petrol station and souvenir stands, stands a summer terrace where the husband-and-wife owners serve fried sardines, shrimp, scampi and, interestingly, shark. The house speciality is calamari stuffed with squid and parsley. Everything here is home-made and concocted from family recipes.

Trošt

Obala maršala Tita 1A, Vrsar (052 445 197). **Open** 10am-midnight daily. **KK**. **Restaurant**.

Don't be put off by the 1970s exterior or the steep flight of steps leading up to this first-floor location – this is easily the best restaurant in Vrsar. The large terrace has a view out over the harbour. Inside are two dining areas. The smaller rustic one has an open fireplace used for cooking; the other is more formal, with sliding glass doors that open out on to the terrace in summer. The high quality of food and service is matched by reasonable prices, 200kn for an average meal. House specialities include sea bass in salt and fish baked with potatoes under hot ashes. Booking essential.

Nightlife

Casanova Beach Club

Montraker Beach, Vrsar (091 206 2987 mobile). **Open** *June-Sept* 11am-4am daily. No credit cards.

Open until 4am the whole summer, Casanova has DJs and different themes each night. Live acts play on Tuesdays. The nerve centre is a black bar under a canopy with a chandelier. Scattered on a wooden deck and under a disco ball are daybeds and wicker couches.

Dionys Beach Bar

Montraker Beach, Vrsar (091 512 9291 mobile). **Open** *June-Sept* 24hrs daily. No credit cards.

Every place needs one. For Vrsar this is it: 24-hour party central. Dionys has DJs and themed nights through the season. There are also go-go girls and cocktail parties on a hillside among olive trees. There's a rock fountain with goldfish; music pumps from a bamboo hut; Café of Colombia burlap sacks are scattered about; tiki torches surround a wooden deck that gives way to little pebble VIP nooks. The Americana cocktail of Campari and red vermouth is a tasty lubricant for getting the dance gears moving.

Arts & leisure

Excursions Mikela

Vrsar Harbour (091 5769 382 mobile, www.vitontours.hu).
You'll find several operators in the harbour offering day trips to the Limski kanal. Expect to pay 120kn per head for a two-hour trip. There are also five-hour excursions (200kn), which include a picnic and tour of the archipelago.

Sports Centre Montraker

Montraker Beach, Vrsar (091 577 4819 mobile). **Open** *Summer* 9am-8pm daily.
Rents out kayaks, pedal boats, windsurf rigs, waterballs, ski tubes and boats from the main public beach.

The Limski shell game

Emil Sošić is the owner of the only shack at the mouth of the Limski kanal. But this isn't how he'd introduce himself – he would likely call himself a businessman. And as it happens his business, **Istrida**, an oyster farm in operation since 2002, perches here on stilts over the water. Ideal growing conditions determine the location. His oysters are in cages, clinging to ropes suspended from the deck behind the wooden hut in this 12-kilometre (seven-mile), knife-shaped harbour that's protected by law from people, and by nature from the elements.

Sošić takes care of every detail, from growing to storage to shipping, and can guarantee fresh goods, including mussels, on restaurant tables within a few hours of a phone call.

'I produce 50,000 European oysters per year,' says Sošić. 'Paris eats that in one day. But quality is our bingo. That's why I am in this kind of business.'

Such a perfect end product is pricey, sometimes twice the cost of the heartier, less risky but less tasteful Atlantic variety. But that very taste and his attention to detail is why restaurants keep calling – and why visitors knock on his shack's door to purchase oysters at 7kn a piece. Mussels are 20kn per kilo.

'Oysters aren't for everyday meals. They're too expensive. But when visitors do treat themselves, they know they have treated themselves to the real thing,' Sošić says.

Limski kanal

The **Limski kanal** drives a dramatic, narrow, 12-kilometre sliver of sea straight into the heart of the peninsula. The scene of cliffs – forested and rising to a height of 150m – and green, crystal-clear water below could be mistaken for a Scandinavian fjord. Hollywood banked on the fact. The Limski was the location for 'The Long Ships', a 1963 film about Vikings off on their rape and pillage jaunts, starring Richard Widmark.

As a protected area, the canal is restricted to licensed sailors but you can take private guided boat trips from Rovinj or Vrsar. A viewing platform by the main road offers a spectacular, panoramic view of the canal and surroundings.

The Lim valley stretches 35 kilometres (21 miles) in total, nearly reaching the central town of Pazin. A couple of kilometres inland from the canal's end you'll find one-time settlement **Dvigrad** ('Two Towns'). Once there were two communities here, Parentin and Montecastello,

which the Romans referred to as Duo Castar. The name stuck although Parentin was destroyed in the 14th century, a casualty of fighting between Venice and Genoa. Dvigrad was abandoned in 1631. Research reveals that this was a major settlement with at least 200 residential buildings and fortified walls. Locals claim it has buried treasure. For more on that, travel another three kilometres to the tiny village of **Mrgani**. According to legend, Mrgani was founded by swashbuckler Sir Henry Morgan. This famous British captain-turned-pirate is said to have used the canal as a bolt-hole to escape enemies and stash his ill-gotten gains. A surprising number of people in these parts bear the Welsh-sounding name of Morgan.

Eating & drinking

Fjord

Limski kanal (052 448 222). **Open** 11am-11pm daily. **KKK. Shellfish restaurant**.

Open since 1963, Fjord is a big restaurant with seating for 250 and caters to big groups. Don't let this put you off. On an open terrace overlooking the canal, it serves oysters, sea bass and delectable mussels cooked with garlic and white wine. Inside there's a massive aquarium and formal dining room.

Viking

Limski kanal (052 448 223). **Open** *Mar-Dec* 11am-4pm, 6-11pm daily. **KKK. Shellfish restaurant**.

This fine venue has huge plate-glass windows and a terrace affording un-interrupted views of Limski's green waters. Oysters are the speciality, but the seasonal range of fresh shellfish is formidable. Particularly good is the lobster, served *buzara* style on a bed of pasta. Viking also specialises in white-fleshed sea-fish such as sea bass, dentex, john dory, gilthead and grouper.

Limski oysters

Decumanus

Poreč

Poreč is something of a cross between Pula and Rovinj, although neither as street-smart nor as bohemian. It can be hard at first to recognise its real self or true value.

It's easier to groan at the hordes of visitors filling the treasured, sixth-century, UNESCO-protected **Euphrasian Basilica**, an ancient square built by the Romans, and the scores of restaurants, cafés and package hotels. Restaurateurs attempt to pull you in for a meal in the pedestrian-only Old Town, and tacky souvenir shops cram the 2,000-year-old, stone-paved thoroughfare of **Decumanus**. But look past the crowds and you'll find a lot of history. Decumanus, **trg Marafor** square, and the ruins of the temples of Neptune and Mars are evidence of the Roman occupation. The harbour contains reminders of Venetian dominance until the 18th century, when Poreč was ruled by Napoleon then the Habsburgs. The Venetians built a town wall which stretched from the harbourside Round Tower, now a bar, to the Pentagonal Tower, now a restaurant. The resort hotels are outside of town to the south, where pine forests run up to the beach: **Plava Laguna** and **Zelena Laguna**. They can be reached by an open-air tourist train.

Sights & museums

Aquarium Poreč
Franje Glavinića 4 (052 428 720). **Open** *Apr-Nov* 9am-11pm daily. **Admission** 40kn; 20kn. **Map** p73 C2 ❶

By and large, this won't make little Cousteaus out of your youngest travellers. Having said that, its attractive, curved blue walls house 25 tanks filled with Adriatic sea life.

Euphrasian Basilica & Bishop's Palace
Sv Eleuterija (052 431 635). **Open** *Basilica* 7am-9pm daily. *Museum* 10am-5pm daily. **Admission** *Church* free; *Belfry* 10kn; *Museum* 10kn. **Map** p73 C1 ❷

See box p74.

Istrian Assembly Hall

Matka Laginje 6 (052 432 263/ www.poup.hr). **Open** varies. **Map** p73 B1 ❸

This Baroque building was once the 14th-century Gothic Franciscan church of St Francis. Behind it, the floor mosaics of the fifth-century St Thomas Church give a sense of deeper history. Today, the painting-filled ceiling above Habsburg walls of marzipan yellow provides the backdrop for the local district parliamentary sessions. For the general public, there are choral concerts and August's contemporary art show, held since 1961, with paintings, installations, multimedia, sculpture, photography and performance art.

Eating & drinking

Atelier

Obala Maršala Tita 3A (091 52 48 514 mobile). **Open** June-Sept 10am-2am daily. **Bar**. **Map** p73 C3 ❹

This popular bar is tucked away behind the seafront by a flight of steep steps. By day, it's dark and neglected, only starting to kick up by early evening. This is a contemporary venue also known for hosting photo exhibitions and live music. The fake zebra-skin sofas, red wall and broken mirror shards on the bar look so much better after a couple of draught Stellas.

Cardo Restaurant

Cardo Maximus 8 (052 452 742). **Open** noon-midnight daily. **KK**. **Restaurant**. **Map** p73 B1 ❺

This restaurant on the corner of Cardo Maximus and Eufrazijeva is, like many, of the fish variety, just nicer than the many common touristy ones nearby. The dining area is a terrace with wrought-iron tables. Beneath a green awning, look for the quaint streetlamps and hand-painted signs advertising fish, scallops, risotto and oysters; select from the display set on ice by the entrance. Fish baked in salt is the house speciality.

Comitium Cocktail Bar

Marafor 15 (no phone). **Open** 6pm-2am Mon-Sat; 5pm-2am Sun. No credit cards. **Bar**. **Map** p73 B1 ❻

A garish, oversized cocktail sign alerts passing tourists to a beautiful garden bar with 20 tables amid the Roman ruins of Marafor. The atmosphere is slightly classier, if more pretentious, than the neighbouring joints, though still fun. Cocktails, cold Bavaria on tap and an upscale, polished wood and marble interior set this place off from the nearby competition.

Dvi Murve

Grožnjanska 17 (052 434 115, www. dvimurve.hr). **Open** Feb-Dec noon-11pm daily. **KK**. **Restaurant**. **Map** p73 E1 ❼

Outside the more touristy part of town this is a popular *konoba* tavern with a large, pleasantly shaded terrace and a busy grill operating in one corner. It cooks up excellent seafood and has a regular following to prove it. Here you can expect standards and local specialities such as sea bass baked in salt and lobster with spaghetti. But this is also a good place to opt for traditional Istrian dishes such as stew with dried lamb, goulash and noodles, wild game or a plate of grilled meats.

Epoca

Obala maršala Tita 24 (no phone). **Open** 8am-2am daily. No credit cards. **Bar**. **Map** p73 A2 ❽

Good music, friendly staff and a sociable buzz make this place a stalwart among harbourside spots for a drink and meet-up with friends. Near the tip of the peninsula that holds the Old Town (and across from the newly opened Palazzo Hotel), at the start of the busy strip of cafés and restaurants, Epoca offers a spacious indoor bar area and sea views. Dancing may break out in the evening, though the crowd you'll be schmoozing with will be mostly fellow travellers. There is a fine choice of cocktails on offer too.

Poreč

Nikole Tesle
Mlinska
Nikole Tesle
Zagrebačka
Obala Matije Gupca
Decumanus
Euphrasiana
Sv. Eleuterija
Epulonova
M. Bernobića
J. Gaja
Sv. Mauro
Obala Maršala Tita
Trg M. Gupca
Trg Marafor
Trg Slobode
Narodni Trg
Ribarski Trg
A. Negrija
V. Nazora
Bože Milanovića
Karla Huguesa
Vukovarska
Pile /rm/ Kandlera
Istarskog Razvoda
Pionirska
V. Gortana
Prvomajska
Trg J. Rakovca
Otokara Keršovanija
Jože Šurana
Žurnica
Parik Olge Ban

Euphrasian
Basilica

Marina

© Copyright Time Out Group 2010

200 m
200 yds

- Sights & museums
- Eating & drinking
- Shopping
- Nightlife
- Arts & leisure

Istria's Byzantine gem

Even for the most hardened of travellers, the **Euphrasian Basilica** and its offerings are breathtaking – and a welcome surprise after wading through the ice-cream and souvenir hawkers.

One of the most important historic sights in Croatia, the Basilica was built in the sixth century by Bishop Euphrasius and dedicated to Saint Mauro and the Virgin Mary. It represents a rare surviving example of Byzantine art – a point the United Nations conceded when it gave the church UNESCO status in 1997.

Standing inside its awe-inspiring interior, it is hard to fathom how much work must have gone into its apse, walls and even floor. You find people sitting in pews staring straight ahead with jaws hanging open. And, happily, as packed as the streets can get in summer, the church always seems to be calm and free of crowds. The main attractions are the finely preserved gold-gilt and mother-of-pearl mosaics, which shine with a brightness that belies their age.

The largest and most stunning is in the apse, above and behind the altar, depicting a procession of saints and angels around the Virgin Mary, who is holding the baby Jesus. Euphrasius, who can be seen bearing a depiction of the church, built his three-nave basilica on the foundation of a fourth-century church. Mosaics from earlier churches are still visible in the floor of the Basilica's northern nave.

The surrounding complex offers impressive sights too – you can absorb the best in 20 minutes or linger for a couple of hours.

Alongside is an eight-sided baptistery, and beyond a belfry, which you can climb (10kn) for a view of the seaside and the surroundings. Next to the church is the former Bishop's Palace, part of its original fifth- and sixth-century walls preserved, housing a museum that contains mosaics gathered from earlier churches.

Guided tours in English are provided every day except on religious holidays.

Fish Food

Eufrazijeva 8 (099 21 22 023 mobile).
Open *Mar-Jan* 11am-midnight daily.
Fast food. Map p73 C1 ❾

A novel idea, though it shouldn't be.
Fish Food is fast-food fish. On the way
to the Basilica, this is a spot to fix your
seafood jones without breaking the
bank. Patrons sit at painted picnic
tables atop a walkway of white stone
and dive into squid (fried and grilled),
mussels and fried sardines. It draws a
sophisticated crowd even though many
end up eating with their fingers.
Domestic beer and decent table wine
are served.

La Cioccolata

*Obala maršala Titu 13 (052 434
276).* **Open** 8am-2am daily. **KKK**.
Restaurant/bar. Map p73 B2 ❿

A posh restaurant and lounge spilling
onto the waterfront promenade, La
Cioccolata has an expansive terrace
stretched out under a white tent. The
cushy leather-esque chairs and low
wicker couches are perfect for relaxing
with cocktails (around 40kn), Bavaria
beer on tap and a choice of wines. The
equally snooty restaurant on site has
an indoor dining room and its own terrace for gnocchi with truffles, steaks
and grilled fish.

Lapidarij

*Sveta Maura 10 (052 431 595,
www.jazzinlap.com).* **Open** *Summer*
noon-midnight daily. No credit cards.
Bar/club. Map p73 C2 ⓫

Lapidarij is a sophisticated sanctuary
from the Old Town crowds. Within the
garden of the City Museum (closed for
reconfiguration until 2012) is this
pleasant bar-cum-nightspot with a
tiered courtyard framed by palmettos,
its space shared with the broken
remains of history – stone basins and
column capitals – piled about like some
antiquarian garage sale. Lapidarij
hosts regular music events such as
Wednesday's jam sessions which
range from swing to acid jazz.

Mali Caffè

Narodni trg 4 (091 443 3222 mobile).
Open 7am-2am Mon-Sat; 10am-2am
Sun. No credit cards. **Bar/club**.
Map p73 C2 ⓬

Commonly acknowledged to be the
best place to grab a drink in town, Mali
Caffè has live music on Mondays,
Wednesdays and at weekends, but it's
the daytime atmosphere that wins over
the locals. Easygoing funk sets the tone
for cocktails, fine coffee roasted at the
renowned Eli's Caffè in Zagreb and
Istrian wines served on a white-tiled
terrace. Mali also offers several *rakija*
grappas and Croatian Velebitsko beer,
a rarity in these parts. This is the spot
to watch outdoor shows on the steps of
the theatre across the square. The interior, filled with overstuffed leather
armchairs, is strewn with rally memorabilia from the owner's days as a professional driver.

Maslina Konoba

NEW *Ribarski trg 4 (095 891 9015
mobile).* **Open** *Summer* 9am-1am daily.
Winter 9am-1am Mon-Sat. No credit
cards. **KK**. **Restaurant**. Map p73
C2 ⓭

A peaceful spot in a quiet square sheltered from the sun and the more
touristy venues, Maslina, which
opened in time for the season in 2009,
is a budget-minded option for fish and
calamari. Though the staff can be a little surly and less than timely with
orders, this is a solid place for pizzas,
pastas and salads. When dining on the
stone terrace on a steamy day, ask
Bosnian-born owner Goran to fix a
refreshing Tangerine Dream: tangerine
Schweppes and red wine on ice.

Mozart Caffè

Rade Končara 1B (052 432 317).
Open 6am-2am daily. No credit cards.
Bar. Map p73 D3 ⓮

This terrace bar really shouldn't be the
busiest location in town. Not only is it
set behind the bus station and Hotel
Poreč and separated from the marina

by a small park, but Mozart also plays dubious Italian pop and the fashion channel on the TV. But, for all that, it's strangely popular, partly because it faces the pine-shaded beaches near the Hotel Hostin, partly because it's patronised by (loud, young) locals only.

Old Time

Marafor 12 (052 453 340). **Open** *Jan, Mar-Dec* 6pm-2am daily. No credit cards. **Bar**. Map p73 B1 ⑮
This is the place to get biker-rowdy. There is, according to owner Rade, always live music, and it is always rock 'n' roll. 'We play whatever the people want – whether it's Johnny Cash or old time rock.' The terrace, with wicker chairs and marble tables, is big enough to handle a crowd until it eventually overflows into the square of Marafor. Inside, there's a long wooden bar and a real barman, not just a student on holiday. Cocktails of merit include sex on the beach and the Sex Machine: vodka, peach liqueur, orange juice and apricot liqueur. Most run in the 40kn range.

Parentino Bar

Obala maršala Tita (052 400 800). **Open** 8am-2pm; 6pm-midnight. No credit cards. **Wine bar**. Map p73 B2 ⑯
Below the Hotel Neptune, this is a slick little wine bar with a terrace facing the yacht end of the marina in town. For holiday sailors, Parentino serves croissants and coffee in the morning; Stella and Slovene Union beers by day; and champagne and many wines after dark. Inside it's marble, glass and leather to suit the clientele.

Peterokutna kula

Decumanus 1 (052 451 378). **Open** noon-midnight daily. No credit cards. **KKK**. **Restaurant**. Map p73 C2 ⑰
A history lesson and meal at the same time, Peterokutna kula is located in a Gothic, pentagonal tower, featuring a relief of a Venetian lion, built in 1447. Near the entryway to the Old Town,

it offers indoor and outdoor seating in nicely restored spaces. As a 170-seater, it's clearly touristy, but the atmosphere is novel and the cuisine is designed to show off the best of Istria; truffles feature in many dishes, including steak.

Sveti Nikola

Obala maršala Tita 23 (052 423 018, www.svnikola.com). **Open** 11am-1am daily. **KKK**. **Restaurant**. Map p73 B2 ⑱
A seafront location, magnificent cuisine and an elegant ambience have helped Sveti Nikola build a reputation as one of the top tables in Poreč. The terrace is right on the harbour, the meticulously designed interior has great sea views and the food features creative interpretations of Istrian classics. The fish carpaccio appetiser is an unusual and tempting mix of scampi, frogfish and octopus. The meat carpaccio comes with truffle, parmesan and rucola. Fancy main courses include fish fillet with asparagus and black truffles, lobster and steak. A sommelier sees to the frequently changing wine list and scores of heavy-hitting VIPs and politicians often drop by.

Ulixes

Decumanus 2 (052 451 132). **Open** noon-midnight daily. **KK**. **Restaurant**. Map p73 C2 ⑲
The speciality of this cornerstone of Poreč cuisine is the Istrian version of surf and turf: seafood and truffles. Surf includes calamari, octopus salad, scampi, shells and fresh fish, plus less common varieties such as ray and sole. Truffles can be had in pasta or as part of starters such as sheeps' cheese or carpaccio. There are usually interesting daily specials on offer as well. To find it, step off crowded Decumanus, down a few steps, and into a cool, cavernous old stone room, charmingly cluttered with antiques and old shipping paraphernalia. The garden behind, in a secluded courtyard, is equally attractive.

Yesterday

Park Olge Ban 2 (098 323 954 mobile).
Open *Summer* 7am-1am daily. *Winter*
7am-11pm daily. No credit cards. **Bar**.
Map p73 E1 ⓴

Out of place and yet somehow it works.
Yesterday is a Beatles theme bar run
by the son and daughter of an Oldham-
born fan who gave Paul McCartney a
loveheart necklace backstage in 1965.
Two years later, Jackie Carnihan met a
hotel receptionist while on holiday
here, got married and had two children.
Macca couldn't have written it better.
The interior features a wall-sized
album cover image of 'Abbey Road'.
Unplugged local acts play on Fridays.
There are also two terraces and plans
for a garden nook.

Shopping

Atelier No 7

NEW *Eufrazijeva 19 (no phone).* **Open**
June-Sept 9am-2pm, 4-11pm daily.
Map p73 B1 ㉑

Artists from Zagreb, Pula and Labin
fill this modest space with their water-
colours, oils and tempura creations.
Opened in 2009, the gallery has a tasteful smattering of sunny scenes and the
expected tourist magnets. It also specialises in a refined combination of
pieces that sell and those that chal-
lenge; abstract and impressionistic ver-
sions of fish and salty harbours. The
paintings are beautifully framed and
many are the perfect size to take home
as souvenirs.

Bacchus

Eufrazijeva 10 (095 902 3999 mobile).
Open *Summer* 10am-midnight daily.
Winter 10am-midnight Sat, Sun. No
credit cards. **Map** p73 C1 ㉒

After several years of tourism it seems
Croatia has woken up to the fact that
visitors might actually want something without a 'made in China' label
on its underside. Just along the pavement from the Euphrasian Basilica,
Bacchus, a shop with a rather homely

stone-meets-wood interior, sells only
home-made products. For sale and on
display are truffles, olive oil, wine, prosciutto, cheeses and a decent selection
of locally made trinkets.

Big Blue

Eufrazijeva 45 (052 433 228). **Open**
Summer 9am-midnight daily. *Winter*
10am-5pm Mon-Sat. **Map** p73 B1 ㉓

Part of the Aqua chain found across
the country, Big Blue is something like
the IKEA of beachwear. With styles
reminiscent of Gap or Benetton, the
quality is many times higher than what
you'll find in the touristy stalls – as
reflected in the price. You'll find swim-
suits, hats, flip-flops, shirts, towels
and bags, all with the store's branded
stripes or fish design.

Enoteca Per Bacco

*Trg slobode 10 (052 451 600/091 427
0521 mobile).* **Open** 8am-midnight
Mon-Sat; 9am-midnight Sun. **Map** p73
D2 ㉔

On the left of this rustic boutique, there
is everything wine. Among the labels
are well-known Istrian bottles such as
Kabola and Kozlović. To the right are
wine glasses and ceramics. The store
also provides tobacco products, jams,
spirits, olive oil, truffles, honeys, pastas, lavender and soap goodies, and
sweets such as biscuits made from
apricots and figs.

Gallery Potočnjak

Eufrazijeva 14 (098 32 9090 mobile).
Open *Apr-Oct* 10am-2pm, 6-10pm
daily. **Map** p73 C1 ㉕

Beside the Basilica is a courtyard filled
with art created by Ante Potočnjak.
Customers mill in and out of multiple
rooms and among the stockpile in the
courtyard. Pieces by the thousand
hang on walls and rest on the floor. The
more touristy ones Potočnjak can create in no time. The more abstract ones,
which he favours, are in a room signed:
'Please do not enter without a minimum of 5,000 euros ready to spend'.

Poreč

These tend to stick around for a while. Still lifes, seascapes and so on carry a 50kn to 5,000-euro-plus price tag – you're bound to find one that appeals to your taste and budget.

Handmade Art Jewellery

Sv Mauro 9 (052 431 150). **Open** *May-Oct* 9.30am-11pm daily. **Map** p73 C2 **26**

This lovely shop is set south of Decumanus, near the courtyard of the city museum. Slip through the stone entrance and you are met with purple walls and a big driftwood branch from which puppets hang. Offerings include unique jewellery from Iva Stojkić, combinations of smooth, coloured stone bobbles and silver accents with charms. The shop also displays masks, driftwood paintings and sculptures.

Koza Unikati

Eufrazijeva 28 (no phone). **Open** 10am-3pm, 6-11pm daily. **Map** p73 B1 **27**

The brother and sister who run this family-owned leather shop make all the products themselves. The tiny place is stuffed with bags, briefcases, shoes and journal covers, all handmade. In the middle is a display of colourful sandals. There's so much here even the cash till is hidden and buried.

Sole Luna

Eufrazijeva 45 (052 434 325/091 520 3999 mobile). **Open** *Summer* 10am-11pm daily. **Map** p73 B1 **28**

The owner of this somewhat unusual mask-making atelier set on gallery street studied at the Venetian School of Sculpture. Walking into the off-kilter space is like walking into Mardi Gras, with representations of Volto, Joker, Colombine, the bird Pulcinella and Bauta. Made of recycled paper, these are the same masks used in Venice for the Carnival, and available here for less. The result: a mask in Venice that runs at 38 euros goes here for 27. With their purchase, customers receive a certificate of authenticity and a guarantee.

Vinoteque Epvlon

Eufrazijeva 31 (052 431 011). **Open** 10am-1pm, 6pm-1am daily. **Map** p73 B1 **29**

In a 300-year-old building with floor-to-ceiling shelves chock-full of top wines, Epvlon, named after the last Histrian King, should be your first stop for picking up a bottle. Owner Raivoj Stipanović is happy to share his expertise and suggest a purchase from the 350 labels. In the back, handcrafted benches surround framed mosaics and a bar made of heavy stone and wood.

Nightlife

Byblos

Zelena Laguna (091 113 3221 mobile).
Open *June-Sept* 11pm-6am Mon-Sat.
Admission 50kn-200kn. **Map** p73
C3 ③⓪

Opened in 2007, this is the club that
Poreč had been waiting for. Quality
sound system, quality cocktails and a
quality agenda: David Guetta, Deep
Dish and Roger Sanchez, for example.
Marko Lucchi designed the 4,000-sq-m
interior, to accommodate several thousand clubbers, in a simple but effective
decor of black and white. Set near the
Hotel Delfin, it has a beach lounge bar
too. Ladies' night is Monday, while
international DJs appear on Fridays.

Paradiso Beach Bar

*Zelena Laguna, Hotel Delfin Beach
(091 892 3008 mobile).* **Open** 8am-
8pm daily. No credit cards. **Map** p73
C3 ③①

Owned by the folks who run the landmark Byblos, Paradiso Beach Bar is
not a late-night club, rather a place
where nights begin or end. Unusually,
it closes at 8pm and opens at 8am,
allowing it to use the motto: 'Where the
party never stops'. This posh spot has
DJs, a covered terrace, a sandy beach
and daybeds. People come to see and
be seen, or just to work off a hangover
with pricey hair-of-the dog cocktails.

Plava Club

*Plava Laguna (091 202 0399 mobile,
www.clubplava.com).* **Open** 10pm-4am
daily. No credit cards. **Map** p73 C3 ③②

Plava is one of the oldest clubs in Istria
– and one of the wildest. Theme nights
include male and female stripteases
and full-nudity lesbian shows every
Wednesday. Thursday is for '70s-'90s
tunes. Fridays are Latino, and
Saturdays are ladies' nights. Pole dancing, go-go girls, young oglers, older
folks hoping to fit in – this is the whole
shebang. Best not to leave your date
unattended. Free transport from town.

Saint & Sinner

*Obala maršala Tita 13 (099 221 1811
mobile, www.saint-sinner.net).* **Open**
Summer 9am-2am daily. **Map** p73
C2 ③③

There's a DJ every night at S&S playing house, techno and the like. During
the day it's more of a Gypsy Kings
scene on a waterfront terrace. Inside,
there's a glossy nightclub feel with
beautiful barmaids, lit crystal, VIP
alcoves, mirrored columns, disco lighting and uncomfortable-looking but
chic barstools. The cocktail menu is
extensive. Dark and light Leffe beer
comes by the bottle. Worth a visit
before hitting an all-nighter.

Villa Club

*Rade Končara (099 214 9003 mobile,
www.villa-club.net).* **Open** 10am-5am
daily. No credit cards. **Map** p73 C3 ③④

This is an all-in-one stop in front of the
Hotel Hostin. In the morning sip coffee
among secluded pines on lounge
couches and bamboo, egg-shaped,
swinging loveseats at the beach bar: a
rope-meets-wood-and-wicker creation.
In the evening, order champagne and
cocktails (cosmos at 38kn) in the downstairs bar near the DJ stand and dancefloor done up in lavender and pink.
There is also live music to go with
nights of R&B and house. To move up
to the VIP lounge upstairs, you'll need
to order a bottle of spirits, something
in the 600kn range. No entrance fee to
dance and drink with the hoi polloi.

Arts & leisure

Poreč Theatre

*Narodni trg 1 (052 432 263, www.
poup.hr).* **Open** times vary. No credit
cards. **Map** p73 C2 ③⑤

Opened in 1886, this theatre mounts
some 15 stage shows a year from
autumn to spring, plus films in summer. Shows and times can be found on
the board at the entrance. In high season, current films are shown every
night but Fridays on the open-air stage.

Novigrad

Novigrad

Located north towards Italy, its compact centre attracting occasional day trippers from over the border, **Novigrad** can seem humble in comparison to the busier coastal spots of Rovinj and Poreč.

The emphasis here is on quality: the recently opened four-star **Hotel Nautica** with its own marina; the deservedly reputable restaurants lining the small, picturesque harbour; and the new boutique hotel **Villa Cittar** with its equally boutique eaterie **Pepenero**.

Instead of being crammed with kitsch souvenir stalls and tourist traps, the seaward tip of the Old Town peninsula has a shaded park and a waterside walkway. And for a discerning community of fewer than 4,000, Novigrad has a surprising number of decent bars, hotels, restaurants and places to shake it up a little. The more modern part of town stretches less than a kilometre east, as far as the bus station and a package-hotel complex tucked out of the way.

Besides this, inside the Old Town – connected with the marina via the pleasant seaside promenade of Rivarella – and around the harbour is the **Museum Lapidarium**, built specifically for Roman remains.

The Venetians gave the town its most elegant sights. The campanile beside **St Pelagius** rises over the modest network of streets. Here in the main square, **Veliki trg**, and the main street of **Velika ulica**, stands a landmark Venetian loggia, site of the Town Hall. North of town at Karpinjan, near the new marina, the **Rigo Palace** (1760) hosts exhibitions and a permanent display of historic items.

Sights & museums

Gallerion Naval Museum

Mlinska 1 (052 720 866, www.kuk-marine-museum.com). **Open** *Nov-May* 10am-noon, 5pm-midnight daily. **Admission** 20kn. No credit cards. **Map** p81 C2 ➊

Just around the corner from the city harbour, Gallerion is dedicated to the Austro-Hungarian presence in the

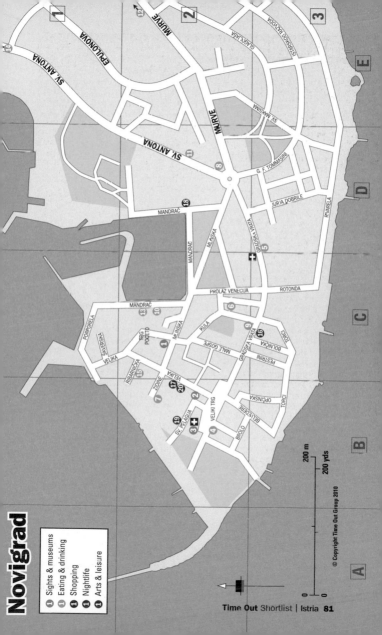

Novigrad

- Sights & museums
- Eating & drinking
- Shopping
- Nightlife
- Arts & leisure

200 m
200 yds

© Copyright Time Out Group 2010

Adriatic 1815-1918, a fascinating look at history from a non-traditional, non-Croatian view. The two-storey display is stuffed with explanations of battles, model ships, uniforms and weapons. The well-crafted exhibits attempt to outline the area's nautical tradition in as objective a way as a town on the sea can. The curator is expert in the field and adroit in multiple languages.

Museum Lapidarium

Veliki trg 8A (052 726 582, www.muzej-lapidarium.hr). **Open** *Summer* 10am-1pm, 6-10pm Tue-Sun. *Winter* 10am-1pm, 5-7pm Tue-Sun. **Admission** 10kn; 5kn reductions; free under-14s. No credit cards. **Map** p81 B2 ❷

Istria's first purpose-built museum is a first-class example of successfully siting modern architecture within the context of an old town. Lapidarium was built to house Roman architectural remains, dating from the first century AD, found in the locality. As well as temporary shows, there are also items from local Romanesque churches.

Parish Church of Sts Pelagius & Maximus

Veliki trg. **Map** p81 B2 ❸

This three-nave church has its origins either around the fifth century or late eighth. The first theory is supported by recent findings of Early Christian window frames. The building has been renovated at least four times, hence the Neo-classical exterior and Baroque interior. Beneath the altar lies a Romanesque crypt dating back to 1146. The campanile next to the church was constructed in 1883, modelled after St Mark's in Venice.

Eating & drinking

Caffè Bar Divino

NEW *Veliki trg 12 (no phone)*. **Open** *Summer* 7am-2am daily. *Winter* 7am-midnight daily. No credit cards. **Café**. **Map** p81 C2 ❹

Opened in July 2009 around a slew of similarly posh-ish cafés in the centre, Divino serves sandwiches – including the all-Istrian prosciutto, cheese and truffles – ice-cream, cakes and pancakes. The terrace spills onto the main square with town hall facing and the campanile beside. Relax after sightseeing with a coffee or a glass of Tuborg.

Cocktail Bar Code

Gradska Vrata 20A (095 877 7767 mobile). **Open** 8am-midnight Mon-Thur, Sun; 8am-2am Fri, Sat. No credit cards. **Bar**. **Map** p81 C3 ❺

This slick, urban, black-and-white cocktail bar stands out from nearby low-key cafés. House music and jazz blares from the speakers while hip-hop videos flash on a wide screen. The bartender is ready to give a showy shake to 30 basic types of cocktail, averaging 40kn each and served in generous portions. DJs play on Saturdays.

Cocktail Bar Cubano

Prolaz Venecija 14 (no phone). **Open** *Summer* 9am-2am daily. No credit cards. **Bar**. **Map** p81 C2 ❻

At this bamboo spot lost in the pines, cocktails and Caribbean beats predominate on a terrace of cheetah-covered chairs, tiki torches and chandeliers draped in satin. A bouncy group of cocktail hawkers take your order.

Damir i Ornella

Zidine 5 (052 758 134). **Open** noon-3pm, 6.30-11.30pm Tue-Sun. **KKK**. **Restaurant**. **Map** p81 B2 ❼

Acknowledged to be one of the best places to eat on the coast, this 22-seat diner should be booked well ahead. Signposted on Velika ulica, it's set in a narrow sidestreet near the seafront. Inside, a bare-brick interior is a comfortable setting for fish and shrimp specialities. Whatever comes in fresh is served. Damir and his daughter, the sommelier, run the floor. Ornella runs the kitchen. The grilled lobster is superb. Desserts include kiwi flan.

Pepenero p84

Konoba Čok

Sv Antona 2 (052 757 643). **Open** noon-3pm, 6-11pm Thur-Tues. **KK**. **Restaurant**. Map p81 D2 ⑧

While his son Viljan runs the kitchen, Sergio Jugovac takes care of guests and the Istrian wines on offer. This simple, well-run seafood eatery offers fresh sea bream, sea perch and sole, lobster and sundry shellfish, including oysters. Black and white truffles top the steaks and pasta. Meals are bookended by a complimentary grappa. You'll find the place by a roundabout just out of town.

Little Caffè

Gradska vrata 15 (098 939 7573 mobile). **Open** 8am-midnight Mon-Thur; 8am-1am Fri, Sat. No credit cards. **Café**. Map p81 C2 ⑨

A young crowd hangs out in this swish café in the heart of Novigrad, with a decent choice of whiskies and Istrian bitters, and Guinness and Kilkenny by the bottle. Though typical, it's a cut above most bars in the Old Town and worth visiting for a drink with locals.

Mandrač

Mandrać 6 (052 757 369). **Open** noon-midnight daily. **KK**. **Restaurant**. Map p81 C2 ⑩

The walls at the back of the 40-year-old Mandrać are covered in gastronomic awards and even though there are seats for 215 diners, reserve in summer. Framed against the 600-year-old city wall, fresh fish and grilled meats are well presented on warmed plates, garnished according to the friendly advice offered by the waiter.

Pepenero

NEW *Sv Antona 4 (052 758 542)*. **Open** noon-3pm, 6-11pm daily. **KKK**. **Restaurant**. Map p81 D2 ⑪

The new heavy hitter in town, this spot has been given gourmet appeal by renowned chef Marin Rendić. One of the best gastro artists around, Rendić serves monkfish with a sparkling white-wine sauce; home-made ravioli stuffed with sea bass in a black truffle sauce; and salmon fillet with a cauliflower and basil cream sauce. The wines are international but tilted to Istrian choices. Wicker chairs and a nice terrace provide comfort.

Restaurant Giovanni

Stancija Rozelo 30A (052 757 122). **Open** 11am-3pm, 6-11pm Mon, Wed-Sun. **KK**. **Restaurant**. Map p81 E2 ⑫

Konoba Čok

Vitriol

On the road to Poreč, Giovanni is an old-school seafood restaurant. Expect top white fish as well as lobster, squid and shellfish. The speciality is seafood pasta. This is the kind of place local politicians gather for lunch so as not to be seen in trendier fusion restaurants. Dining is done beneath shelves of hunting and skeet-shooting trophies in a room with retractable windows that let in cross-breezes.

Restaurant Sidro

Mandrać 5 (052 757 601). **Open** *Summer* 11am-11pm daily. *Winter* 11am-11pm Mon, Tue, Thur-Sun. **KK**. **Fish restaurant**. Map p81 C2 ⑬

In its third generation, this family-run classic has been around since the start of modern Istrian tourism. Sidro ('anchor') only uses fish from the immediate vicinity, heavy on shellfish and sole as the sea is shallower here. It's right on the fishermen's marina and locals show up to eat. For the best shells, come in October. The fishplate Nostromo is a solid tip: white fish, squid, grilled scampi, potatoes and spinach. Same goes for the lobster with spaghetti, which runs to 200kn. There's a nautical interior and terrace – ignore the neon sign and pictures of the food.

Taverna Sergio

Šaini 2A (052 757 714). **Open** *Summer* 11am-3pm, 6-11pm daily. *Winter* 11am-3pm, 6-11pm Mon, Tue, Thur-Sun. **KK**. **Restaurant**. Map p81 E1 ⑭

A family business for two decades, this was opened by ex-footballer Sergio Makin. Lobster with tagliatelle, risotto with scampi and asparagus, *fuži* pasta with truffles and manestra soup are house specialities. Oysters and quality white fish are also served. The garden terrace is secluded from the street by thick shrubs, palms and vines. An accordion is provided for guests as is a list of top Croatian wines. Rooms are let upstairs – note the pool and sauna.

Vitriol

Ribarnička 6 (052 758 270). **Open** 8am-midnight daily. **Bar**. Map p81 C2 ⑮

Best bar in Novigrad by a country mile. Its terrace lapped by the sea, overlooking the setting sun, the Vitriol is trendy enough to appeal to passing Italians without losing its young, lively character. Concoctions have a distinct Italian flavour (Negroni, Garibaldi) but include a zingy Novigrad Beach made of gin, Campari and orange juice. Local wines are chalked up outside, beers include Kriek and Kilkenny, and there are enough hot chocolates to fill an entire menu.

Shopping

La Gusta

Velika ulica 12 (no phone). **Open** *Apr-Oct* 9am-11pm daily. No credit cards. **Map** p81 C3

The place looks like a cheap perfume shop because that's what it is. There are 250 scents on hand in the tiny wooden shop filled with glass bottles. Ask for Chanel No 5, Hugo Boss or Poison and the attendant fills big jugs with the stuff. Prices are super-low.

Rigo

Velika ulica 5 (052 758 681). **Open** *Summer* 9am-11pm daily. *Winter* 9am-5pm Mon-Sat. **Map** p81 B2

Goodies from around Istria – wine, food and souvenirs – are displayed in terracotta roof tiles around the tiny store. There are also marmalades, honey, *rakija*, maps, lavender, framed paintings, etchings, baskets, glasses and decanters. Owner Alek will exchange money in all currencies.

Vinarija Novigrad

Vinarija Novigrad

Mandrać 18 (052 726 060). **Open** 8am-10pm Mon-Sat; 8am-2pm Sun. No credit cards. **Map** p81 D2

At the end of the promenade bordering the fishermen's harbour, look for the sign above battered, blue, wooden doors of this wine shop. Inside are wooden shelves loaded with jugs of wine with basketwork covers. In the back, a clerk fills plastic bottles from wooden barrels. A litre of table Malvasia is 15.50kn, Merlot 16.50kn. It also sells its own Muškat and other off-site labels. Thirsty locals and visitors stream in continuously at all times of the day and evening.

Nightlife

Waikiki Sunset

Gradska Plaža (098 434 699 mobile). **Open** *June-Oct* 10am-4am daily. No credit cards. **Map** p81 B2

Under the campanile on the city beach, the town's ancient walls frame the palm-frond roofed bar and tables of the Waikiki. Milkshakes, coffee drinks and beer are served by cheery waitresses by day while water-polo goes on in the sea out front. DJed house, R&B and hip hop plays at night on the packed concrete dance floor. Cocktails include a Viagra of vodka, Curaçao, apricot liqueur and Red Bull.

Arts & leisure

Gallery Rigo

Velika ulica 5 (052 726 582/ www.galerija-rigo.hr). **Open** varies. **Admission** free. **Map** p81 B2

Located in a Baroque building built by the local Rigo nobility in the late 18th century, this complex was restored in 1994. It is now one of Istria's most important independent galleries, with a fast-moving programme of challenging, contemporary exhibitions all year round. The permanent display features ancient tombstones and fragments from Byzantine times.

Buje

Umag & surroundings

The towns of **Umag**, **Savudrija**, **Brtonigla** and **Buje**, along with Novigrad, are grouped together. You can drive between them hardly realising you have done so – but each has a distinct personality.

Umag has the chief role. Known today as the host of the **Croatia Open** at the **Stella Maris Tennis Centre**, Umag dates to Roman times. Today its population is 13,000, who share 70 tennis courts, 500 kilometres of biking paths and 4,000 sq m of spa centres.

Little brother Savudrija (Salvore in Italian) is an unspoiled fishing village where Croatians relax. A frontier land, it was part of Piran (now Slovenia) until the war. The main landmark is the **Lighthouse**, built in 1818. The town's rising popularity is based on its lodging options, most notably the four-star seaside **Villa Rosetta**, and the **Kempinski Hotel Adriatic**, which opened in 2009 and brought in Croatia's first 18-hole golf course. Four more courses are planned.

Buje is set on a hill, 200 metres above a fertile region of olive oil and wine. Its Old Town, though, has a ghostly feel. Brtonigla is the classic overachiever. A well-preserved, compact village, first written about in the 1200s, today it is a gastro enclave. Three of the best kitchens in Istria – **Konoba Morgan, Konoba Astarea** and **San Rocco** – are found here.

Sights & museums

Boat cranes
Savudrija
South of Savudrija Lighthouse, and on the water near Istarska and the tourist office, are lines of boats hanging above the rocks and water. Suspending these skiffs from the tops of poles via a pulley system and ropes is the traditional local way of protecting them from the harsh Adriatic winds that could toss them against the shore. Though used elsewhere, this method is most associated with Savudrija, and forms the perfect postcard shot.

Buje Ethnographic Museum
Trg slobode 2 (052 773 075).
Open 9am-noon, 6-9pm Mon-Sat.
Admission 10kn.

Viva Mulino!

Mulino, located north and west of Buje close to the Slovene border, is a high-end casino, hotel and restaurant, well situated to enjoy all of Istria's delights – if you can pry yourself away from the slot machine or whirlpool.

The casino was built in 1996 and has 260 slot machines and 20 tables where dealers serve up blackjack, Caribbean stud poker and Texas hold'em. There is also French and American roulette on the floor. And, like any high-end casino, there are dance shows and revues. But that only tells part of the story. Built next to the salt flats between the two countries, Mulino is arguably the most impressive hotel on the peninsula, if a little over the top.

For the most part the clientele is Italian and those with big budgets, but any traveller with the means would do well here. Rooms start at around 120 euros. The hotel is within shouting distance of the coast, ten kilometres (six miles)

from Umag, and near a number of winemakers, olive-oil producers and fine restaurants. When the day is over you can take a dip in the jacuzzi or pool with a cocktail.

Opened in 2007, Mulino should be a five-star but remains only four because some units don't have bathtubs. The 67 rooms and luxury suites set over five floors have everything else. Marble litters the place. Swarovski crystal is used for handles and doorknobs. The ceilings are festooned with paintings. The walls are gilded and there are vast mosaics all over the hotel. There is also a wellness centre and a spa with windows in the saunas.

In addition, there's a fine-dining restaurant serving shellfish, lobster, salmon, roast lamb, pork and steak. To promote both gastro education and the dozens of local wines on the menu, every Friday a different Istrian producer of note is featured, with an accompanying menu drawn up for the occasion.

At the start of the Old Town, the museum is spread over several floors, with displays of kitchens, a loom and crafts.

Savudrija Lighthouse

Savudrija (www.plovput.hr).
Built at the behest of Habsburg Franz I, whose inscription runs around its base, this stands 36 metres (118 feet) high on Croatia's most westerly point. It is the oldest active lighthouse in the Adriatic. Lodging is also available.

Umag Town Museum

Trg sv. Martina 1, Umag (052 741 440). **Open** *Apr-Oct* 10am-11pm Mon-Sat. *Nov-Mar* by appointment only. **Admission** free.
In an old defence tower later converted into the Bishop's Palace, this museum is filled with Roman finds: oil lamps, plates, amphorae and headstones.

Eating & drinking

Belveder

Karigador 51, Karigador (052 735 199). **Open** *Summer* 11am-11pm daily. *Winter* 11am-11pm Mon, Wed-Sun. **KK. Restaurant**.

Opened in 1974, this family-run restaurant is in the tiny village of Karigador, five kilometres (three miles) north of Novigrad on the coast. This is the classic fish restaurant; sea bass, lobster, scampi, squid, mussels, clams and shrimp are served on a terrace hanging over the sea, shaded by a mulberry tree. Order the mixed platter and pair it with a quality red or white.

Goldfish Beach Club

NEW *Stella Maris Bay, Umag (091 462 9413 mobile).* **Open** *June-Oct* 9am-2am daily. No credit cards. **Cocktail bar**.
Opened in July 2009, the Goldfish is a welcome addition to the beach cocktail scene. On wooden planking, DJs play lounge music until the après-beach soirée kicks in and MCed parties go on until morning. Beautiful staff serve cocktails to folks lounging on wicker couches under white sun umbrellas with water on both sides.

Konoba Astarea

Ronkova 9, Brtonigla (052 774 384, www.konoba-astarea-brtonigla.com). **Open** 11am-11pm daily. Closed Nov. **KK. Restaurant**.

Konoba Buščina, Umag p90

ISTRIA BY AREA

Konoba Astarea, Brtonigla p89

Astarea's interior is as cosy as a living room with old photos, a piano and an open fire where most of the menu is cooked, giving your meal a great smoky taste. The menu is fish-centric with some meat alternatives. Amiable owner Anton talks you through the day's menu – don't fret about the bill, three courses with first-class fish and quality wine will be around 350kn per head, or you can eat and drink well for less. This is traditional food done well: fish soup, scampi *buzara*, and a whole fish cooked under the coals (*ispod peke*) with potatoes and a bottle of a good Malvasia. Astarea rightfully attracts a loyal following and booking is recommended. Pick your designated driver; after the meal you'll be offered home-made grappas to drink as you wish.

Konoba Buščina

Buščina 18, Umag (052 732 088, www.konoba-buscina.hr). **Open** *Summer* noon-midnight daily. *Winter* noon-midnight Mon, Wed-Sun. **KK**. **Restaurant**.
Wine, truffles, olive oil, shellfish, wild game and asparagus are among the goodies Buščina offers at *konoba*

prices. Owned by Fabiana Mijanović, this is a family-run restaurant in which son and daughter work the floor and in the kitchen. Lamb, veal and beef are cooked under a roasting bell; fish is too, or grilled. Everything is home-made: bread, pasta, gnocchi, desserts. Outside, two terraces seat about 70. As well as serving their own olive oil, the family has a wine menu with the best local labels, including Clai and Kabola.

Konoba Morgan

Bračanija 1, Buje (052 774 520). **Open** *mid Oct-mid Sept* noon-10pm Mon, Wed-Sun. **KK**. **Restaurant**. See box p92.

Konoba Nono

Umaška 35, Petrovija (052 740 160). **Open** *Summer* 11am-11pm daily. *Winter* 11am-11pm Tue-Sun. **KK**. **Restaurant**.
In a village three kilometres (two miles) north of Umag, Nono offers excellent food, good prices, a rustic atmosphere and a staff who are genuinely pleasant. There's a fireplace for cooking lamb and veal under the roasting bell. On the terrace, steaks are grilled beside farm

implements. The Nono makes its own sausages and has a certificate to sell *boškarin* (Istrian oxen) steak. The home-made pasta with asparagus, *pršut* ham and cream is simple and delightful. Finish with caramelised figs atop sweet ricotta cheese with the word Nono stencilled in cinnamon.

San Rocco

Srednja ulica 2, Brtonigla (052 725 000, www.san-rocco.hr). **Open** 1-10pm daily. **KKK. Restaurant**.

This is luxury. Enjoy a swim and massage then tuck into truffle-flavoured dishes prepared with San Rocco's own-made olive oil – proximity to the sea means that the fish is very fresh. Accompanying wines such as Matošović and Kozlović will be carefully chosen, living up to Brtonigla's reputation as a gastro hub. San Rocco has a pizzeria and wine shop nearby.

Taverna Vili

Savudrijska, Umag (052 752 145, www.taverna-vili.com). **Open** *Apr-Nov* 11am-12.30am daily. **KK. Restaurant**.

This veteran establishment of 20 years' standing is good and its prices reason-

able. It serves seafood spaghetti, john dory, lobster and a handful of shellfish, but excels in grilled beef, pork, lamb and scampi.

Villa Rosetta

Crvena Uvala 31, Savudrija (052 725 710, www.villarosetta.hr). **Open** noon-11pm daily. **KKK. Restaurant**.

As well known as a four-star hotel as a place to eat, Rosetta is a must-stop in Savudrija for gourmets. The restaurant on the ground floor has a fine-dining atmosphere and a wicker-laden terrace that looks on to a field rolling down to a private hotel beach. Decor, food – every detail is laboured over. The family has been in the business since 1938 and have a good few recipes up their sleeves. The mainly Mediterranean menu includes shrimp carpaccio, home-made pastas with lobster, and brodetto fish stew.

Nightlife

Bamboo

Zlatorog Beach, Umag (no phone). **Open** *May-Oct* 24hrs daily. Closed Nov-Apr. No credit cards.

Captain Morgan's

Konoba Morgan provides the quintessential Istrian dining experience. It's not well signposted: to reach it, take the main road out of Buje, then a track on the left-hand side a kilometre (half a mile) before Brtonigla.

Marko Morgan, its young owner, has a simple mission. The classically trained musician (flute, guitar, piano) aims to excite guests by producing simple dishes based on authentic Istrian recipes. Italians love it, travelling regularly to eat here, enjoying the large covered terrace with a view of the vines and bucolic countryside.

The self-effacing Morgan lets the top-quality ingredients, all locally sourced, and attention to detail take centre stage. The business, now more than a decade old, involves the whole family. Morgan senior hunts for the wide selection of game. His mother and sister work in the kitchen. 'It all started when my father would go off to hunt and my mother would make meals for the hunting party,' says Marko.

There's no fixed menu. Morgan relays to customers what is available that day, and invites them to take an aperitif or a glass of sparkling wine. He then presents only what's fresh. 'We serve very simple food,' Marko explains. 'So each ingredient has to be good.'

Reservations are a must. Time-tested specialities are based on the season. They include home-made polenta with game (rabbit, pheasant, wild boar, venison or quail); pasta stuffed with chestnut purée; and *krestine*, red pasta filled with white cockerel meat. Slow-cooked and marinated local *boškarin* ox is another favourite. When it's summer, expect black truffles. In spring, there's asparagus. In the late autumn, white truffles may accompany.

To complete the experience, Morgan makes sure to blend the right wine with the right food. The restaurant has Istria's finest vintages including rare varieties like Plavina and Hrvatica, a strong and little-known rosé.

Just south of Umag on the coastal road, look for the big wooden sign at the edge of the woods, then trek the last 50 metres to Bamboo, situated on the beach with a sand volleyball court. There are, naturally, bamboo tables and chairs scattered about. The whole is shaded by big oaks and palm-frond umbrellas. Slovene Laško is on tap and they also serve cocktails, as DJs spin by day and rock bands play at night.

Daylight Cocktail Bar

Katoro, Umag (099 505 7113 mobile). **Open** *June-Oct* 11am-4am daily. No credit cards.

A rotating crew of DJs keep this club pumping under a vast thatched roof on the water near the Katoro resort. Renowned bartenders, one voted the best in Croatia, supply the drinks from two bars as a lightshow sparkles in the pines. Thursday nights are theme nights and there are drink specials on Fridays. Expect go-go dancers.

Jimmy Woo Club Lounge

NEW *Stella Maris Bay, Umag (091 462 9413 mobile, www.jimmywoo.hr).* **Open** *Summer* 10pm-4am daily. *Winter* 10pm-4am Fri, Sat. No credit cards.

Near the tennis centre and the water, JW instantly became the place to go when it opened in July 2009. A nightly theme keeps everyone happy: funky destination Tuesdays, sexy house Wednesdays and Studio 54 Sundays. The cocktail menu lists hundreds of drinks and the entrance fee is minimal, if not free. The word is that the owners, who also run Papaya on Pag and Piranha and Gjuro 2 in Zagreb, have just signed an MTV party contract.

Arts & leisure

Aleksandar Rukavina Memorial Gallery

Aleksandra Rukavine 1, Brtonigla (052 774 307). **Open** 4-6pm Sat, Sun. **Admission** free.

This gallery contains 47 sculptures by Aleksandar Rukavina, of wood, stone and bronze, focusing on soldiers and peasants. He was also dedicated to restoring villages to their former glory.

Mulino Lux Casino Hotel

Škrile 75A, Buje (052 725 300/ www.mulino.hr). **Open** 24hrs daily. See box p88.

Stella Maris Tennis Centre

Savudrijska, Umag (052 710 888, www.croatiaopen.hr).

Every year in late July, Umag becomes the focus of this tennis-obsessed country. Croatia's biggest pro event has taken place here at the north-west tip of Croatia for two decades. And though it is overrun with tennis devotees for the ATP tournament, Stella Maris has its share of racket-toters all summer long, waiting for spots on approximately 30 courts, 14 of them floodlit. Set on a green stretch of seaside north of town, Stella Maris is generally considered the best centre in the country.

Jimmy Woo Club Lounge

Pula Forum p100

Pula & the South

Southern Istria, for the purposes of this guide, extends from **Bale** at its northernmost extreme to **Kamenjak**, a protected mini-peninsula which dangles from the big peninsula like a pristine appendix. In between sit Istria's only real city, Tito's playground, beaches, a sardine academy and mummies. This swathe of land and sea also provides a needed rich urban flavour and balance in Istria, arguably best known for its sleepy interior and bucolic landscape of wine, olives and truffles.

Focal **Pula** dominates this region. With around 60,000 residents, this is by far Istria's biggest single populace. What's more, Pula actually feels like a city. Traffic moves slowly. People are in a little more of a hurry. There is a wide choice of clubs, bars, restaurants and cafés. It even has its own resort area to the south. These places – **Medulin** being the largest – are known for their beaches, water sports, package-tourism offers and, to a lesser degree, their food and mainstream nightlife. All are within easy reach of Pula by car and by local city buses from the city centre.

The area to Pula's north starts to have more of an inland vibe. The towns here have preserved medieval squares, cobbled streets and traditions that draw heavily on Roman and Venetian influences. This section includes the aforementioned Bale; **Vodnjan** and its sacred mummies; **Fažana** and its sardine industry; and, the **Brijuni Islands**, which form a barrier archipelago and once played host to movie stars and diplomats in Tito's Yugoslavia. This National Park is the must-visit of the region; along with Pula's Roman remains, in particular the Amphitheatre, home of the Pula Film Festival, the region's main cultural event.

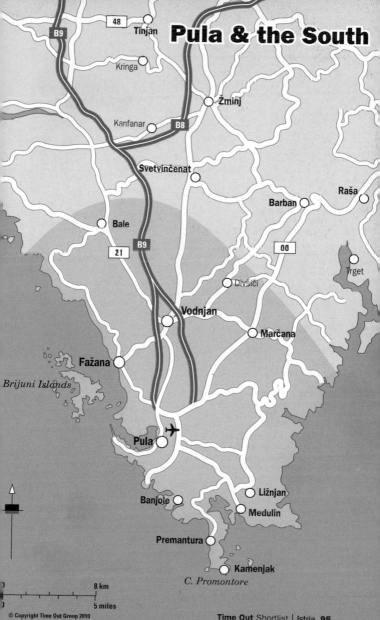

Pula & the South

B9

48

Tinjan

Kringa

Žminj

Kanfanar

B8

Svetvinčenat

Barban

Raša

Bale

Trget

21

B9

00

Divšiči

Vodnjan

Marčana

Fažana

Brijuni Islands

Pula

Ližnjan

Banjole

Medulin

Premantura

Kamenjak

C. Promontore

8 km

5 miles

© Copyright Time Out Group 2010

ISTRIA BY AREA

Pula

If it is not your first port of call, **Pula** can be a jolt back to reality. Although not the county town of Istria – that honour rests with Pazin – Pula is certainly its hub. With around 60,000 citizens, Pula houses nearly a third of Istria's population. For shopping, art or arrival by air, Pula is the place. What the city lacks in an attractive waterfront it makes up for in terms of antiquities, quality places to eat and nightspots.

Pula's **Roman Forum** remains the key meeting-point, while the **Amphitheatre** hosts concerts and the annual **Film Festival**. Building on this old-meets-new philosophy, Pula is hoping to develop itself as a major cultural destination. Municipal plans outline a cultural ring interspersing new, contemporary venues with the town's existing historical sites.

Just about everything else of interest lies south of the city centre, on or off the main Veruda road

leading to the hotel hub and best beaches of **Verudela**. Halfway to the two nearest beaches, at Stoja and Valsaline, is the ornate **Naval Cemetery**, constructed by the Habsburgs, the perfect spot for a stroll on a hot summer's afternoon.

Nearer town, on Gajeva, parallel to the sea and the main road of Arsenalska, stands another military remnant, the **Karlo Rojc** barracks. This has recently been transformed into a multi-purpose arts centre where exhibitions, DJ nights and concerts are held on a regular but ad-hoc basis. This is Istria's leading venue for alternative culture.

The city's sprawling waterfront includes a port handling close to one million tons of cargo every year, a marina for yachters, a forested stretch of beach with a promenade and, outside the centre, resorts built in the 1960s and '70s in Verudela and neighbouring Medulin. Now slowly reviving, Pula is one of those rare coastal towns where life goes on in winter.

Greater Pula

Sights & museums
Eating & drinking
Shopping
Nightlife
Arts & leisure

See p99

VERUDELA

ULICA VERUDA

VALSALINE

SISPLAC

BARAKE

ULICA STOJA

STOJA

RIZZIJEVA ULICA

MONTE RIZZI

TOM SINEVA ULICA

ULICA FRATALICA I PRETOVA

MARSOVA ULICA

PRAGRANDE

MUTILSKA ULICA

MONTE ZARO

MARULICEVA ULICA

RADICEVA ULICA

ARSENALSKA ULICA

RADOUSOVA ULICA

GREGOVICA

KASTANJER

MONTE SERPO

CESTA PREKOMORSKIH BRIGADA

ISTARSKA ULICA

MLETACKA ULICA

MORVIDA

KOPARSKA ULICA

ULICA 43 ISTARSKE BRIGADE

RIVA

MONTEGNURO

TRSCANSKA ULICA

ULJANIK

N

1 km
0.5 mile

© Copyright Time Out Group 2010

Airport

Chapel of St Maria Formosa

Sights & museums

Amphitheatre

Flavijevska (052 219 028). **Open**
Summer 8am-9pm daily. *Winter*
9am-4pm daily. **Admission** 40kn.
Map p99 C2 ❶

Called 'the Arena' by locals, the
Amphitheatre was built in the first century BC under Augustus and then
added during Claudius's rule in the
first century AD. The sixth largest in
the Roman Empire, the Amphitheatre
is made of local limestone and could
seat 25,000 spectators. Today its outer
walls are intact and the complex is still
in use beyond the simple provision of
tours for its many visitors. The 13,000-
square-metre structure, a short walk
north of the city centre, provides a
backdrop for the Film Festival and big-
name concerts in summer. The inside
is a mess of green plastic seating and
clumps of stone but you do get a sense
of the gladiatorial contests held here
until 400 AD, particularly when you go
down to the corridors on the sea-facing
side where the lions were kept.
Through a tunnel lined with Roman
masonry you'll find displays about
olive oil and a map of Via Flavia that
linked Pula with Trieste.

Archaelogical Museum of Istria

Carrarina 3 (052 218 609, www.
mdc.hr/pula). **Open** *Summer* 9am-8pm
Mon-Sat; 10am-3pm Sun. *Winter* 9am-
3pm Mon-Fri. **Admission** 20kn. No
credit cards. **Map** p99 B3 ❷

Many local Illyrian and Roman finds
are on display here in this three-storey
venue established in 1902 as the municipal museum, opened to visitors in
1930, the primary information source
in a town that is an open-air museum
in its own right. Inside you'll find jewellery, coins and weapons from Roman
and medieval times, ceramics and fos-
sils from pre-history, mosaics and sar-
cophagi. New finds mean that the halls
are extended every so often.

Chapel of St Maria Formosa

Flaciusova. **Open** times vary.
Map p99 A4 ❸

A well-preserved three-nave church
from the sixth century AD, St Maria
Formosa is an architectural wonder,
inside and out. Layers of stone once
housed mosaics; some can be found in
the Archaeological Museum. In its heyday, it was one of two chapels belong-
ing to a Benedictine abbey torn down

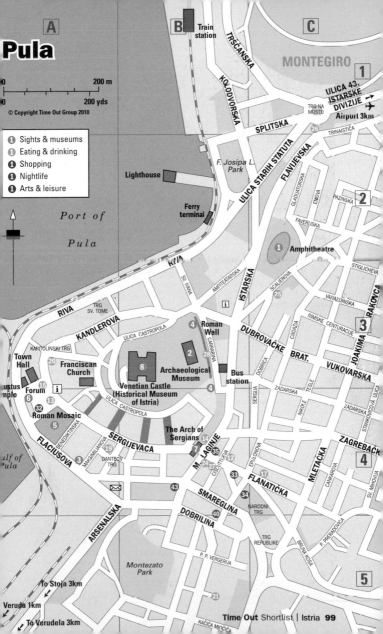

Pula

200 m
200 yds

© Copyright Time Out Group 2010

- **1** Sights & museums
- **1** Eating & drinking
- **1** Shopping
- **1** Nightlife
- **1** Arts & leisure

A **B** Train station **C**

MONTEGIRO

TRŠĆANSKA

KOLODVORSKA

SPLITSKA

ULICA 43.
ISTARSKE
DIVIZIJE
Airport 3km

TRG NA
MOSTU

TRINAJSTIĆA

FLAVIJEVSKA

ULICA STARIH STATUTA

F. Josipa L.
Park

GLADIJATORSKA

EMONIA

PAZINSKA

FAVERIJSKA

Lighthouse

Ferry terminal

Port of
Pula

1 Amphitheatre

AMFITEATARSKA

ISTARSKA

SCALIEROVA

STIGLICHEVA

25

VLAŠKA DINSKA

CROATIA

RIMSKE CENTURIJE

RAKOVCA

JOAKIMA

RIVA

TRG
SV. TOME

SV. IVANA

KANDLEROVA

ULICA CASTROPOLA

4 Roman Wall

CARRARINA

DUBROVAČKE BRAT.

VUKOVARSKA

KAPITOLINSKI TRG

Town Hall

20 Franciscan Church

2

8

Archaeological Museum

28 CARRARINA

Bus station

DABRICA

SERGIJA

ZADARSKA

TESLE

NIKOLE

ZADARSKA

STANKOVIĆEVA ULICA

ZAGREBAČK

ustus
mple

Forum

6 **32** **15** **13**

i

5

Roman Mosaic

Venetian Castle
(Historical Museum
of Istria)

ULICA CASTROPOLA

BENEDIKTINSKA

MAKSIMILIJANOVA

19

DANTEOV
TRG

SERGIJEVACA

3

FLACIUSOVA

ulf of
ula

M. LAGINJE

The Arch of
Sergians

14

35

12

CISTERTIJEVA

33

FLANATIČKA

17

MLETAČKA

CANKAROVA

SV. MIHOVILA

43

SMAREGLINA

34

Narodni
TRG

DOBRILINA

40

EPULONOVA

TRG
REPUBLIKE

P. P. VERGERIJA

BRIJUNI KOSA

P. PRERADOVIĆA

ARSENALSKA

Montezato
Park

To Stoja 3km

Veruda 1km

To Verudela 3km

21

KAČIĆA MIOČIĆA

Time Out Shortlist | Istria **99**

Temple of Augustus

in the 16th century. Today the chapel stands as evidence of just how much ancient wealth Pula has hidden about.

Hercules & Twin Gates
Carrarina 1 & 3. **Map** p99 B3 ④
The two gates are located on either side of the Archaeological Museum and on opposite sides of Carrarina. The Gate of Hercules is so named because of a carving of the half-god, half-mortal hero's head at the top of the stone archway. Built in the first century BC, it is the oldest town gate and helps to shine a light on the origins of Pula as an urban settlement. The Twin Gates are beautifully preserved and were built between the second and third centuries AD. They served as the main entry through the walls that surrounded Pula, most of which were demolished in the 19th century.

Mosaic
Sergijevaca. **Open** 24hrs. **Admission** free. **Map** p99 A4 ⑤
This floor mosaic was discovered two metres under the floors of destroyed buildings after World War II. Dating back to the second century AD, in the remains of a Roman house, it's a gem of design and detail. The tiled scene,

amid 40 other squares of different intricate geometric patterns, is the representation of the 'Punishment of Dirce' by twins Amphion and Zethos.

Pula Forum/Temple of Augustus
Forum (052 218 609). **Open** *Summer* 9am-3pm Mon-Fri; 9am-3pm Sat, Sun. **Admission** 10kn. **Map** p99 A4 ⑥
The Forum has acted as Pula's main square since the Romans. This space, a hop from the sea and below the castle hill, houses the tourist information office, cafés, boutiques and the Town Hall, or Communal Palace. Built upon the remains of two ancient temples, the palace has been the site of the government seat here since 1296. On the Forum's western edge stands the Temple of Augustus, begun in 2 BC. Six classical Corinthian columns surround a building with a modest collection of Roman stone and bronze sculptures. Once part of a threesome of temples here, this was the lone survivor until World War II, when it was bombed and rebuilt afterwards.

Triumphal Arch of the Sergi
Sergijevaca. **Map** p99 B4 ⑦

Also known as the Golden Gate, this Roman attraction at the southeast entrance to the town centre provides a dramatic welcome to the ancient city. Built between 29 and 27 BC by the Sergi family, the Triumphal Arch is said to have inspired Napoleon's construction of the Arc de Triomphe. Its most notable aspects are the reliefs of grapes and winged victories on the inner façade. Passing through the arch and past the statue of James Joyce, marking where the author taught in 1904-05, you walk down the Roman-era high street, Sergijevaca.

Venetian Castle & Historical Museum of Istria

Gradinski uspon 6 (052 211 566, www.pmi.hr). **Open** *Summer* 9am-9pm daily. *Winter* 9am-4pm daily. **Admission** 15kn. **Map** p99 B3 ❸

Atop a leafy hill looking over the town sits a star-shaped castle constructed in 1630 at the behest of the Venetians, on the site of a Roman fortress. Built to protect the harbour, today it houses the Historical Museum of Istria. The collection dates from medieval times to the present. On display is a compilation (40,000 pieces) of photographs, postcards, uniforms, maritime equipment, coins and maps.

Eating & drinking

Bass

Širolina 3 (no phone). **Open** *Summer* 8am-midnight Mon-Thur; 8am-1am Fri, Sat; 10am-midnight Sun. *Winter* 8am-midnight Mon-Sat; 10am-midnight Sun. No credit cards. **Bar**. **Map** p97 C2 ❾

A great bar set between town and Verudela, Bass has a slew of beers, reasonably priced cocktails, sangría and *rakija* brandy. You'll know you're in the right place if you feel like you are trapped in an Alan Ford cartoon. On the terraces are wicker, teardrop-shaped chairs and the rocking variety. DJs play funky rock on Fridays.

Days out

Central Pula has no beaches but you'll find a handful within an easy bus journey from the city centre. The nearest ones at **Stoja** and along Lungomare between **Veruda** and **Valsaline** are perfectly acceptable, but if you're taking a city bus (Nos. 1 and 4 respectively) to get there, you may as well grab the Nos. 2A or 3A to Verudela, for nicer shingle beaches and more convivial lunching options.

If you've come specifically for a beach holiday, leave Pula and head south for nearby **Medulin** or the windsurfing mecca of **Premantura**, both a quick and regular bus journey from Pula, on the Nos. 25 and 26. Both have ample to offer the outdoor sports enthusiast. Beyond Premantura is the pristine and protected **Kamenjak**, with its secluded beaches spanning across an area of 395 hectares at the very southern tip of Istria.

Another day-trip option is **Fratarsko Island**. In summer locals decamp here almost permanently, spending nights under canvas among the shady pines and commuting to the city by ferry. There are free showers. Ferries from Bunarina, heaving with sun worshippers for the ten-minute crossing, run every 20 minutes or so in season.

The other major excursion from Pula is to the National Park of the **Brijuni Islands** – Tito's playground, where villas, exotic animals and Roman ruins take centre stage. Boats only set off from Fažana, seven kilometres north-west of Pula, by bus No. 21 every hour.

ISTRIA BY AREA

Borghese

Monte Paradiso 21 (052 392 111).
Open *Summer* 11am-midnight daily.
Winter 11am-midnight Tue-Sun. **KKK**.
Restaurant. Map p97 D1 ⑩

Borghese is a reputable seafood restaurant in Verudela with prices to match. Starched white tablecloths await the diner in an interior embellished with natural light. The fish is that-day fresh and finely prepared, but don't miss out on the recommended starter of mixed salad with fruits de mer and the speciality main dish of scampi ravioli.

Bunarina

Verudela 9 (052 222 978). **Open** *Summer* 8am-midnight daily. *Winter* 8am-10pm daily. **KK**. No credit cards.
Restaurant. Map p97 E1 ⑪

A down-home popular spot, this is a local fishermen's haunt on the jetty of Bunarina. In high season tables cover every square inch of the limited space as customers watch the boats or wait for a ferry to Fratarsko island. It provides food in season on the terrace, as well as live music.

Caffè Bar Nautika

Flanatička 11 (no phone). **Open** 7am-10pm Mon-Sat; 7am-2pm Sun. No credit cards. **Café**. Map p99 B4 ⑫

Locals come to this car-free promenade to check out who is wearing what and to woo potential significant others. The produce and fish markets are to one side in the train-station-like Austro-Hungarian complex, and the Golden Gate is to the other. Coffee and stronger liquids are served on a terrace under a big, yellow umbrella. Inside the little bar and above a stone-stacked wall is a flatscreen TV for football.

Caffè Diana

Forum 4 (052 214 779). **Open** 7am-11pm daily. No credit cards. **Café**. Map p99 A4 ⑬

Diana, opened in 1973, is the classic café on the Forum looking directly at the Town Hall and the Temple of Augustus – note the wood-and-marble interior and big, white, sun umbrellas. Also sited by the Tourist Office, it's a good place to pull out your map and plan your attack.

Caffè Uliks

Trg Portarata 1 (052 219 158). **Open** *Summer* 6.30am-2am daily. *Winter* 6.30am-11pm daily. No credit cards. **Café**. Map p99 B4 ⑭

If there is any question whether you are in the right place, the statue outside gives it away. A century ago James Joyce taught here by the Roman arch. He and his eloper are also honoured with a Joyce cocktail (Jameson's, Martini Bianco and Krašokova pear) and a Nora of Bailey's, Bacardi and cream. There are bottled Guinness and Kilkenny, and Irish coffee, in this otherwise standard bar that plays up Pula's most famous Irish resident.

Cvajner

Forum 2 (052 216 502). **Open** 8am-11pm daily. No credit cards. **Café**. Map p99 A3 ⑮

Or, to give it its official title, the Kunstkafe-Cvajner. Either way, it's a splendid bar on the main square. Part gallery, part junk shop, the Cvajner presents mismatching furniture, sculptures and an old carriage, placed around a spacious, high-ceilinged interior where one wall is dated AD 1928. Bottles of Chimay and dark Laško beer complement standard cocktails, best partaken on the Forum terrace.

Gina

Stoja 23 (052 387 943). **Open** 11am-11pm daily. **KKK**. **Restaurant**. Map p97 D3 ⑯

Along with fish and hearty meat dishes, the Istrian-style menu features seafood – fresh daily – and pasta combinations such as ravioli stuffed with crab. The pasta is home-made and the bread is baked in a stone oven on site. There is a qualified sommelier on staff, and the wine list features 60 mostly local choices, many from Istria. Stone walls, polished wood, the sea air washing in through the big windows, plus the Istrian-style fireplace, create a cosy space for this family-run venue just uphill from the Lungomare promenade by the forested peninsula of Stoja.

Kantina

Flanatička 16 (052 214 054). **Open** 8am-midnight daily. **KK. Restaurant**. **Map** p99 C4 ⑰

Hidden behind the main market, this lovely terrace restaurant serves Istrian delicacies in a converted Habsburg villa. The decor, like the food, is a combination of contemporary with age-old touches. Truffles feature heavily, either with steak or, more traditionally, with *fuži*, Istrian pasta twists. There are plenty of greens, rocket particularly, some 100 types of wine and the homemade cake selection is outstanding. New this year: jazz on the terrace at weekends and a wine bar where you can taste and buy your favourite labels.

Milan

Stoja 4 (052 300 200, www.milan 1967.hr). **Open** *Summer* noon-11pm daily. *Winter* noon-11pm Mon-Sat. **KKK. Restaurant**. **Map** p97 D2 ⑲

Considered one of the top three spots in town, Milan is set in a family-run, modern, three-star hotel by the Naval Cemetery. A display case heaves with riches fresh from the sea, duly listed on a long main menu. Most dishes are reasonably priced considering the quality on offer. Shellfish come in all types, though risotto portions are (in Croatian terms) quite small. The wine cellar has 700 types, running up to 1,000kn a bottle; your waiter will advise.

Mushroom Pub

Prolaz kod Zdenca 4 (052 210 686). **Open** *Summer* 2pm-2am daily. *Winter* 7am-midnight daily. No credit cards. **Pub. Map** p99 A4 ⑲

A mix of alternative types, students and Hajduk fans keeps this charming terrace and bar – set on an picturesque old-town square – buzzing with a friendly vibe until late. It's a good place to catch the game on TV or warm up before the clubs start hopping.

Orfej

Konzula Istranina 1 (052 214 405). **Open** 8am-11pm Mon-Sat; noon-10pm Sun. **K. Restaurant**. **Map** p99 A3 ⑳

Tucked behind the Forum, Orfej is a place you won't immediately think is

Valsabbion p107

Milan p103

worth a stop when you pass it. It is. The bread is home-made and served with excellent sandwiches, burgers and salads. There are also pastas and pizzas delivered to a big stone terrace with room for about 80. The interior across the street is old stone meets marble, with jazz on the radio and an artsy crowd bustling about. A locals' spot.

P14

Preradovićeva 14 (052 382 987).
Open *Summer* 8am-midnight Mon-Thur, Sun; 8am-1am Fri, Sat. *Winter* 8am-midnight daily No credit cards.
Bar. Map p99 B5 ㉑
Jožo Čurković's alternative haunt at the far end of Flanatička attracts an arty clientele for impromptu stand-up performances and one-off events. Centre-pieced by a snake-shaped bar table, decorated with mushrooms and a lit-up globe, P14 is a spot like no other downtown bar. Leffe, Hoegaarden and Istrian spirits flow from a bar propped up by friendly regulars.

Piazzetta

Rizzijeva 9 (052 214 286). **Open** 11am-11pm Mon-Fri; noon-midnight Sat, Sun.
KK. Restaurant. Map p99 C2 ㉒
A solid Italian restaurant, this. The interior is a swirl of painted grape leaves on smoked glass framing wooden streetlamps. Piazzetta serves pasta – baked cannelloni, home-made ravioli with truffles and tagliatelle with salmon – plus steak in a green pepper sauce, and beef medallions wrapped around *pršut* ham with a red wine and balsamic reduction.

Podroom

Buducinova 16 (no phone). **Open** 9am-midnight daily. No credit cards. **Bar.**
Map p97 C2 ㉓
Podroom used to be one of the truly solid bars in Pula. Sadly a recent fire destroyed part of the outside area of the bar but the leafy garden, with its stone waterfall, is still in play. Inside are a picture of a woman pulling a gun from

Culture club

Many know the **Rojc** complex as an alternative space slamming with rave parties. True, these exist, but the Rojc, an innovative town-sponsored project housing a myriad of non-governmental associations, is so much more.

Built in 1870, the Karlo Rojc building was originally an Austro-Hungarian military school. After the Yugoslav Army vacated the premises in the early 1990s, it was pressed into service for war refugees. Following the conflict, the building fell into disrepair until 1998. It was then the town council did something quite radical: it allowed NGOs – with agendas as varied as drama workshops and an orchestral group – to make use of the building. In one stroke the government converted a crumbling behemoth (avoiding both an environmental and city-planning nightmare) and gave noble causes a place to call their clubhouse.

By 2004 the city council and the newly established Department for Culture and Co-ordination had a system in place: qualifying organisations could apply for rooms to use free of charge with only the expense of restoring the space they occupied. Today 100 NGOs use 100 per cent of the rooms within the complex's two buildings. Theatre of Art, an NGO specialising in costumes, sets and anything related to stage productions, moved into one of the last two available rooms.

'With many creative groups in one place, ideas can easily be shared,' Kristina Nefat, the group's director said, in front of hallways given over to muralists. 'If I need be, I can walk down to the stage to see if something I am putting together works.'

Live music has also given Rojc its alternative following. There are DJed parties, music events, the yearly punk festival Monteparadiso and experimental theatre by Dr Inat. Check the website for upcoming happenings.

Cvajner p102

her purse, red walls and velvet pillows, all as dark as a basement – which is what the bar's name means.

Qpola Bistro

Trg Porlarata 6 (052 210 322). **Open** *Summer* 8am-2am daily. *Winter* 8am-midnight daily. **KK**. No credit cards. **Bar-restaurant**. Map p99 B4 ㉔

On the second floor of a shopping centre, this fashionable cocktail bar and restaurant lends itself to chilling out or starting a night on the town but is most notable for its view of the Golden Gate arch. A decent seafood menu can be perused from the balcony terrace. A pleasing mix of new music is supplemented with lounge DJs on weekend nights. It's also a good call for breakfast or a snacky lunch.

Rock Café

Scalierova 8 (052 210 975). **Open** *Summer* 8am-2am daily. *Winter* 8am-midnight daily. No credit cards. **Bar**. Map p99 C3 ㉕

A boisterous young crowd necks beers, shoots pool, cruises the long bar or roomy booths and sometimes breaks into dance as Elvis, Boston and metal classics rock the speakers of this institution. Set near the Amphitheatre, it is dressed up in old posters, music memorabilia and murals. Mirko, the enthusiastic owner, hosts Friday gigs (mainly in winter): jazz, blues and rock, mostly from Croatian combos.

Scaletta

Flavijevska 26 (052 541 599, www. hotel-scaletta.com). **Open** *Summer* 11am-midnight Mon-Sat; 6pm-midnight Sun. *Winter* 11am-2pm, 6pm-midnight Mon-Sat. **KK**. **Restaurant**. Map p99 C2 ㉖

This restaurant and charming hotel just up from the Amphitheatre is a splendid option for its location – and its kitchen. A risotto Scaletta with fruits de mer is delicately seasoned. Steak comes with white truffles, lobster with Istrian noodles, *rezanci*. Malvazija

and other Istrian tipples are the customary accompaniments, although you can order up an Erdinger wheat beer – Scaletta is German-owned.

Scandal Express

Ciscuttijeva 15 (052 212 106). **Open** 7am-midnight Mon-Thur; 7am-2am Fri; 7am-2pm, 6pm-2am Sat; 7am-2pm, 6pm-11pm Sun. No credit cards. **Bar**. Map p99 B4 ㉗

A tiny dive where local bohemians and in-the-know visitors meet, this place sits near the theatre at the Giardini end of Flanatička. There's no room around the bar at all, so regulars hug the corners by the entrance or, more usually, spill out on to the narrow street.

Sorso Wine Bar

Carrara 1 (052 222 532, www. velaneera.hr/winebar). **Open** 8am-midnight daily. **KK**. No credit cards. **Wine bar/restaurant**. Map p99 B3 ㉘

In the Italian community building in front of the Archaeology Museum, Sorso ('sip' in Italian) specialises in wine. There are 80 varieties of reds and whites from Istria, South Africa, Italy and France, as well as champagne and dessert wines. On the terrace and mezzanine you can accompany them with sandwiches and salads; eggs, croissants and Illy coffee comprise breakfast. The building and bar act as the HQ during the Pula Film Festival.

Valsabbion

Pješčana uvala IX/26 (052 218 033, www.valsabbion.net). **Open** *Feb-Dec* 10am-midnight daily. Closed Jan. **KKKK**. **Restaurant**. Map p97 D1 ㉙

The best table in town, and one of the top five in Croatia. Attached to the hotel of the same name, Valsabbion comprises two-dozen tables, half on a bay-view terrace under a white canopy, half in a tasteful, art-deco interior of refined pastel colours. The food is inventive and satisfying. If money is not an issue, try the tasting menu of ten

ISTRIA BY AREA

gourmet creations, truffle carpaccio or wild asparagus, all finely presented. A la carte, Kvarner Bay shrimps and Premantura crabs are teased with touches of greenery. The wine list is 200-strong.

Vela Nera

Pješčana uvala (052 219 209, www. velanera.hr). **Open** 8am-midnight daily. **KKKK**. **Restaurant**.
Map p97 D1 ㉚
Next to a supermarket, its terrace overlooking Marina Veruda, this is a very decent restaurant. Its modern, spacious interior is a refreshing change from the starched-white formal approach common elsewhere in town. Informal, too, are some of the combinations adventurously thrown together – the salmon and whisky carpaccio as a cold starter, for example, or the peaches and champagne mingled with scampi in the house risotto. Dining partners can dip into the fish or meat platters.

Vodnjanka

D Vitezíača 4 (052 210 655). **Open** *Summer* 10am-5pm, 7-10pm Mon-Fri; 10am-3pm Sat. *Winter* 10am-6pm Mon-Fri; 10am-3pm Sat. **KK**. No credit cards. **Restaurant**. **Map** p97 C1 ㉛
This family-run restaurant near the Rojc arts centre is popular with Pula's cultural movers and shakers – note the waiter's multicoloured goatee. The food is based on traditional Istrian cuisine with fresh fish and game. The must-try is the house aperitif: three layered herbal brandies topped with a lid of ice and a hole in the middle.

Shopping

Enoteka Istriana

Forum 11 (091 400 8440 mobile). *Summer* 10am-2pm, 6pm-10pm daily.
Map p99 A4 ㉜
Here Duška stocks hand-made ceramics as well as olive oil, truffle oil, honey and wine from across Istria in a tiny shop on the main square, a welcome respite from the tacky souvenirs. On a barrel tasting-table you can try local *rakija* brandy. Rooms for hire upstairs.

Heruc Galeria

Flanatička 10 (052 216 406). **Open** 8am-9pm Mon-Fri; 8am-1pm Sat.
Map p99 B4 ㉝
On the main pedestrian drag, Heruc is a designer shop for women. Under a high ceiling with high-end threads covering every available shelf and hanging space, the featured designers include Gil Bret, Strenesse Gabriele Strehle, Betty Barclay and Coccinelle.

Pula market

Narodni trg. **Open** *Vegetable market* Summer 7am-8pm daily. Winter 7am-4pm daily. *Fish market* 7am-2pm Mon-Sat; 7am-noon Sun. *Meat market* 7am-1.30pm Mon-Sat; 7am-noon Sun.
Map p99 B4 ㉞
Pula's main market is a Habsburg marvel, built in 1903. Well-ordered rows of stone tables outside groan with fresh produce. Along the sides, retractable wooden kiosks sell flowers, oils, liqueurs and sundry kitsch. The fish and meat markets sit next door, jammed with lamb, pork, veal, squid, sardines, salmon, octopus and shells.

Tisak Media

Flanatička 1 (052 213 601). **Open** 7am-10pm Mon-Sat; 7am-2pm Sun.
Map p99 B4 ㉟
Opposite the Golden Gate, this is the spot for maps, magazines and every trinket for electronic devices: headphones, batteries and the like. They also sell foreign papers, and DVDs and CDs to back up your files and photos.

Nightlife

Ambrela

NEW *Ambrela Beach, Verudela (052 215 585).* **Open** *Apr-Oct* 9am-3am daily. No credit cards. **Map** p97 E1 ㊱
Ambrela combines a terrace overlooking a stone beach with DJs thumping

hip hop, house, techno, R&B and broken beats from 10pm. Renovated in 2009 and near the Hotel Brioni, it has a daytime café and restaurant upstairs and cocktails down.

Aruba Club

Šijansku 1A (no phone). **Open** *Summer* 7am-1am Mon-Fri; 7am-3am Sat; 9am-11pm Sun. *Winter* 7am-11pm Mon-Thur; 7am-1am Fri; 7am-3am Sat; 9am-11pm Sun. No credit cards.
Map p97 A1 **37**

Expect commercial house and R&B here in the basement and ground floor. Thursdays are salsa nights. The decor is exposed wooden beams, satin yellow drapes, throw pillows and wooden plank floors. Among the two terraces are palms and stone fountains that help you forget the location at the corner of a mall on a busy thoroughfare. As well as cocktails, you can order up tortillas and cheeseburgers.

E&D

Verudela 22 (052 213 404). **Open** *Summer* 9am-2am daily. *Winter* 9am-midnight daily. No credit cards.
Map p97 E1 **38**

At E&D you sit in a sculpted hilltop garden, with a small pool and terrace seating, enjoying fine views of the sea while sipping sunset cocktails or morning coffee. Above the Lungomare promenade, in greenery near the resort hotels, this stunning café can get hopping from happy hour onward. DJs spin lounge and dance music in summer, when a full seafood menu is offered at reasonable prices. It's a 60kn taxi from town and worth every lipa.

Stella

Valturska 71 (052 380 035). **Open** *Summer* 7am-midnight Mon-Sat; 9am-midnight Sun. *Winter* 7am-midnight Mon-Thur; 7am-5am Fri, Sat; 9am-midnight Sun. No credit cards.
Map p97 A1 **39**

This is the locals' disco, open late-night only in winter. In summer it's a relaxed café, next to a busy road, forgotten about when you step into the open-air bar with mosaics. Big screens show sports events. The mood on the terrace, with velvety and wicker chairs, is governed by funky daytime music. Kids frolic in the grassy playground.

Uljanik

Dobrilina 2 (092 236 8289 mobile). **Open** *Summer* 10pm-5am Wed-Sat. *Winter* 10pm-5am Thur-Sat. No credit cards. **Map** p99 B4 **40**

Open since 1965, this is the old standby and standard. Uljanik has a huge dance floor with heavy-duty concert lighting and two bars. Outside are a stage and expansive courtyard. Locals sink *bambus* (red wine and coke) or *gemišt* (white wine and soda). Half-litres of tap beer run at 12kn. There are theme parties and DJs spin everything.

Zen Club

Dukićeva 1 (052 535 468). **Open** *Summer* 8am-2am Sun-Thur; 8am-4am Fri, Sat. *Winter* 8am-midnight daily. No credit cards. **Map** p97 A1 **41**

Zen dives completely into the zebra-skin-and-wicker motif. As well, there are Buddhas and provocative paintings of naked women with wild animals. There's a nice outdoor terrace, cocktails, DJs rocking R&B and house – and free entry. You can also order croissants, fruit plates and frappés.

Arts & leisure

Aquarium Pula

Verudela (052 381 402/052 381 403, www.aquarium.hr). **Open** 9am-10pm daily. **Admission** 30kn. **Map** p97 E1 **42**

There are 40 tanks and pools within this Habsburg fort turned aquarium. Inside are Adriatic plants, fish and crustaceans. Decorated with old fishnets and implements of seafarers, this is also a centre for turtle rehabilitation. Guided tours of the the old fort are laid on, as well as birthday parties for kids.

Istrian National Theatre

Laginjina 5 (052 222 380/www.ink.hr).
Map p99 B4 **43**
Catty-cornered to the Golden Gate, the
National Theatre building has been
restored several times since the late
1800s. As well as drama, there are concerts, children's shows, workshops and
dance studios.

Karlo Rojc

Gajeva 3 (www.rojcnet.hr). **Map** p97
C2 **44**
See box p105.

Around Pula: South

Go to Pula to get your city fix.
For beaches head south seven
kilometres to **Medulin**, built for
mass tourism in the 1970s. The
main town and administrative
centre of the Medulin Riviera –
which also includes the nearby
communities of **Pomer**,
Premantura, **Pješčana Uvala**
and **Banjole** – is a working fishing
port at its heart. Its old centre
remains quaint and picturesque
with alleyways winding between
tall, Venetian-style buildings and
a central piazza housing the tourist

office, post office and the Church of
St Agnes. And even though the
carnival rides and the throngs
crowding the harbourside
promenade may indicate otherwise,
it's hard to foul up 70 kilometres of
indented coastline, the region's only
sandy beach, a bevy of watersports
and family-based beach activities.

Medulin prides itself on its
sports facilities: beachside tennis
courts; volleyball courts; grass
football pitches; athletics facilities;
and mapped-out cycling routes.
Add six diving schools, two
equestrian centres and parasailing,
water-skiing, jet-skiing, beach
canoeing and sea kayaking, and
you can see why this is a popular
training destination for full-time
sportsmen. Sailing and windsurfing
are also popular pastimes.

Medulin's long, sandy beach,
Bijeca, with waterslides, is a
magnet for young families. Many
head for the islands of **Ceja** and
Levan in Medulin Bay, reached by
regular ferry. Other small islands,
served by water taxis, suit secluded
sunbathing.

Until recently, Premantura was a
sleepy little fishing village. Facing

Medulin

Batelina

Medulin, and a far cry from the busy beaches across the water, its little coves offer secluded, if rocky, access to the sea, its shady pines protection from the midday sun. Such splendour could not go unnoticed. Today Premantura has burgeoned with modern holiday apartments and hacienda-type private houses. In the centre a tall, stone bell-tower acts as a mini-roundabout – this is the gateway to **Kamenjak**, the protected tip of southern Istria.

Nearby Ližnjan is worth a visit for its big pebbly beach, **Marlera**, hidden from the crowds.

Eating & drinking

Barracuda Beach Bar
Bijeca Beach, Medulin (no phone).
Open *Summer* 10am-2am daily.
Bar-club. No credit cards.
Right on Medulin's big sandy beach, Barracuda is the place to party. Set on the sand, tables are tree trunks sawn in half and the chairs are stumps covered in cloth. There are boats you can climb into and enjoy an intimate strong cocktail. The bar itself – run by a gregarious team led by owner Rino Matković

– sits under a thatched roof. The weekend DJ starts at 10pm, when you can play night volleyball, dance among the tiki torches, or skinny dip.

Batelina
Čimulje 25, Banjole (052 573 767).
Open 5-11pm daily. **KKK**. No credit cards. **Fish restaurant**.
Generally considered to be one of the best fish restaurants in Istria – reserve your table at Batelina days in advance. The owner is a professional fisherman and the menu depends entirely on what he and his friends managed to land that morning. It's a small venue with only 26 inside covers, with 40 seats outside in summer. Try the mixed marinated fish as a starter, small portions of half-a-dozen types, crab, sardines and tuna. No lunchtime service.

Konoba Ankora
Selo 144, Premantura (052 575 642).
Open 7am-11pm daily. **K**. No credit cards. **Restaurant**.
The only *konoba* in Premantura to serve cut-price cooked daily lunches, this place stays filled all year round. Cheap and cheerful, it has a large, shady terrace complete with a barbecue and, of course, old anchors.

ISTRIA BY AREA

Premantura fisherman

Konoba Galiola

Ližnjan 578, Ližnjan (052 578 323).
Open *Summer* noon-11pm daily.
Winter noon-11pm Tues-Sun. **KKK.**
Restaurant.
Galiola's owner, who lived in Sweden,
has managed to combine Scandinavian
and Croatian architectural influences –
heavy wooden vaulted ceilings meeting shore-side stone – but the fare here
is all Istrian. The octopus filled with
shrimp, salmon and calamari is baked
under the *peka* (a cooking bell covered
in charcoal). White fish is grilled fresh
every day. Turf fans can choose lamb
or young pig. All in all, this is well
worth the diversion to Ližnjan.

Konoba Mižerija

Brajdine 106, Medulin (052 576 711).
Open 7am-midnight daily. **KK.**
No credit cards. **Restaurant.**
The basic harbourside food in this
konoba (tavern) includes spaghetti
with seafood, grilled squid, sardines
and mussels, served in a no-fuss atmosphere of rough-sawn wooden beams
above a stone terrace with wicker
chairs around card tables. This is classic old Yugo tourism, complete with a
waitstaff who care just enough and
fishermen sitting among diners.

Konoba Porer

Krše 1, Premantura (091 736 5761
mobile). **Open** 4pm-midnight daily.
KK. Restaurant.
A handy spot with a sea view from the
big wooden tables on the expansive terrace, Porer has a grassy kids' play area
and is dog-friendly. Besides Istrian
standards, the menu includes beef
medallions cooked in seasonal sauces,
wild mushrooms, cheeses and wild
asparagus. Owner Sandro also serves
barbecue ribs, fresh fish, ravioli and a
can't-miss seafood risotto.

Konoba Stare Užance

Premantura 127A (052 575 163).
Open *Summer* 5pm-1am daily.
Winter 5-11pm daily. **KK.** No credit
cards. **Restaurant.**
Inside an old stone house, a young couple pamper a few lucky guests every
evening. With only four tables indoors
and precious more in the garden, reservation is essential. Sanja and Sandro
Frančula strive to give customers the
best an Istrian-style *konoba* tavern can
provide. It's an informal spot with
hearty fare, including truffles with
bacon or cheese; pasta with truffles or
fish; local *pršut*; *manestra* bean soup;
Boškarin beef; and *supa*, a *bukaleta* jug

Fourteen islands, fourteen pearls.

**PUBLIC INSTITUTION
BRIJUNI NATIONAL PARK**

Post: Brijunska 10
52212 Fažana, Croatia
Tel +385 (0)52 525 888
www.brijuni.hr

BRIJUNI

Istria
Green Mediterranean

CROATIA

Istria's Finisterre

The southernmost point of the Istrian peninsula, **Kamenjak** is a little-known protected nature park of 360 hectares (900 acres), of which 30 kilometres (18 miles) is coastline. From dinosaur footprints to black widow spiders and tiny endemic orchids, Kamenjak is full of rare finds, both flora and fauna. In total, scientists have identified around 550 plant species here – around 35 of which are on Croatia's endangered plant list. Orchid lovers will be knocked out. If you're into things paleontological and botanical you can follow an educational trail with information boards pointing out Kamenjak's singular riches.

If, however, your main concern is peace and relaxation then you'll find Kamenjak a veritable haven with its numerous private little coves and crannies for sunbathing and swimming, far from the madding crowds of Medulin. Forget your costume – skinny dipping is the way to go, as any local is bound to show you.

Access to Kamenjak is from the south side of Premantura. You can drive here but there is now a small fee to bring a vehicle in and all cars must leave the area by 9pm. Unless you're driving a 4x4 you'll not be inclined to exceed the 20-kilometre speed limit – even in a hire car. Most people prefer to walk or cycle – you can hire bikes from the campsite in Premantura.

Wooden signposts allow you to orientate yourself instead of wandering around in search of painted rocks. Look out for the **Safari Bar**, a bohemian hangout worth the trip all by itself. This cult spot is perched on a cliff at the very southernmost point. The view is spectacular, the bar appropriately equipped to play host. Everything is made from objects washed up by the sea. There are stone tables and wooden block chairs. Lanterns hang from trees, there's a fishing-net slide for the little ones, and a café that serves sandwiches and is stocked with beer, wine, lemonade, tea and a daily sangría.

of warm red wine, toasted bread, pepper, olive oil and sugar. Fresh seafood includes fish grilled over a fire, cuttlefish and octopus salads.

Marea Caffè Bar
Brig 17a, Premantura (098 984 1061). **Open** 8am-midnight Mon-Thur, Sun; 8am-1am Fri, Sat. No credit cards. **Café**.

This is a spiffy modern café with cute barmaids just up the road from Camp Stupice. It's an ideal place to sip an espresso and read the paper on a multi-tiered terrace before heading out to catch some rays; it's ideal for après-beach cocktails too. Look for the sandwich board on the corner advertising frappés and smoothies.

Pizzeria Nina
Glavica 1, Banjole (052 573 457). **Open** 5pm-midnight daily. **KK**. No credit cards. **Pizzeria**.

One street north of the village's main harbour and west of the best beach, the Nina is so good that people wait patiently outside the gates until they open. Big and cooked in a stone oven, the pizzas don't disappoint. The *speciale* (45kn) comes with ham, salami, green peppers, olives, mushrooms, tomatoes and artichokes. They also serve salads, fried calamari, steaks and vegetarian options. There are pool tables inside. Outside there's a giant terrace with family-sized tables and enclosed, padded trampolines for the little ones.

Poli Čeha
Ližnjan 152, Ližnjan (098 367 135 mobile). **Open** 7am-11pm Mon-Thur; 7am-midnight Fri, Sat; 7am-2pm Sun. No credit cards. **Café**.

A salty locals' café in the snoozy centre of Ližnjan, this has a terrace with views of the sea and beer, wine and harder choices behind the bar. Ice-cream is served from below an antique bike hanging on the outside patio wall. Darko, the owner, has fashioned a cosy

wood-and-stone interior; he also runs a bar on a sandy beach on the island of Levan opposite Medulin.

Restaurant Vanga
Burle 47, Medulin (052 576 046). **Open** 8am-midnight daily. **KK**. **Restaurant**.

Wade past the many plastic-looking venues clustered about Medulin harbour and settle in the 25-year-old Vanga for top-notch white fish and unexpected treats like sole in creamy shrimp sauce. For meat eaters there's roasted veal in a spicy red sauce and roasted pork wallowing in Med herbs. Vanga plates breakfast from 8am in a tasteful white stone interior or on the terrace as Italian romantica wafts from speakers. Owner Gino Šverko lets out rooms in the pension above.

Nightlife

Caffè Bar Marina
Sad 11, Medulin (052 576 639). **Open** 8am-2am Mon-Thur, Sun; 8am-3am Fri, Sat. No credit cards.

A rare late-night venue, Marina plays music while projecting videos. Murals of Medulin backdrop locals throwing darts or dancing. Tunes and atmosphere suit a younger bunch but can be great fun with the doors open; the patio lets out onto the street. There's no good explanation for the stuffed dog or chipmunk behind the bar.

Summer Club Dali
Kraška 9, Medulin (052 223 792). **Open** *Summer* 10pm-5am daily. No credit cards.

This disco is of the classic holiday variety: young crowd, mixture of beats, nightly DJs and drinks that are somewhat more expensive than they should be. The entrance fee is 30kn. For that you can fraternise with international boppers in an aqua bar and shake it beneath the open sky and palm fronds flecked with disco-ball lighting. Look out for the giant sign behind the

ISTRIA BY AREA

Bebop
Bale style

The **Last Minute Open Jazz Festival** bounces improv beats off Bale's old stones and brings the best new players from abroad – just the type of event that the peninsula is starting to become famous for. Always staged between August 1 and 5, the festival (052 824 235, www.kameneprice.com) is free of charge and sponsor-free. There are no banners covered in supermarket logos, soft-drink mottos or mobile-phone coverage maps. This is just about one man's dream to bring jazz to Bale. 2010 marks its fourth year.

The man is Tomislav Pavleka, a photographer who spent 16 years in Amsterdam and came back to Croatia with 'no plan at all'. That no plan turned into the ownership of a string of houses in Old Town Bale. He then cleared out the centre area of that string to make a courtyard, which acts as a planned and sometimes impromptu stage for musicians and patrons – such as Tom Waits – in his restaurant-bar Kamene Priče.

At the festival, you can expect to find about 120 musicians from the United States, Latin America, Africa, and all over Europe. It is a raucous affair where younger players cut their teeth and earn their wings against old veterans. In 2009 some 5,000 spectators showed up for the five-day event that's also loaded with wine, local food, workshops, a youth festival and a jazz camp.

amusement park and right inside the entrance of Camp Medulin: 'After Beach Party & Aqua Bar'.

Arts & leisure

Diving Centre Shark
Autokamp Medulin, Medulin (052 894 2741/www.diving-shark.hr).
The area around Medulin is one of the most sportif in all of Istria; many come here for diving and windsurfing alone. The DCS has a diving school and also offers the chance to go deep in scores of locations around Istria's southern tip – including shipwrecks.

Premantura Windsurfing
Hotel Belvedere beach, Medulin (091 512 3646 mobile/www.windsurfing.hr).
Rents bikes, kayaks, and boards for windsurfing, plus surfing courses for every level. There's a branch at Camping Stupice in Premantura.

Around Pula: North

Bale, on the old road towards Rovinj from Pula, is a superbly preserved, picturesque, medieval Venetian-style town built around the 15th-century, two-towered Castle Bembo. This tight collection of cobbled streets five kilometres from the sea has its roots in Roman times, when it was Castrum Vallis and served as a stronghold between the port cities of Poreč and Pula. Today the most historic spectacle is the dinosaur remains found outside of town and displayed in the Gallery Ulika (trg La Musa 1).

Further south, between Bale and Pula, is **Vodnjan**: another spot with Roman roots and medieval stylings. Vodnjan (Dignano in Italian) is one of the best examples of an Old Town that still functions as the true centre of community activity. The main square, Narodni trg, around the Town Hall (one of eight palaces on the main street),

Fažana

buzzes with cafés and stage shows all summer long. Vodnjan is most associated with top-notch olive oil, spurred on by a 380-producer association, the first in Croatia.

The seaside town of **Fažana**, the site of an amphorae workshop in the first century AD and the vogue spot for Roman aristocracy, is the gateway to the **Brijuni National Park**. Tito's off-limits, luxury getaway for celebs and heads of state is an archipelago forming a calm setting for sardines to thrive. This is celebrated with the sardine fishing academy: free lessons in traditional techniques are given in July and August.

Sights & museums

Brijuni National Park
Office *Fažana (052 525 807/ www.brijuni.hr)*. **Admission** *Train tour with a guide* 210kn.
See box p118.

Church of St Blaise Sacral Art Collection
Župni trg, Vodnjan (052 511 420).

Open *Summer* 9am-7pm Mon-Sat; 2pm-7pm Sun. *Winter* by appointment.
Admission 35kn.

With nearly 1,000 pieces dating from the fifth century, the collection in Vodnjan's parish church is one of the most important in Istria. Among the pieces are paintings, stone reliefs, reliquaries, jewellery and sculptures. Stranger and more intriguing is the church's collection of saintly belongings. The artefacts include a piece of Mary's veil and a thorn from Jesus's crown. Even more notable are the bodies (or parts of bodies) of six saints, the Vodnjan mummies. They attract 15,000 annual visitors because of their supposed magical healing powers.

Eating & drinking

Al Fondaco
Narodni trg 4, Vodnjan (no phone).
Open 7am-11pm Mon-Sat; 7am-2pm Sun. No credit cards. **Café**.
Located in the Italian community centre building, this café is also by the town hall and stage where shows take place in summer. You can hear Italian singers practising next door.

ISTRIA BY AREA

Tito's playground

A rarity among tourist attractions, **Brijuni National Park** is ideal for kids and adults alike. For the grown-ups, Brijuni has been an important stage for historical events for 5,000 years, most recently as the pleasure palace of post-war Yugoslav leader Josip Broz Tito, who rubbed shoulders with movie stars, drove about in his 1953 Cadillac and chummed around with a parrot named Koki. For children, there are dinosaur footprints, a little tourist train and exotic animals otherwise seen in zoo cages.

The oldest remains of human habitation date from 3,000 BC. After 177 BC, the Romans built villas, a summerhouse set on three terraces, a series of temples, thermal baths and a freshwater fish pond, as well as facilities for processing olive oil: the last of their olive trees, dating from AD 400, still flourishes on the main island. Their working harbour remained in use well into the sixth century.

After the Romans, Byzantium added fortified walls, breached in 788 by Frankish King Carlo the Great. In 1312, plague wiped out the population, so when the Venetians claimed the islands in 1331 there was no one to resist. Brijuni was used for its quarries, the stone transported to Venice. The area became marshy and a haven for mosquitoes. When Napoleon arrived, he ordered a full survey with a view to draining and developing the area. Austrian steel magnate Paul Kupelwieser bought Brijuni as real estate for 75,000 gold florins. His dream was to create an English-style country park – today's Brijuni is Kupelwieser's legacy.

Kupelwieser excavated the archaeological treasures. He built villas. He planted trees. He landscaped gardens. He built Europe's first 18-hole golf course. He established a zoo. He created his own Xanadu but sadly didn't live long enough to see it. After World War II, Brijuni, along with the rest of Istria, became part of Tito's Yugoslavia. He used Brijuni as his base, setting up the Non-Aligned Movement with India and Egypt here in 1956 and inviting the rich and famous to his idyllic playground.

As you step onto Veliki Brijuni's quayside, you are following in the footsteps of Queen Elizabeth II, her sister Margaret, JFK and Sophia Loren, all documented in the 'Josip Broz Tito on Brijuni' exhibition housed in the main museum. Tito was regularly presented with exotic animals; you can still see many of them, including Indira Gandhi's elephants Sony and Lanka. Those who died were stuffed and placed in Brijuni's Natural History Museum, part of a three-museum complex near the harbour.

Brijuni National Park p117

Bar Brioni

Titova Riva 20, Fažana (052 525 522).
Open 7am-10pm daily. No credit cards.
Café.

Bar Brioni's harbourside terrace is the place for a civilised drink before getting the ferry to Brijuni. Inside, a golf theme hints at Europe's first 18-hole course awaiting you there: golf balls topped with glass act as coffee tables while black-and-white photos show golfers playing a round in Tito's pleasure park. Wines include Teran and Malvasia, cocktails a Monte Carlo of champagne, gin, mint and lemon.

Girotondo

Istarska 1, Vodnjan (052 511 120).
Open 5am-2am Mon-Thur, Sun; 5am-4am Fri, Sat. **KK**. **Restaurant**.

Vodnjan's all-in-one stop, Girotondo is a decent restaurant. Expect excellent fish soup, home-made pasta, risotto with lobster, big salads and pizza with truffles. It's also a spot to come for drinks late into the evening. The interior is modern with old touches: white stone and brick columns. Two terraces on the ground floor and one rooftop give patrons space to spread out.

Gostionica Kod Kancelira

Istarska 3, Bale (052 824 445). **Open** noon-11pm daily. **KK**. **Restaurant**.

Located on a street leading into Bale, this *konoba* tavern serves fresh shells from the Limski kanal: mussels (60kn a portion) and sea truffles, for instance. As well as lobster, fresh fish and beefsteak in green-pepper sauce, the place prepares fine pizzas on a shaded back terrace or on the front patio.

Kamene Priče

Kaštel 57, Bale (052 824 235).
Open *Apr-Nov* 10am-11pm daily. **KK**.
No credit cards. **Restaurant/bar**.

First, Kamene Priče is a *konoba* (tavern): fresh food only and no menu, just owner Tomislav travelling to Rovinj every day to pick up fish, steak, lamb and vegetables. It's also a bar: a hodge-podge of comfy furniture strewn about the interior with random bouquets of lavender. In front and on the cobbled street are benches and chairs but the back courtyard is where the magic happens. Under the stars, arty, bohemian types surround a makeshift stage in use all summer – as part of August's jazz festival. Tomislav also lets rooms upstairs. (See box p116).

Konoba Bembo

San Zuian 24, Bale (no phone). **Open** *Summer* 8am-midnight daily. *Winter* 8am-10pm daily. No credit cards. **K**.
Restaurant.

This is a family *konoba* (tavern) that puts on no airs. Inside there are old pictures of Bale and a wooden deer head on the wall. The terrace across the street is filled with wooden benches and surrounded by flowers in old pots. The food is solid *konoba* fare: home-made sausages, *fuži* pasta and gnocchi with beef goulash. Bembo also has top fish such as sea bass. Ideal for an inexpensive midday *marenda* brunch.

Konoba Feral

Trg stare škole 1, Fažana (052 520 040). **Open** 8am-midnight daily. **KK**.
Restaurant.

Konoba Feral is the classic spot to taste Fažana's sardine prowess. Inside and on the terrace, the decor is classy *konoba* (tavern): big bay windows, lanterns hanging from the roof before stone walls, fishing-nets, ropes, spears and a stone fireplace meet white tablecloths and roses in little vases. 'Savor' style is a good choice: sardines cooked with white wine and garlic, and served cold. The menu also has tagliatelle with truffles, seafood spaghetti, veal with truffles and mussels. Good, domestic litres of white wine run at about 40kn.

Konoba Istra

Trg La Musa 18, Bale (052 824 396).
Open *Summer* 6.30am-11pm daily.
Winter 6.30am-11pm daily. **KK**.
Restaurant.

Located in the middle of the modern centre of Bale and run by the Janko family, Istra serves a vast range of dishes, from *ćevapčići* grilled meat to fish, most good, fresh and reasonably priced. On a big back patio framed by a vegetable garden, with red flowers overflowing from boxes and fishing-nets hanging from the rafters, patrons eat *minestra* soup, omelettes with asparagus and *pršut* ham, and steak with truffles and lobster.

San Rocco

Zagrebačka 2, Bale (098 966 6357 mobile). **Open** *Summer* 8am-10pm daily. No credit cards. **Café**.

This sweet shop has ice-cream, cheese-cake, tiramisu, yoghurt cake, chocolate cake and vanilla cream cake topped with fruit – all home-made. Right in the middle of Old Town Bale, the interior is tiny with marble floors; the mojo is on the outdoor terrace, with a wooden deck on the old stones, brown wicker chairs and tables under white sun umbrellas. Ideal to start a tour of Bale.

Vodnjanka

Istarska, Vodnjan (052 511 435). **Open** *Summer* 11am-midnight Mon-Sat; 5pm-midnight Sun. *Winter* 11am-11pm Mon-Sat. **KKK**. **Restaurant**.

Certainly the best restaurant in the vicinity and rivalling the best tables on the peninsula, Vodnjanka has been around for over four decades but only became a true Istrian eaterie in 1979 thanks to owner Svetlana Celija. Her menu changes with the season, her philosophy being to cook only with what is grown within a ten-kilometre radius. The result: wholesome, delicious meals delivered to the simple dining room or panoramic rooftop terrace. Home-made pastas are accompanied by wild asparagus, wild mushrooms and wild game. Snail goulash with polenta is a favourite. For dessert, there's almond cake with lavender. Accompany the meal with a litre of fine house wine or one of many top Istrian varieties

Arts & leisure

Small Fishing Academy Pilchard

Fažana Harbour (052 383 727, www.istra.hr/fazana). **Open** July & August. **Admission** free.

From the first Friday in July until the last Friday in August, the fishing village of Fažana puts on a free-of-charge fishing fair in honour of the humble sardine, or pilchard. Much as Lübeck was made for marzipan and Montélimar for nougat, so Fažana lives for sardines. There's a sculptors' promenade along the harbour dedicated to the little fellows. All the restaurants specialise in them. There are weekly fishermen's festivals and weekly academies, where you'll learn everything from the traditional way to preserve your catch in salt to mending and painting nets in resin. Expect everything to be accompanied by copious lashings of wine and outbreaks of hearty a-cappella singing.

ISTRIA BY AREA

Mirna Valley, Motovun

Inland Istria

Inland Istria is the larder of the peninsula. In the north-eastern part truffles cover everything. In the western half, the wine comes in all shades. In the central region, the smell of *pršut*, Croatian prosciutto, wafts from houses and restaurants. And, in the area to the south, olive oil is king.

As for sightseeing, fresco-filled medieval churches dot the area. Cobbled streets line well preserved towns and villages; hiking and biking trails criss-cross the surrounding green rolling hills. Festivals feature all summer.

The most famous of these hilltop towns is **Motovun**, the gastro hub of **Livade** below. To the east, a string of modest villages – **Hum**, **Roč** and **Draguć** – make for ideal day trips and fall under the administrative purview of **Buzet**, the City of Truffles.

West of Motovun, the lead attraction is **Grožnjan**. With its easygoing style, month-long jazz fest and bevy of galleries, it is always a visitor favourite. Within its ambit, **Momjan**, to the north, is a wine lover's haven. **Oprtalj**, to the east, will attract those with a yen for church tourism – as will the town of **Vižinada**, due south of Grožnjan. **Višnjan** is like a combination of the whole group with a Venetian Old Town and vineyards at every turn.

In the very central part of the peninsula, **Pazin**, featuring a castle constructed in 983, is the chief locale among a lovely grouping of towns and villages. **Žminj** and **Gračišće** are just a short ride away and make great stops for day-trippers interested in seeing ancient places of worship. At the edge of the interior region, **Svetvinčenat** has a preserved castle in which it hosts the popular annual **Dance & Non-verbal Theatre Festival**.

Motovun

Motovun is the main attraction away from the coast. Nearly everyone, locals and tourists, has a story about their favourite angle from which to see the most beautiful and best preserved of the peninsula's medieval hilltop settlements. This might involve driving along the River Mirna at night and seeing the lights of the town like an illuminated snow globe, appearing at once. It may involve an early misty morning, your head seemingly in the clouds. Whatever, it will be memorable. Montona to the Romans, Motovun is best known for its **Film Festival**, which transforms this sleepy spot into a party hub for one week every summer.

Motovun is on the summit of a 277-metre (910-foot) hill in the middle of the Mirna Valley, surrounded by a truffle-rich forest. When the prehistoric settlement was founded, it would have been surrounded by water. The estuary stretched right up to the 'Gates of Buzet' at the head of the valley. It was down this ancient inlet that Jason and his Argonauts are supposed to have fled after capturing the Golden Fleece.

From its strategic position, Motovun controlled the merchant routes across the valley floor out to the coast. Although depopulated after the Italian exodus in 1945, it later became home to a new wave of inhabitants, many of them artists and writers. The result is the Motovun Film Festival, started in 1999. Recently local expats have reopened the Kino Bauer on the main square to screen movies from arthouse to kids' favourites, in English or with subtitles. There is talk of open-air films in summer.

The trek to the Old Town can be something of a slog but the top is ample reward for all the climbing. A stroll along the original 13th-century walls reveals a stunning 360-degree panoramic with the whole of inland Istria laid out before you, including tiny Livade on the other side of the river below, best known for truffles.

Motovun

Walk the walk

The walls of Motovun give views of the surrounding area and a sense of Istria's interior spread. The strategic nature of this position, nearly 300 metres high, will give you an idea of why Motovun has stayed so perfectly preserved.

Two sets of fortified walls divide the town into three sections – the higher you climb, the older it gets. Non-residents may not drive in the narrow cobbled streets; there's a car park at the bottom of the hill. As you climb up, past dilapidated, 16th- and 17th-century Venetian-style houses, you pass shops selling wine, truffles and grappa.

As the road levels, it passes through the main city gate from the 15th century. Its walls are hung with Roman tombstones taken from the cemetery of Karojba, a village five kilometres (three miles) away.

Within the gate is a museum of antique weaponry. Also here is the town's art gallery. Next door is a café, the **Caffè Bar Montona Gallery**, its terrace sited on the other side of the street, against the first set of fortified walls. Sitting here you have a view to the Adriatic. A telescope has been provided. There's a cashpoint alongside, the only one here.

A few steps more and, facing the town loggia, is the 13th-century gate into the original heart of Motovun. Pass through the steep, slippery archway by using the handrail. This entrance houses the restaurant **Pod Voltom**. Turn left onto the main square, **trg Andrea Antico**. Dominated by a 13th-century belltower, the piazza is sited over a water collection pit. You can still see the 14th-century well. Next to the tower is the **Church of St Stephen** and, facing it, a Renaissance palace citadel, housing the local cinema. Here is Motovun's only hotel, the **Kaštel**. The last lap takes ten minutes, just beyond the post office on a gravel walkway round the back of town, giving views of vineyards, forest, and the Mirna river and valley.

Eating & drinking

Caffè Bar Antico

Pietra Kandlera 2, Motovun (052 681 697). **Open** 10am–1am daily. No credit cards. **Bar**.

A locals' dive behind the main square in the Old Town, Antico has beers by the bottle and Favorit on tap. The interior is dark with brick walls in one room and stone in the other – but you'll likely be on the patio anyway. Here wicker chairs spread across a two-tiered space with the clock tower alongside soaring straight above.

Caffè Bar Montona Gallery

Trg Josefa Ressela 2A, Motovun (052 681 754). **Open** 8am–1am daily. No credit cards. **Café**.

Run by friendly local couple Claudio and Lela, this relaxed café atop the hill has stunning views of the Mirna valley from its expansive front terrace. It is the kind of place where you can expect to fall into immediate conversation with a local then exchange shots of local intoxicant *biska*, the grappa made of mistletoe. Tables lining the terrace attract passing tourists, while regulars gather inside for long winter huddles.

Caffè Bar Mure

Mure 7, Motovun (098 191 0758 mobile). **Open** *Apr–Nov* 9am–9pm daily. No credit cards. **Bar**.

Mure is a secluded terracotta-roofed hut of a café on the walls of the Old Town. It seems temporary but it isn't. Great views of the river, vineyards and valley below can be had from the picnic tables hugging the stone fortifications. Owner Savo serves Stella on tap plus white Malvasia and *rakija* (grappa) flavours including *biska* mistletoe. This place pops during the film festival. A great spot to catch the sunset.

Gostionica Tartuf

Livade 5, Livade (052 664 107). **Open** noon–10pm Mon, Wed–Sun. KK. **Restaurant**.

Opposite Zigante, the famous and expensive truffle restaurant, Tartuf has all you need for a complete truffle experience. It has the 'Tartufo Vero' sign outside, which means it has met Istria's high standards of handling, serving and pairing truffles with appropriate wines, for instance. A low-key patio of ten tables is complemented by a modest dining room. The menu is also simple, combining the tasty tuber with steak, omelette and pasta. They serve a good *manestra* soup, and *pršut* prosciutto and cheese.

Konoba Dolina

Gradinje 59/1, Livade (052 664 091). **Open** noon–10pm Mon, Wed–Sun. No credit cards. KK. **Restaurant**.

A short drive from Motovun (head into Livade and take a right at the only roundabout), Dolina is a perfect example of superb, simple, local food in a superb, simple, local place. Many Italians drive down just for the night. It's slightly off the beaten track, not touristy or flash – and all the better for it. It's also very good value. The secret is the quality of the fresh ingredients: huge plates of meaty porcini mushrooms served with olive oil; *fuži* pasta with truffles; squid with chips; cabbage salad; and beans. Dolina fills with locals sat at wooden tables, repeat guests and chattering elderly Italian ladies from the nearby spa. There are tables outside too.

Konoba Dorijana

Livade 4A, Livade (052 664 093). **Open** 11am–11pm Mon, Tue, Thur–Sun. KK. **Restaurant**.

This is a great little spot. Across the turnabout from the better-known Zigante, it has a perfectly homely dining room with a somewhat of a French feel – dainty wallpaper, wooden ceiling, black-and-white photographs and a refinished bar made of stone. Run by Dorijana Basanese and family, it serves traditional food with unique touches: turkey stuffed with truffles; pasta with

Church of St Stephen p125

Propeler Pizzeria

wild mushrooms; seasonal asparagus soup; suckling pig; and snails with polenta. Outside on the pavement, there is a string of tables nicely positioned under the welcome shade of a large, old tree.

Konoba Mondo

Barbacan 1, Motovun (052 681 791). **Open** *Summer* noon-3.30pm, 6-10pm daily. *Winter* noon-3.30pm, 6-10pm Mon, Wed-Sun. No credit cards. **KKK. Restaurant**.

Mondo divides opinion. Praise from the *New York Times* recently led to a frenzy in the local media, partly driven by a positively spun translation. Soon after a renowned Croatian restaurant critic described the risotto as the worst he had had since being in the Yugoslav army. Our recent visit here was nothing to write home about – whether that means it's on the decline or ascent is unclear. You can expect to find a menu of standard Istrian *konoba* fare: steak with walnut or almond sauce, Istrian veal with a white-wine Malvasia sauce. In summer try and get a spot on the pleasant little terrace.

Pod Voltom

Trg Josefa Ressela 6, Motovun (052 681 923). **Open** *Summer* noon-11pm daily. *Winter* noon-11pm Mon-Tue, Thur-Sun. **KK. Restaurant**.

This is the classic place to grab a bite in Motovun. 'Under the Arch', by the old city gate, serves a selection of honest, regional fare, including truffles, and can be relied upon to have a fire blazing in winter and terrace seating in summer. The terrace is dramatic, overlooking the Mirna Valley. A crew of veteran waiters serves some of the best meat in Istria.

Propeler Pizzeria

Jozef Ressler 8, Motovun (095 903 2666 mobile). **Open** *Mar-Nov* 11am-11pm daily. **K.** No credit cards. **Pizzeria**.

This hub just opened just before the 2008 Film Festival, and offers a welcome variety to Motovun's truffle-centric dining options. At the top of the Old Town, it dispenses a steady stream of thin-based pizzas and interesting salads. Prices are good value: a mid-morning mozzarella, basil and tomato panini (warmed in the pizza oven) is 13kn. The owners are a mix of local and London-trained, so pizzas feature organic spicy rocket, with chunks of Parmesan and chilli oil. Salads include roasted red peppers with local sheeps' cheese. Pizzas may take a while when busy, but the view compensates.

Vidik

Divjaki, Motovun (no phone).
Open *Summer* 7am-midnight daily.
No credit cards. **Bar-diner**.

On a sharp turn along the road to Pazin and Poreč, this is a perfect spot for an afternoon beer or wine with a view of the valley and Motovun above. The entirety of the enterprise is a terrace with wooden tables and benches – thus its summer-only status. As well as suds, they serve table wine, sandwiches and Balkan *ćevapčići* rissoles.

Zigante

Livade 7, Livade (052 664 302).
Open *Summer* noon-11pm daily.
Winter noon-10pm daily. **KKKK**.
Restaurant.

A short drive down from Motovun to Livade, this famous formal restaurant is a heavy hitter and the base for an industry centred on a world-record event a decade ago. It was then that Giancarlo Zigante (and dog Diana) were said to have discovered the biggest white truffle in history, weighing 1.31kg. Fame spread, and this restaurant was opened in 2002. Zigante runs truffle factories, makes truffle paste, runs a truffle festival and has his own shops. And the restaurant? Set in a beautiful house with outdoor seating, it offers very expensive if impressive dishes (some truffle-free) to an exclusive clientele.

Shopping

Art Studio Isabella

Mure 11, Motovun (052 681 513).
Open *Summer* 10am-7pm daily.
No credit cards.

On the path that leads around the walls, Isabella is a nifty gift shop, which majors on the non-perishable end of the souvenir trade. Inside the two-room boutique, you'll find handbags, T-shirts, ancient-looking maps, painted plates and antiques: a trunk, an old basin. It also sells music boxes with songs such as 'Stairway to Heaven' and 'Imagine' programmed in.

Atelier m

Gradiziol 11, Motovun (052 681 560).
Open *Summer* 9am-7pm daily. No credit cards.

Run by photographer Eni, here the highlight are his shots of inland Istria, mainly in black and white, available framed and unframed in a variety of sizes, and great value from 200kn upwards. His work captures misty mornings in the vineyards, rusting *konoba* signs, village houses with the fading red paint of a Communist star, and deserted churchyards. Also on sale are hand-printed T-shirts (with a distinct Corto Maltese theme) and handmade bracelets and necklaces.

Etnobutiga Ča

Gradiziol 33, Motovun (052 681 767).
Open *Mar-Dec* 10am-10pm daily.
Closed Jan, Feb.

On the main steep stone path, this is a store with a classy little restaurant and wine bar thrown in, a labour of love for owner Livio Lanča. The basement has top wine labels; the ground floor is filled with tasteful, home-made knick-knacks, as is the floor above. These include knitted items; lavender products; local pasta; hand-woven baskets; wooden sculptures; jewellery; and liqueurs. Beyond, the eatery has an Istrian menu centred on truffles, and includes home-made pasta with venison, and sausages. On offer are also salted sardines, *manestra* soup and big salads. The best bits are the breezy terrace for dining and tasting wine and olive oil and the view soaring over the valley, the river and the forest. Because

Roman holiday

At Istria's main spa resort, visitors have been healed since Roman times. Amazingly, given Istria's Central-European inclinations, **Istarske Toplice**, is the *only* real full-service spa resort on the peninsula. Located just off the road between Motovun and Buzet, set under a dramatic cliff, the centre takes advantage of on-site thermal springs, which were used regularly in the Habsburg days. Today Istarska Toplice boasts a complex of two hotels with 250 rooms. One was built during the Yugoslav era and still has a dated quality. The other is a four-star finished in 2008.

The two pools, outdoor and in, are filled with the sulphur-rich waters from the spring. People come from across Europe to rest in the pungent baths, which stay around 32-34 degrees, to seek relief from a variety of ailments from rheumatism to respiratory. They come for the five different saunas, massage, inhalation and fitness rooms to receive treatments such chocolate peels and vitamin facials.

Also on the premises you will find ear, nose and throat doctors, rehab specialists and experts for minor plastic surgery. Hiking, horse-riding, tango and salsa nights can also be arranged at or around the main hotel. In fact, there are a slew of package options for nearly every combination of treatment and adventure. Autumn and winter tend to be the busiest times – always phone ahead.

there is no wall to peer over, it feels as if you are on top of the world, suspended above the panorama.

Miro Tartufi

Gradiziol 1, Motovun (052 681 724).
Open *Summer* 9am-8pm daily.
Winter 9am-8pm Sat, Sun.
A good place to come for everything from kitsch to quality. Miro Tartufi stocks many *rakija* grappa varieties: *biska* mistletoe with truffles, for instance. There's also cheese with truffles and regular truffles, plus olive oil, picture frames and sundry souvenirs.

Motovun Gallery

Borgo 11, Motovun (052 681 791).
Open *May-Nov* 10am-6pm daily.
No credit cards.
Zagreb-born Renata uses her contacts in the Croatian arts-and-crafts scene to display an interesting selection of pottery, paintings, sculptures, jewellery and crockery from the ground floor of her family home. Prices start at 50kn, with the signature paper mâché doves going for 200kn. She also sells inventive ornaments with lavender, etchings and hemp creations. Artists and artwork come from a 30-kilometre radius of Motovun.

Primizia Shop

Gradiziol 15, Motovun (052 681 666).
Open *Summer* 10am-8pm daily.
Winter varies.
Orderly Primizia has a wall of wooden shelves with wine from all over Istria, and a wall of truffle products. Somewhere in between, again in an orderly fashion, are guides, T-shirts in ancient local Glagolitic, shot glasses and postcards. The back window has a gorgeous view of the Motovun forest.

Arts & leisure

Istarske Toplice

Sv Stjepan 60, Livade (052 603 410, www.istarske-toplice.hr).
See box, left.

Draguć p132

Inland Northeast

Snuggled beneath the **Ćićarija mountains**, which form a border between Croatia and Slovenia, **Buzet** is the first place of any size you reach when travelling west from Rijeka. It's also one of the few towns with a business centre, supermarkets and petrol stations. It is the governmental seat for several villages, many worth a trip for their eateries. Known to the Romans as Piquentum, and the governmental centre of Venetian Istria, Buzet is publicised as the 'City of Truffles' because of the high concentrations of the delectable fungi that crowd oak roots in the forest surrounding the town and nearby Mirna river. Buzet bolsters this claim with its gourmet **Subotina** festival on the second weekend in September.

Hum sits at the end of a seven-kilometre country road known as the **Glagolitic Avenue**. The road contains 11 stone monuments to Glagolitic script, a forerunner to Cyrillic. It begins with the Pillar of the Chakavian Parliament and ends at the town's huge metal gates. With only a single, circular street to traverse, it takes little time to explore this charming place, mostly unchanged for nearly a millennium. Hum calls itself the smallest town in the world, because even with barely more than a score of citizens it meets all the governmental criteria for such status: a school; a church; a post office; a town hall and a pub. Squeeze in a dozen houses and that's Hum. Traditionally it's been home to just two families, with the priest also the publican. Inside its thick medieval walls there is a small museum-cum-souvenir store and the **Imela Shop** that offers Hum's mistletoe grappa *biska*. Just outside the walls is the only restaurant: **Humska Konoba**.

At the head of the Glagolitic Avenue, along the Buzet-Lupoglav road, lies the lovely town of **Roč**, considered the centre of the ancient Glagolitic alphabet. The **Roč Missal**, the first Croatian book, dated c1483, was produced by Jurij Zakn, whose bust stands in front of the Roč parish church. Roč's other claim to fame is the **Accordion Festival** in the first half of May.

East of Hum is the modest community of **Draguć**. It is also somewhat incongruously called Istria's Hollywood, mainly because it has been the site of several film productions, such is the pristine condition of its intact medieval architecture. Tourists are drawn to its peaceful location with views across terraced vineyards and to the frescoes in the 12th-century Romanesque **St Elisium Church** and the 16th-century **St Rok**, where biblical scenes cover every inch of the tiny vaulted interior. Ask for the keys in the **Buffet Zora** café and they'll point you in the right direction.

Sights & museums

Buzet Regional Museum

Trg rašporskih kapetana 1 (052 662 792). **Open** *Summer* 9am-3pm Mon, Wed, Thur; 9am-3pm, 5-8pmTue, Fri; 10am-2pm, 5-8pm Sat, Sun. *Winter* 11am-3pm Mon-Fri; by appointment Sat, Sun. **Admission** 10kn; 5kn children.

Housed in the 17th-century Bigatto Palace, this museum was founded in 1961, reflected in its collection and ambience. It displays a range of interesting artefacts from the Buzet area, including ethnographic pieces, stone monuments, pottery from Hum and an exhibition called 'Anti-fascist battle in the Buzet area'. Most interesting are the preserved craftsmen workshops – the machine which made combs from-local *boškarin* ox horns is great fun. The museum also hosts concerts, workshops and temporary exhibitions such as photography.

Hum centre

A walking tour of Hum begins at the town's massive metal doors, which have ox horns for handles and calendar medallions showing monthly tasks across its top. From here you enter a cave-like antechamber hewn straight

out of the rock. Above is the town hall. On the walls are stone tablets inscribed in ancient Glagolitic. Ahead is the main square; to the left is the large Church of the Exalted and Blessed Virgin Mary with its magnificent crenulated belltower. The consecration chapel of Sv Jeronima in the graveyard houses 12th-century frescoes covered with Glagolitic graffiti. Left is a Lilliputian house with a picturesque loggia. This is the only street inside the walls.

Eating & drinking

Agrotourism Karoca

Sovinjak (052 663 039, www.karoca. com). **Open** 2-10pm Tue-Fri; 11am-10pm Sat, Sun. **KK**. No credit cards. **Restaurant**.

In Sovinjak, a village south and west of Buzet, Karoca is a gem worth a few hours. Everything is made on the premises, bread, sausages, pasta and wine. The menu sports wild boar, venison and veal and all amply layered with truffles. You can take your meal on the stunning terrace – pass through a stone arch by the old wooden carriage to a big grass landing with views of Oprtalj, Motovun and Vrh.

Buffet Zora

Draguć 30, Draguć (052 665 182). **Open** 11am-10pm Tue-Sun. **KK**. No credit cards. **Café**.

On the main square, Zora manages to serve several functions in Draguć. The only real place for a coffee, a drink or food, it serves prosciutto, cheese, sandwiches and *manestra* soup; beer, *rakija* grappa and domestic wine. A general meeting place, it has a pleasant terrace with the clock tower and the valley in view. The interior has pictures of actors – Michael York, Karl Malden– who have been filmed here, to name but two. (There is rumour of an upcoming George Lucas production.) After the meal, you can ask here for the key for the beautiful frescoed churches nearby.

Humska Konoba

Hum 2, Hum (052 660 005,
www.hum.hr). **Open** 11am-10pm
daily. **KK**. **Restaurant**

After you finish the circuit around
town, step out of the main gate and into
Hum's single restaurant. A lovely, covered, summer terrace features burly
wooden tables, red-and-white che-
quered tablecloths and stone flower
boxes with roses looking over a beautiful view down into the valley. This is
the setting to share a *bukaleta* jug of
traditional Istrian *supa*: red wine
topped off with warm, toasted bread
sprinkled with olive oil. There is also a
tasty corn soup with sausage, goulash
and pasta with truffles.

Konoba Paladin

Franečiči 25, Buzet (052 662 061).
Open 9am-9pm Mon-Sat; noon-7pm
Sun. **KK**. **Restaurant**.

Open for 15 years, this family business
(parents and two daughters, all cook)
serves solid Istrian fare – asparagus
with pasta, pasta with truffles, mushrooms and cream sauce – with other
options. For baked veal ribs (150kn),
call a day in advance; suckling pig is
100kn. The family lives above the
restaurant, a simple dining room centred around a fireplace and pictures of
Istrian oxen on the walls. The terrace
is peaceful, surrounded by fruit trees.

Konoba Roč

Roč 14, Roč (052 666 451). **Open**
noon-10pm Tue-Sun. **KK**. No credit
cards. **Restaurant**.

This family-run restaurant is the only
place to eat in Roč. The waiters are
friendly, and the food is tasty and
fortifying. The classic meal is scram-
bled eggs with truffles and *pršut* prosciutto. Konoba Roč also serves shish
kebabs, pork steak and pork loin. The
wooden-walled interior is covered in
Glagolitic memorabilia; on the patio log
picnic tables stand next to a tiny grass
and palm park with a stone sculpture
double bass.

Konoba Sveti Ivan

Sv Ivan, Buzet (052 662 898). **Open**
10am-11pm Mon-Sat; 1-11pm Sun.
KK. **Restaurant**.

At the entrance to Buzet, this is a
restaurant where you're likely to end
up in a beer-soaked chat with a regular. It also serves good local cuisine
such as *manestra* soup, *boškarin* ox,
mushroom-and-truffle soup, and steak.
Sveti Ivan has a terrace, three indoor
dining rooms and two fireplaces for
cooking. There's a stone oven for pizzas. For dessert, order the sweet cheese
with ice-cream, honey and fruit, a special 50-year-old recipe.

Konoba Volte

Kozari 16, Kozari (052 665 210).
Open noon-11pm Mon, Wed-Sun
KK. **Restaurant**.

In the village of Kozari near Buzet,
Volte serves real domestic food to a discerning, mostly local clientele. There is
roasted veal with mushrooms,
omelettes with asparagus, and *manestra* soup. The wine list contains a dozen
or so well chosen Istrian labels. The
cooks not only cook, but make their
own bread and pasta, and grow their
own vegetables. The dining room is a
rough-sawn-wood affair with baskets
and tulips in vases, while the terrace
looks through arched columns onto a
lavender-surrounded grassy area.

Konoba Zlatni Breg

Prodani 33, Prodani (052 665 180).
Open noon-11pm Tue-Sun. **KK**.
Restaurant.

Opened in 2008 five kilometres (three
miles) south of Buzet, Zlatni Breg is a
konoba tavern in name but a restaurant
in spirit, with a painstakingly thought-
out decor and an inventive menu.
Davor and Jasminka Črnak's philosophy lies in presentation. There must be
four or five colours on each dish, and
every ingredient has to be in-season;
they use their own vegetables and
herbs, they buy eco-friendly chickens
and eggs from villagers and every-

ISTRIA BY AREA

thing is home-made. You'll taste the difference with concoctions such as prosciutto and cheese wrapped and rolled with slices of oranges and tomatoes; sage gnocchi prepared with a ham-and-sage sauce; and shrimp with wild asparagus. They also serve the classic truffle dishes, steak and pasta, and *boškarin* ox. As well as having a long list of top wines, and home-made cakes, they have a lovely terrace that looks toward Vrh.

Restaurant Stara oštarija

Petra Flega 5, Buzet (052 694 003, www.stara-ostarija.com.hr). **Open** noon-10pm Mon, Wed-Sun. **KKK**. **Restaurant**.

The big hitter in Buzet, this is the only place to eat in Old Town. It has the region's 'Tartufo vero' stamp; dishes include brown trout with truffles and a thick mushroom soup with truffles. There's a slow food menu for 690kn that is a truffle-laden treat, with truffle cheese and *pršut*, pasta, steak and crepes. An extensive wine list features peninsular varieties. The interior dining room has terracotta tiles for lamps, red-clothed tables on brick floors and scientific charts of the famous tuber mixed in with paintings of the town. And all surrounded by big windows and panoramas of the countryside: Hum, Roč and the Ćićarija mountains.

Restaurant Vrh

Vrh 1, Vrh (052 667 123). **Open** *Mar-Feb* 1-10pm Tue-Sun. **KK**. **Restaurant**.

Located in the peaceful hilltop town of Vrh, south of Buzet, this restaurant has been a family business for 30 years. Owner and cook, Ondina Petohlep, masterfully makes home-made bread and dishes such as lamb roasted under the cooking bell (250kn per kilogram), and ravioli with asparagus and broccoli. The menu also includes game with pasta, beefsteak with truffles, and *boškarin* ox simply but expertly complemented by salt, pepper and thyme.

The stone-walled spot has daisies in jug vases and a terrace looking down over a lush valley.

Veli Jože

Opatija 20, Buzet (052 669 141, www.kastelvelijoze.com). **Open** noon-midnight Tue-Sun. **KK**. **Restaurant**.

Six families live in this community below a castle on the road to Buzet from Motovun; halfway between is a sign along the river. Turn left and head up a hill to the lone business sitting in a clearing. Veli Jože serves wild boar (order in advance) and fish, an oddity inland. They also offer lamb, suckling pig and marvellously meaty, piquant goulash. There are truffles for many dishes. Vegetarians can tuck into big salads. After dinner and a local glass of wine on the big stone terrace, order the apple stuffed with blueberries served with ice-cream.

Shopping

Hum Museum

Hum (052 660 054). **Open** *Summer* 10am-7pm daily. *Winter* 10am-7pm Sat, Sun.

Though this is more souvenir shop than museum, it does house a small collection of old Istrian furniture and artefacts inside a rustic interior, to the right as you enter. Turn left and there's a big boutique selling tasteful and easily portable keepsakes: honey; marmalade; brandies; paintings; maps, and cookbooks. You can also pick up a handy Glagolitic alphabet chart.

Imela Shop

Hum 2, Hum (052 660 001). **Open** 11am-7pm daily.

Owned by the same hard-working folks that run the Humska Konoba, Imela is a perfect little gift shop. It sells only native items and has the best *biska* mistletoe grappa in the area. You may also sample and then buy grappa along with local wine, organic hon and, of course, truffles.

Nightlife

Club 190

Il Ist. Brigade 1, Buzet (052 662 617).
Open 8am-midnight Mon-Thur; 8am-
4am Fri, Sat. No credit cards.
For late-night carousing in Buzet town,
this is it, funky and appropriately
kitsch for you to have a good time. Pink
walls, mirrored ceiling, gold-framed
mirrors with angel wings, zebra pillows and a chandelier are surrounded
by stone walls: all in all, it's pretty
heavy on the ornamental. An above
VIP section has white leather couches
and a flat-screen fireplace. Below, the
marble bar sells standard cocktails,
beer, wine and *rakija*. House and R&B
pump out at weekends.

Old River Grill

*Most Bračana, Buzet (091 681 0000/
098 360-823 mobiles, www.old-river.
net).* **Open** 7.30am-11pm Tue-Thur;
7.30am 3am Fri; 7.30am-4am Sat;
9am-10pm Sun.
All things to all people, the Grill is first
an ideal place to grab a sandwich on
the way to Buzet (it's by the river on
the road from Motovun). The terrace-
only restaurant with wooden floors,
retractable windows and a terracotta
roof also offers slightly more formal
options like a mixed grill, bruschetta
with truffles and 18 quality wines. On
weekend evenings. the Old River Grill
becomes cocktail central with a DJ mix-
ing house and disco. Part pit-stop, part
nightclub – and with a wonderful river-
side location.

Arts & leisure

Raspadalica

*Slum, Buzet (098 167 8737 mobile,
www.raspadalica.org).*
The Ćićarija mountain range rings the
north-east edge of the peninsula and
frames Buzet. After a steep drive up
into the slopes and along the ridge, just
after the village of Slum (a 30-minute
drive from Buzet), you'll come to the
headquarters of Raspadalica, the only
real outfitters in the area. There are no
signs so make sure to have arranged a
meeting ahead of time. After you do, be
prepared for real adventure. The crew
here organises paragliding, hiking,
mountain biking, climbing, caving and
nearly anything else you fancy. They
also lead multi-sport outings – it's sea
and land – as well as cultural visits.

Humska Konoba p133

Grožnjan sits 228 metres (750 feet) above the sea and is loaded with 26 galleries and plenty of studios. One of Istria's prettiest and most lively medieval hilltop towns, it provides spectacular views: the Adriatic to the west and the dramatic landscape of the Mirna Valley to the east. For years after the war it was a ghost town, the majority Italian population having fled Tito. Sundry creatives slowly took it over until by 1965 it was formally declared a 'Town of Artists'.

Grožnjan's street signs are hand-painted ceramics, rather than state-manufactured enamel. The colours of the shutters are subtle but just right. There are ancient-looking stone seats perfectly sited for enjoying the view. And everywhere you look, there's a gallery. In the little town square and outside the town loggia on warm evenings, recitals are given by tenors or jazz players, part of the **Grožnjan Musical Summer** (www.hgm.hr).

A military base during Roman times, **Oprtalj** (Portole in Italian) rests at the top of winding road north of Motovun, 378 metres (1,240 feet) above sea level. Self-styled as a town of frescoes, it has more than a dozen churches in the vicinity with four in the nearly deserted but beautiful settlement proper. Of note is the **Church of Sv Marija** built in the 15th century. Located at the edge of town, it has a rich interior lined with pictures depicting the life of the Holy Mother by four master painters including Clergino of Koper (Slovenia). From the main square there are spectacular views, a *konoba* for a bite, and a gourmet food and wine shop.

Momjan is a tiny town due north of Grožnjan. What it lacks in size it more than makes up for in gastro offerings. This is the spot to try typically white Muškat wine and red Teran, at the Kozlović and Kabola vineyards. For a meal you would be hard-pressed to do better (anywhere on the peninsula) than **Marino**, just below in the village of Kremenje. If you're here in early November, the **Momjan Wine Festival** is a must. The 12th-century, derelict **Momjan Castle** is a minor hike but worth a visit.

South of Grožnjan and west of Motovun, **Vižinada** has a beautiful well built in 1722, around which a yearly festival of regional sweets gathers in mid August. Of the eight churches, **St Barnabas** most merits attention, accessed by a knock on the door of the house opposite. Key in hand, you'll see its 14th-century frescoes and graffiti in old local Glagolitic. The key master will also allow you to climb the 25-metre bell tower of **St Jerome Church** for the panorama.

Višnjan lies on the crossroads between Pazin and Poreč. The Old Town's cobbled streets contain a 16th-century gate with a Venetian lion, and a square featuring 13th- and 14th-century walls. From the 18th-century loggia there are views of the vineyards that have made the region famous. One of the area's top producers is **Peter Poletti**, who makes memorable Malvasia and has a Muškat rosé. Višnjan has at least three other claims to fame. The **Višnjan Observatory** has discovered more than 1,700 minor planets in the last decade, making it one of the most prolific astronomical discovery sites. Sadly it cannot be visited. You may, however, visit the nearby **boškarin farms** to witness the resurgence of this indigenous Istrian ox. Finally the **Baredine Cave** provides a chance to get out of the summer heat and a view of Istria's underground world.

Oprtalj

Sights & museums

Baredine Cave

Nova Vas (052 421 333/098 224 350, www.baredine.com). **Open** *Apr-Nov* times vary; *July, Aug* 9.30am-6pm daily. **Admission** 50kn; 30kn children.

Istria's most spectacular cave complex and an official nature reserve since 1986, Baredine is located between Višnjan and Poreč. The cave has been open to the public since 1995, when it was reconstructed and fortified. Passing through the stalagmites, some up to ten metres long and equally as high, the 40-minute guided tour takes you through five chambers culminating with underground lakes 60 metres (200 feet) below ground level. One pool is home to the proteus anguinus or the albino cave salamander. The Proteus Speleological Society caving club based here can also organise more challenging adventures. There's a terrace restaurant for a post-visit meal.

Fonticus City Gallery

Trg lože 3, Grožnjan (052 776 357/ 052 776 349, www.gallery-fonticus-groznjan.net). **Open** *Summer* 10am-1pm, 5-8pm Tue-Sun. *Winter* varies.

This public two-floor space is a museum, an outlet for Croatian and international artists, and a standard bearer for Grožnjan's 26 galleries. It has a rotating agenda of shows. Also under its purview is a collection of insignia, crests and coats of arms from German, Croatian and Slovenian nobility.

Eating & drinking

Agrotourism Fatorić

Ferenci 36A, Ferenci (052 446 146). **Open** by reservation. **KK**. No credit cards. **Restaurant**.

A traditional *konoba* on the slope of the village Ferenci, which sits between Vižinada and Višnjan, Fatorić serves lamb and pork slow-cooked under the *peka* cooking bell in the traditional way. English is hard to come by here but good domestic fare isn't. It serves delicious home-made pasta, wine, prosciutto and cheese. No opening hours - you'll have to ask a local to call for you and make a reservation.

Agrotourism Tončić

Čabarnica 42, Zrenj (052 644 146). **Open** *Summer* 12.30-10pm Fri-Sun. *Winter* 12.30-9pm Fri-Sun. **KK**. No credit cards. **Restaurant**.

This is what a *konoba* looks like: all stone with a big cooking fireplace and shelves filled with home-made grappa. Before reaching this tiny village near Oprtalj on a country road, call Orjeta

Tončić to see what you'd like them to prepare for you – her mother is a dab hand at lamb, pork and rabbit. The specialities, though, are home-made polenta, *fuži* pasta and *manestra* soup. Only in-season ingredients are used: asparagus, truffles (black and white) and mushrooms. The family has sheep, pigs, rabbits and three dogs for truffle hunting. As you enjoy your cherry *rakija*, notice the pictures of driver Michael Schumacher, who made a special trip via motorcycle to eat here.

Bastia

1 Svibnja 1, Grožnjan (052 776 370). **Open** *Mid June-Aug* 8am-2am daily. *Mar-mid June, Sept-mid Jan* 9am-10pm. **KK**. **Restaurant**.

Under the church tower, this large, imposing traditional restaurant is the main one in Grožnjan. Fabulous local dishes include home-made sausage, rumpsteak with truffles and twisted pasta ties (*fuži*) with wild game. The fish platter is a handy alternative. There's a little bar with a piano in the back and modest rooms, with views of the valley below, for let.

Caffè Bar Vero

Trg Conera 3, Grožnjan (no phone). **Open** 8am-midnight Mon-Thur, Sun; 8am-2am Fri, Sat. No credit cards. **Café**.

Deep in town with a perfect drinking terrace that looks over the hillside and toward Motovun, Vero feels like a real bar. Cheap beer on tap and well priced wine options combine to make this a visitor and local favourite. The multi-level patio has wicker chairs above and big, group-sized wooden tables below. They also serve croissants and frappés.

Konoba Oprtalj

Oprtalj 17B, Oprtalj (052 644 130). **Open** 1-10pm Tue-Sun. **KK**. No credit cards. **Restaurant**.

The interior is classic *konoba*-style with stone walls and framed etchings hung upon them. Set in the main square near the loggia, this is the only place to eat a proper meal in Oprtalj. The food is solid: truffles on polenta, omelettes and ravioli. There is also veal in gorgonzola sauce and pizzas – the pizza Oprtalj has sausage, egg and pork loin. The terrace by the car park looks out over the valley below.

Marino

Kremenje 96B, Kremenje (052 779 047). **Open** noon-10pm Mon, Wed-Sun. **KKK**. **Restaurant**.

Owned by Marino Markežić, who also makes Kabola, some of the best wine in Istria, Marino is a superbly conceived slow-food restaurant with seasonal ingredients of local produce. Spring sees wild asparagus teamed with cured pork and pasta with eggs and tender pork medallions. Black truffles make an appearance in summer. White truffles adorn plates in autumn and winter. As jazz wafts lightly above in the dining room, where degustation menus are wrapped in little ribbons, you can order T-bone steaks, venison and roasted veal prepared by chef Sergi Razman. Marino also lets boutique-style rooms in this village next to Momjan, deep in wine country.

Ponte Porton

Ponte Porton, Kostanjica 67, Grožnjan (052 776 395, www.ponte-porton.hr). **Open** 11am-11pm Mon, Wed-Sun. No credit cards. **KKK**. **Restaurant**.

All alone on the Mirna river, set in a recently refurbished old house, Ponte Ponton sits on a sharp turn along the road between Motovun and Grožnjan towards the sea. It's a little pricier than most *konobas* but the menu is a little more varied and imaginative than most: fish options are rare in inland Istria. Outside, there's a clutch of tables lit by fluorescent strips; inside the two rooms vary in their formality. The presentation is fancier than rustic – food (great chunky chips) comes on square black plates. You can stop off for a beer and there are rooms to rent upstairs

Loggia, Oprtalj p141

Grožnjan p136

Marino, Kremenje p138

Shopping

Galerija AP

Umberta Gorjana 10, Grožnjan (no phone). **Open** *Apr-Oct* 10am-9pm daily. No credit cards.

Run by a mother-and-daughter team, this atelier and gallery, just off the main street in a shop with an arched stone doorway, specialises in silk paintings. Inside you'll find imported silks designed and painted on the premises. There's a demonstration display so visitors can see the process. The products, with geometric shapes and abstract swirls, take many forms, their wonders to behold: skirts; tops; scarves; and even ties. Galerija AP also sells fine hand-made jewellery designed and crafted by daughter Djana – rings, bracelets, necklaces – with stones wrapped in silver.

Khala Energy Design

Vincenta iz Kastva 2, Grožnjan (091 443 3430 mobile). **Open** *Summer* 9am-9pm daily. No credit cards.

Khala is a quirky and interesting boutique offering an alternative to the standard souvenir options by offering energy-based products. It's owned by a much-travelled interior designer who fell in love with Grožnjan. Inside the ethereal space, a mix of exposed beams and chandelier, are necklaces, lavender (oils and the like) and natural incense. Stand-out products are the crystals, amethysts and decanters designed to naturally purify water.

Loggia

M Laginje, Oprtalj (052 644 219). **Open** 10am-7pm Mon, Wed-Sun.

Set, logically, at the town loggia, this all-in-one stop has a range of wines from the immediate region (20 producers and four varieties); the local priest's herbal grappa; sausage; prosciutto; and cheese. Owner Daniel Coslovich also makes his own olive oil and wine. You won't leave without first trying the lavender or olive-oil *rakija*.

Pharos

Umberta Gorjana 8, Grožnjan (091 374 2280 mobile). **Open** *Summer* 10am-2pm, 6-9pm daily. *Winter* 10am-2pm daily. No credit cards.

Pharos is something like a well-to-do souvenir shop that is heavy on artwork. It also carries antique furniture, local landscape paintings, lavender oil and candleholders.

Arts & leisure

Boškarin farm

Fabci, Višnjan (052 462 129/091 556 1021 mobile). **Open** varies. **Admission** 40kn.

In the 1960s there were some 50,000 *boškarin*, Istrian oxen, whose use diminished as families bought tractors. By 1990 there were 100 left. At that time an association of breeders began a campaign to save it. Today, the animals have made a comeback and authorities have tried to increase interest by allowing a controlled number to become highly prized entrée items in restaurants that qualify. Valued for their intense, organic taste, the population today numbers 600 according to Mario Gašparini, a breeder from Fabci outside Višnjan. You can visit his farm and take an hour-long tour during which he'll take the massive animals through all the traditional spoken commands farmers have used to prepare their fields for planting for centuries.

Lavenda Oklen

Vrbani 3, Vižinada (052 446 101/ 098 991 3787 mobile). **Open** varies.

If you're wondering where all the lavender comes from that fills oils in souvenir shops across Istria, visit the lavender fields outside Vižinada. On six hectares of land, the Oklen family has 26,000 plants, the biggest farm in Istria. Owner Djanino is happy to take you on a tour of the grounds; at the gift shop you can buy lavender-infused oil, soap, honey, face wash and potpourri in hand-made bags.

Gračišće

Inland Central

Towns in Istria's central corridor are often considered stop-offs – going south from Motovun, **Pazin**, **Žminj** and **Svetvinčenat** are on the way to Pula. But it would be a pity while you're there not to spend a little time poking around these picturesque and historic spots.

Pazin is big by Istrian standards. Officially the county town for Istria, it has a bus and train station, a working cinema, a theatre, and a department store. But mostly Pazin is in love with Jules Verne, naming streets after the French author, housing the regular meeting place for the local Jules Verne society and holding a Jules Verne Day every June. Strangely Jules Verne never came here. But he did use the beautiful and well preserved **Pazin Castle** as a major location for his 1885 novel 'Mathias Sandorf'; and the venues that interested him still hold good for visitors today. The castle, the river flowing beneath it and the neighbouring 130-metre-(426-ft) deep gorge (Istria's suicide

venue of choice) are just as Verne describes it in the book – he had a local expert scope things out.

A stop in the nearby town of **Beram** and its **St Mary of the Rocks Church** to see the 'Dance of the Dead' fresco is another must.

South and east of Pazin, **Gračišće** was first recorded in 1199 and is almost perfect in its medieval structure. Passing through the loggia, where prominent male citizens dispensed summary justice, you enter through the main gate. To your right is Plac, the main square, with deserted **Palace Solomon** and its high Gothic windows and Renaissance façade. Close by is **Majka Božja na Placu** church ('Mother of God on the Square'), where barren women once hammered nails in the wall in hopes of becoming pregnant. Just outside **St Vitus Parish Church** and its tower (from which great views of the countryside can be had) – ask for the key at Konoba Marino – you will notice spooky gravestones with Celtic names

ISTRIA BY AREA

timeout.com/travel
Get the local experience

Camel racing in the United Arab Emirates

© Bernardino Testa/ITP Im

and ominous Masonic symbols, and a priest's tomb built into the graveyard wall.

Žminj is the centre of Istria, literally. As such, it is the site of the peninsula's old star-shaped intersection, with roads leading to Pazin, Rovinj and Poreč. It is also loaded with old churches for nearly every taste: frescoes, wooden altars and baroque stylings. One in particular, the tiny 14th-century **St Anthony's**, has a circular window above the front door positioned to catch the noon light and throw it against the altar.

Svetvinčenat is a small medieval town dominated by its impressive 13th-century **Grimani Castle** (ask at the tourist office for a tour and they'll open it up for a nominal donation). Gutted by fire in the 1500s, occupied by the Nazis then burned down by the Partisans, the castle has been painstakingly restored to its former glory. These days used as a cultural centre, Grimani hosts the annual **Dance & Non-verbal Theatre Festival** held at the end of July.

Sights & museums

Pazin Castle & museums

Trg Istarskog razvoda 1, Pazin (052 625 040/052 624 351, www.emi.hr). **Open** 10am-6pm daily. **Admission** 25kn.

Built in 983, the Pazin Castle is the 'biggest and best preserved medieval fortress in Istria'. It is, no doubt, a marvellously preserved structure. It is also the site for Pazin's two main museums – Town and Ethnographic – both renovated and well run. The former contains pieces from Pazin's past starting from prehistoric times, including weapons, paintings, stonework and weapons. The latter contains traditional costumes, tools and other artefacts, giving an inside look at local Pazin life through the ages.

Hunting for gold

Tired of reading about truffles? Not sure what all the fuss is about? Well, you could just buy truffles, truffle paste and the like at a shop from a salesperson with only a fleeting knowledge of the stuff – but the only way to find out what these litte beggars are really about is to get out there and find your own gold.

A day spent at the **Karlić** ranch 12 kilometres (eight miles) south of Buzet in Paladini (052 667 304, 091 578 70 16 mobile, www.karlictartufi.hr) will allow you to learn the business from the bottom up, shoes muddy and with a self-righteous sheen of sweat on your face.

The Karlić family is one of the truffle heavies on the peninsula. They hunt and train their own dogs, packaging and selling the valuable fungus without a hint of mystery or pretension. Since 1993, they have serviced some 150 restaurants throughout Croatia. At their shop, you can purchase jarred truffles, truffle pâté, plus truffle-infused honey, biscuits, olive oil, sausages, cheese and even salsa.

By going on a hunting expedition with grand dame Radmila Karlić and the family's dogs, you will get the opportunity to see the process first-hand while romping through their two square kilometres of lush, private forest. Each outing takes approximately three hours, costs 20 euros per person (offered for groups of four or five only) and includes in the price a suitable, quality degustation.

St Mary of the Rocks Church

Beram. **Open** times vary.

Beram is just north and west of Pazin. People come here for one reason: the famous frescoes inside St Mary of the Rocks Church, which stands guard beside a cemetery, a ten-minute walk from the centre of town. Ask at the Vela Vrata restaurant for the key. You'll be directed to a house. With the key you get a guide, whom you should pay ten kunas. Inside the church, she'll explain the scenes, which were painted in 1474 and cover almost every inch of the interior. The money shot is the 'Dance of the Dead', skeletons and humans taking a morbidly beautiful waltz together.

Eating & drinking

Caffè Bar Magnus

Trg maršala Tita, Žminj (052 846 335). **Open** 7am-11pm daily. No credit cards. **Café**.

In the square with a patio beneath the main church, this is the place to come for big coffees and a beer. Inside is no-nonsense with old pictures of villagers, table football and fruit machines. Walk directly across the piazza to the front door of the church, where you can ask for the key to nearby chapels and convince the nun that you are fit enough to climb the campanile.

Djidji

Tinjan 17, Tinjan (052 626 196/091 626 1960 mobile). **Open** 4pm-midnight Mon-Sat; noon-midnight Sun. **KK**. No credit cards. **Restaurant**.

This *konoba* is the most popular place to eat in this little town southwest of Pazin, sitting in the middle of the square. Reservations are recommended at weekends as folks come from all around for the renowned local proscuitto as well as pasta with truffles, pork skewers and steak. On the patio out front or on the fruit-tree-framed terrace out back, you can enjoy first-class red and white wine from Arman and Kozlović. Djidji also has rooms for rent in the 300-year-old building.

Freske

Podberam, Beram (no phone). **Open** *June-Oct* 8am-11pm daily. No credit cards. **Café**.,

St Mary of the Rocks church

Pazin Castle p143

A summer café featuring a cluster of wooden tables on a surrounding terrace, Freske is sited on a clearing at the bottom of the road leading up to Beram, just north of Pazin. If you're spending any time here, you will be stopping in for one of the handful of beers, *rakijas* or coffee drinks served under the leafy vines and green tarpaulin hung for shade.

Kod Kaštela

Svetvinčenat 53, Svetvinčenat (052 560 012). **Open** 10am-11pm daily. **KK. Restaurant**.

Open since 1970, Kod Kaštela, with a pleasant view of the castle walls, is the place to eat when in town. The specialities of the house are asparagus and mushrooms picked in the woods around Svetvinčenat. On offer as well are meat carpaccio, octopus salad, steak with peppers, lamb and a local pasta called *pljukanci*, served with proscuitto, asparagus and mushrooms in a cream sauce. The pancakes with nuts and marmalade is a nice touch for dessert. There's a good wine list of local labels and a relaxed terrace on which to enjoy them.

Konoba Danijeli

Danijeli 76, Tinjan (052 686 658/091 686 6588 mobile). **Open** 2pm-midnight Tue-Fri; noon-midnight Sat, Sun. **Bar**.

Just outside the town of Tinjan, ten kilometres from Pazin on the road to Poreč, in prosciutto country, this is a great place to taste the local dried ham offerings, bought from houses in the village. Owned and run by Mirjana Fabris, Danijeli serves wonderful home-made *pljukanci* pasta and typically complements it with asparagus, truffles and *boškarin* ox. The restaurant also dishes up pork, veal and lamb, which they cook under a roasting bell. There is indoor dining, a terrace and café. There are rooms for let and a swimming pool for guests.

Konoba Marino

Gračišće 75, Gračišće (052 687 081). **Open** 2-11pm Mon, Tue, Thur-Sat; 10am-11pm Sun. **KKK**. No credit cards. **Restaurant**.

Marino is just inside the stone gate leading into this village southeast of Pazin. Inside the stone walls of the dining room, which matches the stony feel of Gračišće itself, the stand-out dishes

ISTRIA BY AREA

Whatever your carbon footprint, we can reduce it

For over a decade we've been leading the way in carbon offsetting and carbon management.

In that time we've purchased carbon credits from over 200 projects spread across 6 continents. We work with over 300 major commercial clients and thousands of small and medium sized businesses, which rely upon our market-leading quality assurance programme, our experience and absolute commitment to deliver the right solution for each client.

Why not give us a call?

T: London (020) 7833 6000

www.CarbonNeutral.com

include ravioli with game, and substantial salads. Marino serves litres of decent house wine for a reasonable 40kn. There are four rooms for let above and the family here will lead you to the village sights, keys in hand.

Konoba Puli Jurića

Jurići 1, Žminj (052 846 678).
Open noon-10pm Mon, Wed-Sun.
KK. **Restaurant**.
On the road between Pazin and Žminj, Konoba Puli Jurića is a snazzy roadside diner with a tree-shaded terrace and a cheery inside dining room. Filled with locals, it serves specialities such as veal stew and ravioli with venison – good food at good prices and a convenient locale to relax between village visits.

Vela Vrata

Beram 41, Beram (091 785 4995 mobile). Open noon-midnight Tue-Sun. KK. **Restaurant**.
A wonderful little restaurant in the centre of Beram, Vela Vrata serves homemade pasta, beefsteak, veal and sausage and cabbage. Of course there are truffles on a number of dishes and a few reds and whites on offer. The interior is typical stone and brick but there is also art hanging and for sale. The flagstone terrace overlooks vineyards. You can get the key for fresco-filled St Mary of the Rocks Church at the house next door.

Vinja

Stancija Pataj 73A, Pazin (052 623 006). Open noon-11pm daily. KKK.
Restaurant.
The speciality here is *pljukanci* rustica: local, home-made pasta served with *pršut* prosciutto, pine nuts, asparagus, mushrooms and black truffles. This high-class *konoba* on the outskirts of Pazin has tile floors and a terrace framed by vineyards, lavender and a big grassy field for the kids. There's an extensive wine and decor that includes candles, wooden baskets and iron napkin rings. The chocolate soufflé, like all the desserts, is made on site and absolutely delicious.

Nightlife

Caffe Bar Vampire

Kringa 32, Kringa (no phone). Open 3-11pm Mon-Thur; 3pm-1am Fri, Sat; 10am-11pm Sun. No credit cards.
This is the area's most mental venue, a blood-splashed pub in the village of Kringa, 15 kilometres (nine miles) southwest of Pazin. Within, one room is a weekend dancefloor with a DJ playing rock and techno. Officially open until 1am, the Vampire often works later as locals and curious visitors give their best 'Thriller' impression while grooving inside the spooky and dark pub. The themed decor echoes the local legend of Juro Grande, a 17th-century vampire whom Kringa's citizens stabbed in his coffin. The cocktail of choice is the Vampirski Orgasm: vodka, gin, Malibu and juice.

Svetvinčenat, p143

Rabac

East Coast

ISTRIA BY AREA

The most remote and least-known area of the Istrian peninsula, the east, centres on **Labin**. Famous for its inordinate number of artists, Labin's Old Town is the perfect place to roam a while and absorb the flavour of a well-preserved medieval settlement – and to open your wallet for some cutting-edge artwork. There is also a good museum, complete with a tunnel exhibit on mining (for which the area was famous), and a decent contemporary art gallery with rotating exhibitions.

Labin has always had attitude. The Romans recorded the presence of unruly pirates here. Local Matija Vlačić was a leading European religious reformer alongside Martin Luther. Labin's miners revolted against Italian rule and declared itself an independent republic.

The hub of tourism is to the east of Labin in the nearby coastal town of **Rabac**. Here, strung along the

harbour, are seafood restaurants to suit any budget. As well, there are fine beaches tucked under the Učka mountain, which provides high drama in the entire panorama. Just the other side is the Kvarner area, and Rijeka harbour, making the rest of Croatia easily accessible by car or ferry.

South and east of Labin, the town of **Raša** was built in the 1930s, when the area was under Mussolini's rule, to house the area's miners. What visitors uncover here is a sense of Italy's fascist efficiency and a sideways glance at the region's former way of life. The place was built to have exactly what residents needed and no more: an identical string of houses, a main square and a post office. Even in prayer, in the church shaped like a miners' overturned cart and with the campanile shaped like a lantern, Il Duce reminded workers of their daily lives.

East Coast

Beram

Pazin

Tinjan

Gračišće

64

66

Kringa

Kršan

Žminj

Brestova

B8

anar

etvinčenat

Labin

Rabac

Barban

Raša

66

Trget

Divšići

Vodnjan

Marčana

la

Ližnjan

Banjole

Medulin

Premantura

Kamenjak

C. Promontore

0   8 km

0   5 miles

© Copyright Time Out Group 2010

Labin, Rabac, Raša & Barban

Istria's east coast feels different to the rest of the peninsula. Wild and isolated between the foothills of Učka mountain and the Kvarner Bay, the region is something of a law unto itself. The only major town in Istria's south-east corner is **Labin**. On a high peak, three kilometres (two miles) from the sea, it is said to have been a fortification founded by Celts in the fourth century BC. They christened it 'Albona' or 'Alvona' ('town on a hill') and this ancient name is still in use.

With a population of 10,000, Labin is an economic centre; the plain beneath the Old Town sprawls with a residential and business community. Known as 'Podlabin' ('Under Labin'), this is where Mussolini built his two new towns to house local miners. You can see a reconstructed shaft at the **Labin Museum**.

As you ascend the steep, cobbled hill to the Old Town you'll pass beautiful villas built to house the white-collar workers. Passing through the first city gate you enter the main square, still named Titov trg, with its brightly painted buildings and Venetian loggia. This is the town's social hub.

In the modern era, Labin's renown is built on its vibrant arts scene, with an inordinate number of home-grown artists and cultural events to bring in visitors. As you continue uphill through the second gate and explore the Old Town, you pass galleries, studios, museums and workshops such as the **Municipal Gradska Galerija Labin** (ulica 1.maja 5, 052 852 464), the City Gallery, which provides a year-round (and free) programme of eight to ten contemporary shows.

It sits just opposite the Labin Museum. These and other public spaces are commandeered for the annual **Labin Art Republic** (www.labin.hr) series of arts events – music, arts, performance – in July and August. Initiated in 2003, it stages live shows, exhibitions, and ad-hoc street entertainment.

On the south side of the old city walls, šetalište San Marco is a terrace providing an unbroken vista out over the Kvarner Bay. Locals claim the shallow depth of the sea here, only 80 metres, encourages the growth of a particular plankton, and thus outstanding seafood. If you carry on to the top of the town, all of eastern Istria spreads out before you. Within immediate view is **Rabac**, a spectacular sea cove three kilometres (two miles) down the hill and to the east.

If Labin is strong on culture, Rabac provides all the summer fun. Much as Labin stages its Art Republic, Rabac is best known for its DJ-oriented **Summer Festival** (www.rabacsummerfestival.com). As you travel down frightening hairpin bends towards Rabac bay, the small town comes into view like something out of the French Riviera. And like the Riviera, seaside gentrification is already underway. If you don't want to laze on the beach, you can explore the nature trails, one leading to the **Tears of St Lucia**, a natural spring whose waters are reputed to heal your eyes. You are also close to the ferry terminal at **Brestova**, for access to Cres and Lošinj and their famed sandy beaches.

South-west of Labin, **Raša** has to be the strangest attraction in the region. Built in the 1930s to house coal miners, the place and its pre-planned architecture remain intact. Beyond, just as you leave Labin for the peninsula's interior, medieval

Labin Museum

Barban – famous for horse-riding knights – provides access to isolated bays and a chance for visitors to climb in the saddle.

Sights & museums

Church of St Barbara

Trg Republike, Raša
The only real sight in town, unless you count the town itself, Raša's church is shaped like an overturned miner's cart – appropriate since the town was constructed for miners. Dedicated to St Barbara, the patron saint of workers, it was built in the mid-to-late 1930s and, like everything else in town, was designed by Gustavo Pulitzer Finali. St Barbara's chiselled image stands in front of the campanile, which is supposedly shaped like a miner's lamp.

Church of St Mary of Consolation

Alda Negrija, Labin. **Open** 10am-4pm Mon-Sat. **Admission** free.
A few minutes' walk north of the central Old Town leads to the Church of St Mary of Consolation, sometimes called the St Mary of Health Church. For tourist purposes, its main value is for its nine oil paintings that date from the early 17th century and are dedicated to the life of the Virgin. The pieces are likely from Baroque master Antonio Moreschi. There is also a series of wooden statues of the Apostles.

Labin Museum

Ulica 1. Maja 6, Labin (052 852 477). **Open** *Summer* 10am-1pm, 6-8pm Mon-Sat; 10am-1pm Sun. *Winter* by appointment 7am-3pm Mon-Fri. **Admission** 15kn; children 10kn.
The Labin Museum combines a little of everything that the East Coast region has to offer. On the bottom two floors, the collection is permanent and contains antiquities and ethnographic pieces: costumes, pots and the like, diligently gathered from ten local villages. On the top floor is a rotating exhibition of contemporary works. But the real hit is the coalmine exhibit, where visitors put on hard hats and walk along cart tracks to the claustrophobic sound of real mining.

Mediterranean Sculpture Symposium

Dubrova (052 852 464). **Admission** free.
Located in Dubrova, a tiny settlement north of Labin, this sculpture park

Mussolini's mining mission

Driving west of Labin you come across a little town tucked into the foothills, near a river and shaded by trees. There's no beach here but **Raša** is worth a visit all the same. It stands as a testament to what mining has meant to southeast Istria. But more than anything it stands as a monument to Benito Mussolini.

Though exploration for coal began in the early 1600s, it wasn't until the 1830s that Labin and its surrounding area became a centre for mining. Over the next century, coal's extraction became the vicinity's reason for being and the basis of its most important events. One such event, which still shapes the attitude of Labin citizens, is the 1921 strike when coal miners of different nationalities came together from in the aftermath of World War I to protest at working conditions after the Italians had taken over Istria from Austria. For nearly five weeks the town held out until the strike was put down militarily. The period is known as the Labin Republic, a name still used today, and one that adds no little spice to the town's rebellious lore.

A decade later, Mussolini left his stamp on the coal-rich region when he commissioned the building of a town with the express purpose of housing miners. He hired Gustavo Pulitzer Finali to build a Narnia-esque village at the foot of the mines and construction began in 1936. It was finished and opened in November 4, 1937. The result was Raša, the youngest town in Istria.

Named after the river that runs close by, the town was built with community needs firmly in mind. Every other family house – all connected – has the same functional façade. There's a hospital, a post office, a town square and a hotel. The church, the piazza's focus, is shaped like an overturned miner's cart and dedicated to St Barbara, the patron saint of miners. That's Raša – part creepy, part practical, part attractive, part ghost town, and all Il Duce.

adds to Labin's reputation as an art vortex. Approximately 90 pieces dot the landscape. This is the locale for the yearly Mediterranean Sculpture Symposium, which has taken place from early August to mid September for the past four decades. International residencies give artists a chance to hammer on Istrian stone and in turn Labin receives new pieces for its collection. Look out for the large, green glass cube, due to be opened at some point in the future as the visitors' centre.

Memorial Collection of Illyricus

G Martinuzzi 7, Labin (052 852 477). **Open** 10am-1pm Mon-Sat. **Admission** free.

Inside the Frankovich Palace on the north-west side of town, this little-known collection of writings from local scholar Mathias Flacius Illyricus (Matija Vlačić Ilirik) displays both his prolific body of work and the importance of his dissident voice. A renowned professor of Hebrew at Wittenburg in Germany, among other places (Jena, Regensburg, Antwerp), Illyricus was a comrade of Martin Luther, who even took part in his marriage ceremonies.

Eating & drinking

Caffè Bar Robinson

Obala maršala Tita, Rabac (no phone). **Open** *Summer* 10am-2am daily. No credit cards. **Bar**.

At this slick little spot, beads hang over doorways, plank wooden flooring supports cane chairs on one terrace and tree-stump stools sit between olive trees atop another multi-tiered balcony hanging right over the Adriatic. Located just off the main promenade between Maslinica beach and the harbour, Caffè Bar Robinson also features an enthusiastically happy waitstaff serving piña coladas, mai tais, tequila sunrises and mojitos. Czech Budvar beer is provided on tap.

Due Fratelli Restaurant

Montozi 6, Labin (052 853 577, www.due-fratelli.com). **Open** *Summer* 11am-midnight daily. *Winter* 11am-11pm Tue-Sun. **KKK**. **Restaurant**.

A beautiful restaurant on the road between Rabac and Labin, Due Fratelli sits in a pretty garden in the wooded foothills above the beaches. In charge since it opened in 1994, these two brothers catch their own fish so it's all fresh. The menu includes shellfish, seafood pasta and châteaubriand. The dining room – with half a boat sticking out of a wall and new wooden beams lining the ceiling – is big. Its fireplace is used for grilling sea bass, john dory and grouper which sit on ice in the entry among scattered amphorae. People travel out of their way to eat here so make reservations.

Gostionica Kvarner

Šetalište San Marco, Labin (052 852 336). **Open** 10am-10pm Mon-Sat; 11am-midnight Sun. **KKK**. **Restaurant**.

Gostionica Kvarner has the best location of any restaurant in Labin. The terrace seating is on šetalište San Marco with stunning views over the Kvarner Bay. The view comes with outstanding food, all produced locally. There's a good, wide-ranging menu, including an Istrian hot plate of small portions of local specialities such as tagliatelle with chicken, *fuži* pasta with beef and gnocchi with wild boar. It also has steak tartare, octopus salad and calamari risotto. Try *krafi*, shaped like ravioli, pasta sweetened with raisins, rum and sugar, and stuffed with four types of local cheese. In summer fish and meat are grilled on the terrace.

Gostionica Primorje

Obala maršala Tita, Rabac (052 872 217). **Open** *Summer* 10am-11pm daily. **KK**. **Restaurant**.

Situated on the water, this is a typical holiday restaurant only a bit nicer. Go past the main walkway of the harbour

Live large at luxury Lino

Spicy lobster and Cres lamb are menu highlights

For an all-around experience a notch above the other harbour-side restaurants on the Rabac Riva embankment, save up and visit **Lino**. It has more than earned its high reputation – Suzana and Lino Hrvatin have been running the place for the last 15 years. Suzana supervises the floor with a drill sergeant's precision and a mother's warmth while Lino, a big man with the heart of an artist, takes care of the cooking.

Lino's general philosophy is to cook seafood dishes all based on garlic and olive oil. The result is memorable. The linguini with clams is savoury. The spicy lobster fra diavolo for two people is sublime and the fettucini Lino with scampi, whipped cream, and a touch of spice is, well, you get the picture. All dishes, from the crab salad to the omnipresent grilled fish, are fresh and lovingly prepared.

As well as fish and seafood, Lino, who worked for years in New York, cooks roasted lamb from the island of Cres across the Kvarner Bay, veal marsala and filet mignon.

Surrounded by pine trees, and with two terraces looking over the water, this is not just a great place to eat but a good place to have a drink and watch the sunset. The wines are for the most part Istrian with the occasional Dalmatian bottle creeping on to the list.

and Primorje sits between excursion boats at rest, with pine trees growing up through the stone terrace. The suggestion is simple: lasagne with shrimp. They also dish out grilled fish and excellent risottos with shrimp, squid and mussels. But this spot differs from many in the number of non-fish meals they create: wild game with gnocchi; steak; pork; and sirloin.

Gostionica Prstenac

Barban 60, Barban (052 567 019).
Open 8am-midnight Mon, Wed-Sun. **K**. **Restaurant**.

The reason for this restaurant's existence, it seems, is as the social centre for the town's horse festival. Located within the city walls, right on the main square, Prstenac is named after the small, round, metal target used in jousting. Friendly staff serve the small dining room and the handful of patio tables. Among the offerings you'll find sheepsina cheese; fish soup; wild-game pasta; calamari; pork chops; and sausages. You'll have to try hard to spend more than ten euros here.

Lino Restaurant

Obala maršala Tita 59, Rabac (052 872 629). **Open** noon-11pm daily. **KK**. **Restaurant**.
See box left.

Martin Pescador

Trget 11A, Trget (052 544 976).
Open noon-11pm daily. **KKK**. **Restaurant**.

In a narrow, natural harbour south of Raša, Martin Pescador in the tiny seaside village of Trget is one of the best restaurants in the area. People flock from all over to eat here. The terrace features tables overlooking the water and between seafoam-green shutters, an old wooden wine press and lanterns. Fishing skiffs sway back and forth in the working harbour. Nets hang from the ceiling. The waiter brings a basket of fish – sea bass, for instance, layered

ISTRIA BY AREA

Labin p150

with fig leaves – around the large, heavy wooden tables. On the menu are seafood risotto and pasta options as well as meat choices but you'd never forgive yourself if you order anything but fish. Wash it down with top Istrian wine – and don't forget to bring your credit card.

Miramare Restaurant

Obala maršala Tita, Rabac (052 872 146). **Open** *Apr-Nov* noon-11pm daily. **KK**. No credit cards. **Restaurant**.
Touristy, sure. But the food is good, it is solid value and there are two balconies with soaring views of the harbour and the sea beyond. Located before you reach the seaside walkway, this family-run restaurant is a good place to bring the tribe. It has pizzas but also pork medallions with mushrooms, Greek salads, a grilled fish plate and mussels.

Nostromo

Obala maršala Tita 7, Rabac (052 872 601, www.nostromo.hr). **Open** 11am-11pm daily. **KKK**. **Restaurant**.
One of the best restaurants in Rabac, Nostromo has a large, roofed terrace overlooking Maslinica beach in Rabac bay. The retractable windows give the feeling that you are outside as the salt air breezes into the interior room. Understandably, the menu majors on fish and seafood specialities. There is, for instance, a mean black risotto and a risotto with crabmeat. But it isn't exclusively surf here. It serves a châteaubriand and a steak stuffed with cheese and mushrooms – and a decent range of local wines.

Rapčanka

Obala maršala Tita 313, Rabac (052 872 784). **Open** *Apr-Nov* noon-11pm daily. **KK**. **Restaurant**.
This place is all things to all people. It's owned by a family who also run an old-fashioned bar, a pizzeria and a slightly posh seafood restaurant, all on the slope this street makes as it leaves the harbour. But everyone seems to end up over on Rapčanka's simple terrace whose 20 tables are filled nightly with folks looking for good and good-value dishes such as sea bass fillet. Grilled eel goes for 55kn. There is also grilled salmon, an excellent beef goulash with asparagus and home-made pasta, and a slew of Istrian reds and whites.

Raša Kavana

Trg Republike 1, Raša (052 874 000). **Open** 6.30am-midnight Mon-Sat; 7am-midnight Sun. No credit cards. **Café**.
For a coffee or something stronger, Raša Kavana hits the spot. There are black-and-white shots of the slightly eerie town during its origins in the 1930s and 1940s. On the main square opposite the church, the café and its terrace serve as the town clubhouse. There is a flat-screen TV for sport, mirrored interior walls, Beck's by the bottle and table wine.

Riva

Obala maršala Tita, Rabac (052 872 347). **Open** *Summer* 7.30am-1am daily. *Winter* 7.30am-11pm daily. No credit cards. **Café**.
This ritzy café on the harbour has wicker chairs on wooden floors, etchings of boats on the walls and little lamps on chair-side tables. Breaking that mood is the big-screen TV and Van Halen over the speakers. Across the promenade, Riva's terrace, with sun umbrellas against the silhouette of green hills beyond the sea, juts into the water. On balmy summer evenings, sex on the beach and margaritas are served along with a whole chalkboard of cocktails.

Velo Kafe

Titov trg 12, Labin (052 852 745). **Open** 7am-11pm Mon-Fri, Sun; 7am-midnight Sat. **Bar-restaurant**.
A combination of three venues in one, all of them busy all year round, give the Velo Kafe centre stage in Labin – located in the heart of town just for good

measure. In the basement, a comfortable, half-trendy, half-rustic restaurant features glowing terracotta walls, plenty of artwork and a traditional open fire blazing on winter nights. The food is typical Istrian fare (no pizzas, despite what the sign says) at very reasonable prices – no wonder you'll see artists filling the place. Above, the café and its two terraces throng in summer. The Rock Café nightspot occupies the first floor and serves as a tourist-season restaurant. Look out also for the Spider Café Bar opposite, another good late-hour drinking haunt, with a regular programme of DJs in summer.

Shopping

Galerija Merania

Ulica 1. Maja, Labin (052 285 2466, www.merania.hr). **Open** *Apr-Dec* 10am-1pm, 6-9pm Mon-Sat. *Dec-Apr* 10am-1pm Mon-Sat.

This ceramics shop is just down from the Labin Museum and city gallery. The husband-and-wife team of Dolores and Masimo do the throwing. This homely space displays their creations, which provide a great alternative to the kitsch souvenirs on sale in kiosks along the coast. There are plates, teacups, ceramic coal lamps, clocks and traditional *bukaletas* for wine, all hand-painted by the owners. Hoteliers from around the peninsula order their place settings here. If you're in Labin for a while, sign up for one of Merania's workshops and learn the techniques for yourself. Check the website for more information.

Sanifor

Stari trg 1, Labin (091 527 2795 mobile). **Open** *mid Apr-mid Oct* 9am-2pm, 7-10pm Mon-Sat; 9am-1pm Sun. No credit cards.

This classy gift shop is set by the Vrata Sanifor, the city gate leading to the Old Town from the tourist office. Inside, owner Franka stocks fine hand-made items: well-priced paintings and sculp-

ture plus olive oil, truffles and Clai wine, perhaps one of the peninsula's best labels. The place is meticulously run and has a 500-year-old olive press on the floor. When renovating this 16th-century house, the owners had to lower the floor to create space. In the process of pulling up the floor stones, a Roman cistern was found. Franka has made it part of the room; there's a window looking down into the ancient water container

Arts & leisure

Art Gallery Valenta

Stari trg 2, Labin (091 513 5095 mobile). **Open** *Apr-Nov* 10am-2pm, 7-10pm Mon-Sat; 10am-2pm Sun.

This establishment is a showcase for Labin's art scene. The Art Gallery Valenta sells pieces that range up to 12,000 euros in price and exhibits the quality one would expect to find in a big-city space. Talking to local artist Goran Valenta is reason enough to come in. He runs the shop where his work as well as that of four other artists – Mate Čvrljak (Labin), Zdravko Djerek (Zagreb), Stjepan Ivanišević (Split), Željko Senečić (Zagreb) – are displayed. Sculpture also finds its way in the door. Original prints start at 100 euros.

Ranch Barba Tone

Manjadvorci 60 (052 580 446, 098 701 377 mobile). **Open** varies.

On the road between Labin and Pula, Barban is a modest village famous for its medieval horse-riding competitions, when knights would joust a tiny target called a *prstenac*. The first contest was held in 1696. Today, horse-riding proficiency is still valued. The competition draws 8,000 spectators for the third weekend in August. Ranch Barba Tone offers guided horseback trips. One is the ride to the sea – once riders reach the Blaz bay they swim, with the help of guides, with their horses.

Get the local experience

Over 50 of the world's top destinations available.

Essentials

Hotel Monte Mulini, Rovinj p171

Hotels & Villas

Like its many landscapes, lodging in Istria takes several forms. On the coast, there are plenty of adequate package-variety resorts. The inland area is a villa and agrotourism hub. Elsewhere are boutique hotels, family-run guesthouses and even the region's oldest nudist colony

Whether you choose the east, west or south coasts, you'll find classic 1970s-era beach resorts with roots in Yugoslav times. Most of these have been given facelifts to meet the rising level of tourists' needs. So, though the shape of these buildings still might say 1973, their accoutrements – contemporary decor, spas, modern cuisine – say 2010, or something close to it. For package tourism and basic digs for holidaygoers, these centres are sufficient, as they cater to families and those whose chief priority is proximity to the sea.

Note that a significant number add a nominal sum, say five euros, for half-board stays, a bargain for the budget-conscious.

For those who don't care for the all-in-one offers, the options are wide-ranging. There are more than a few top hotels, villa possibilities and boutique getaways. In **Rovinj**, for instance, the **Monte Mulini** had a five-star makeover in 2008. The **Valsabbion** in Pula is sheer class. Both also offer don't-miss restaurants. Further up coast, the **Kempinski Hotel Adriatic** near Savudrija is a new five-star with an 18-hole golf course.

In addition, there are countless private lodgings both along the sea and especially inland. You will see signs for *sobe* (rooms) everywhere. Most are inexpensive. The ones to look for are those with an extra sign demarcating them as **Domus Bonus**, which the Istrian tourist board guarantees to meet several criteria: size and quality of room; proprietor on hand; and cutlery that must be stocked (a corkscrew is a necessity, for instance).

In the interior, you can find agritourism destinations. The key here is that your lodging is on a family's farm. Not only will you eat farm-fresh food – as is mandated to gain an agritourism licence, food must come from the farm – but you'll get to check on the crops, the animals and get a sense of what it is to roll up your sleeves in Istria.

South

Dianaville

Dračice 31D, Banjole (052 573 485, fax 052 573 803, www.dianaville.com). **K**. No credit cards.

A quiet, gated getaway hidden from the crowds of the southern Medulin tip of the peninsula, this compound of apartments and rooms is part of the Domus Bonus network, meeting stringent criteria from Istria's tourist board. Dianaville is tucked behind the smaller, sailing-boat harbour of Banjole. There are ten apartments of various sizes (sleeping from two to eight), six doubles and two singles across two nice villa-esque buildings and amid roses, palms, and grapevines. Owner Diana gives guests a tour of the town, pointing out the best beaches, and serves breakfast for a nominal extra. There's a common roofed grassy courtyard for the kids and family barbecues.

Hotel Arcus Residence

Burle, Medulin (052 529 100, fax 052 529 101, www.arcus.hr). **K**.

This year-round hotel makes a nice change from the usual package-tourist blocks. It's smaller in scale, with 84 rooms, double and singles, and two suites, right on the seashore opposite Medulin's main promenade. Facilities and services include air conditioning,

ESSENTIALS

Hotel Scaletta, Pula p163

an indoor pool, a gym, saunas, aromatherapy and massage treatments. The restaurant can make special meals for vegetarians, athletes and diabetics.

Hotel Histria

Verudela, Pula (052 590 000, fax 052 214 175, www.arenaturist.com). **KKK**.
The Histria is a three-star with a panorama of Verudela Bay from the bank facing the Valsabbion. Most of the 240 simply furnished rooms have sea-facing balconies. Facilities include a circular outdoor pool, a heated indoor one (both with seawater) a spa, sauna, gym and disco. Tennis courts and other sports pitches are nearby. It also has a casino and conference centre. Although pricey considering the prosaic nature of the rooms, it has great half-board rates at five euros over the rack rate. A Blue-Flag beach is 50 metres away.

Hotel Medulin

Osipovica 31, Medulin (052 572 001, fax 052 576 017, www.arenaturist.hr). **KK**.
Ten kilometres from Pula, Medulin's only four-star has 178 rooms and 12 suites on four floors. The Yugo architecture may not inspire but the rooms are big and clean, with air-conditioning throughout and balconies. Among the attractions are a club, pool bar, piano bar and internet. There are also two outdoor, salt-water pools and a fitness centre. The hotel is on the sea and only 100 metres from the Bijeca beach.

Hotel Milan

Stoja 4, Pula (052 210 200, fax 052 210 500, www.milan1967.hr). **KK**.
By the Naval Cemetery before you get to the Stoja headland, the Milan is best known for its quality restaurant. Its dozen three-star rooms, equipped with Wi-Fi, are clean and comfortable, and all feature big beds and tile floors. Importantly, the hotel is within easy reach (200 metres) of the modest beach at Valkane Bay.

Hotel Omir

Sergija Dobrića 6, Pula (052 210 614, fax 052 213 944). **K**.
The Omir is a Socialist-style guesthouse with old furnishings and light fittings, and a somewhat discombobulating breakfast room decked out with

art and an aquarium. It is also a handy cheapie in the centre of town, with 19 quiet rooms and a pizzeria downstairs. Around the corner is the ten-room, three-star Galija (Epulanova 3, 052 383 802, www.hotel-galija-pula.com, KK), with 20 rooms.

Hotel Palma
Verudela, Pula (052 590 760, fax 052 214 175, www.arenaturist.com). Closed Mid Oct-Mar. **KK**.
This three-star has 132 rooms over three floors. It shares the facilities of the nearby Histria, the 18 tennis courts, restaurants, tavern, yacht club and piano bar. Guests have the use of three outdoor pools, one with waterslide. Rooms have balconies; half have views of Verudela Bay; half have park views. Attractive half-board rates only add four euros to the price of a double.

Hotel Riviera
Splitska 1, Pula (052 211 166, fax 052 219 117, www.arenaturist.com). **K**.
Classic Habsburg hotel whose grand, 19th-century, neo-Baroque façade and marble lobby belie the fact that its 67 rooms, scattered across five floors, are in need of renovation. It's in the Arena Turist hotel group, so hopefully this won't be far off. But it does have views of the centre and the water – it's a useful base if you're just in by train or bus and only want to see the Amphitheatre and a few sights around town.

Hotel Scaletta
Flavijevska 26, Pula (052 541 599, fax 052 540 285, www.hotel-scaletta.com). **K**.
This German-run hotel and restaurant complex is a short walk towards the station from the Amphitheatre. Set on the main café street, it is well placed for the Pula hubbub as well. The dozen rooms (two singles) are simple and comfortable with air-conditioning and Wi-Fi. A decent breakfast, served in the lounge, is included with the price. It is sited five kilometres (three miles) from the airport and 2.5 kilometres (1.5 miles) from the water.

Neptune-Istra Hotel
Brijuni National Park (052 525 807, fax 052 521 367, www.brijuni.hr). **KK**.
There are several lodging options on Veliki Brijuni, the same island visitors

Stancija Meneghetti, Pula p164

Valsabbion, Pula

private land filled with olives and grapes. The interior is decorated in country-home style with exposed beam ceilings, tasteful artwork, throw rugs and wooden floors framing modernity: plasma-screen TV, DVD, internet. A chef at guests' beck and call is included in the price.

Stancija Negričani

Marčana, Divšići (052 391 084, fax 052 580 840, www.stancija negricani.com). **KK**.
Restored in 2002, Negričani is a farmhouse six kilometres (four miles) from Vodnjan. A cross between an agrotourist lodging and a villa, it has nine rooms sleeping 22 people. These stone-wall bedrooms which once housed livestock have been completely renovated and are equipped with Biedermeier furniture, washbasins on wrought-iron stands and strangely congruent modern touches like massage chairs, Wi-Fi and cable TV. The rooms have views across cherry and plum trees and a pool surrounded by butterfly-laden lavender. Negričani's restaurant is a highlight in and of itself and serves steak with truffles and lamb, veal and octopus under the *peka* roasting bell.

Valsabbion

Pješčana uvala IX/26, Pula (052 218 033, fax 052 222 991, www.valsabbion. net). **KKK**.
A place to be pampered, here ten immaculately conceived rooms comprise the accommodation at the high-class restaurant Valsabbion. Half have sea-view balconies; all are equipped with fine taste. Of the rooms, six are doubles, with the remaining four providing suites of varying levels of space and refinement. The buffet breakfast, not included in the price, is outstanding. You could and probably should opt for the half-board option with a four-course dinner here at one of Istria's finest restaurants. To complete the picture, there's a panoramic pool, gym and beauty treatments.

come to for tours of Tito's star-studded playground. This has 87 rooms (53 doubles, 14 singles and 20 suites), set on the harbour and charming in an updated Yugo-elegant kind of way. Nearby, the 53-room Karmen has a similar feel and is seaside. For real seclusion and five-star holiday comfort, there are also villas for let. The nicest are scattered on the island's south-east edge. The Primorka, the most chic, sleeps eight and comes with a hostess/chambermaid, all transport and a tour of the island.

Stancija Meneghetti

Bale (091 24 31 600 mobile, fax 01 242 2815, www.meneghetti.info). **KKKK**. No credit cards.
One of the nicest villas on the peninsula is near Bale, two kilometres (1.2 miles) from the sea. Sleeping ten, it was once a villa for Austro-Hungarian officers. Today the complex, with an extra guesthouse, comes with an outdoor and indoor pool, gym and steam bath, all sitting on ten hectares (25 acres) of

Hotel Istra, Rovinj p170

West Coast

Agrotourism Sterle

Štancija Drušković 20, Brtonigla (052 774 276, www.agroturizamsterle.hr). **K.** No credit cards.

The quintessential agrotourist destination, Sterle has five rooms on a farm that produces all the food and drink for its guests. Set in the Brtonigla gastro hub, it has ten hectares of grapes, ten of olive trees and a massive room for drying home-made prosciutto. The owners speak an assortment of languages and are as pleasant as they come. The restaurant has a terrace – covered by an ancient tree with an 180-square-metre wingspan – attracting diners from far and wide. As a bonus, Sterle runs the on-site Marble Cave, providing tours of its labyrinth of stalagmites and stalactites.

Casa Garzotto

Garzotto 8, Rovinj (tel/fax 052 811 884, fax 052 814 255/098 616 168 mobile, www.casa-garzotto.com). **KK**. This beautifully restored four-unit boutique hotel (with eight additional in annexes around Old Town) of studio apartments is in the heart of Rovinj. With its old window shutters and classic furniture from the late 1800s, the Garzotto is already winning repeat customers. Two of the apartments are heated by a roaring fire in winter. Breakfast consists of buffet treats partaken in the ground-floor tavern bar. The owners are English-speaking and go out of their way to meet your needs.

Hotel Adriatic

Obala Pina Budičina, Rovinj (052 815 088, fax 052 803 520, www.maistra.hr). Closed Nov-Mar. **KK**. Adriatic is a simple three-star on the harbour that lets 27 rooms for mid-range rates in the middle of town – with a view of St. Catherine's Island to boot. Although it's the oldest hotel in Rovinj, built a century ago, the large, basic rooms are in good shape. The pleasant terrace café is one of many along the busy harbour. The noise from here can be a bit of a problem for early sleepers in sea-view rooms, but this is a great place for couples and anyone looking for fun in town. There is Wi-Fi and a restaurant.

The New Dimension of Vacation

Umag
Istria, Croatia, Mediterranean

Hotels, Resorts, Campsites

Istraturist Umag d.d.
Jadranska 66, HR-52470 Umag, Croatia

Contact Centre:
✆ ++385(0)52 700 700
booking@istraturist.com

www.istraturist.com
www.istracamping.com

Hotel Cittar

Prolaz Venecija 1, Novigrad (052 757 737, fax 052 757 340, www.cittar.hr). **KK**.

With an exterior built into a section of Venetian wall in the centre, the Cittar is one of the best deals in Istria. It certainly has the best location in town. Run by a friendly team under Sergio Cittar, it has 14 perfectly adequate rooms with varnished floors, big beds, bathtubs and air-conditioning. A breakfast of warm croissants, meats and cheeses is laid out in the sunny conservatory. There are also two tennis courts. Half-board is offered in summer, when you should book well ahead.

Hotel Delfin

Zelena Laguna, Poreč (052 414 001, fax 052 451 658, www.plavalaguna.hr). Closed Nov-Mar. **K**.

This low-frills resort offers a decent budget option for families. The huge complex is like a small town unto itself with 793 rooms on a hilltop in a pretty pine-forested peninsula. The rooms are small and plain, but reasonably cool in the pine-shaded building despite the lack of air-conditioning. The pebble and less crowded rocky beaches 50 metres away are quite separate from the rest of Zelena Laguna. There's a sports centre next door plus an outdoor pool with saltwater.

Hotel Filipini

Filipini, Poreč (052 463 200, fax 052 463 201). **KK**.

In the village of Filipini five kilometres (three miles) outside Poreč, this little farmhouse-cum-boutique hotel in the woods is a great find. The eight units have cathedral ceilings, and are filled with antique furniture atop wooden-plank floors. There's an outdoor jacuzzi and tennis courts surrounded by olive groves and vineyards. But, for all that, the best attraction is the restaurant, serving slow food in a traditional Istrian manner. There's lamb in a pine-nut sauce, and veal in a marinade of honey and wild mint. The place fills with lodgers and diners quickly, so book ahead in high season.

Hotel Hostin

Rade Končara 4, Poreč (052 408 800, fax 052 408 857, www.hostin.hr). **KK**.

The Hostin chain only has one hotel in Poreč, and it offers competitive luxury at decent prices. The modern, attractive resort complex, surrounded by pines, is next to the marina beside a strip of seaside greenery that holds all the resorts. The sea is 70 metres away from the hotel's 39 rooms. Amenities include a pool, a sauna, a whirlpool, a steam room, a gym and a nearby pebble beach. Diving, boat and bike rentals are also nearby.

Hotel Istra

Sv Andrea, Rovinj (052 802 500, fax 052 813 484, www.maistra.hr). Closed Jan-mid Mar. **KK**.

Many high-end hotels in Croatia have spa facilities – but only this one occupies a whole island. St Andrew's

Hotel Palazzo, Poreč p173

The latest in luxury

Opened in August 2009, the **Hotel Adriatic**, under the Swiss-based Kempinski umbrella of properties, singlehandedly brought a new category of tourism to the Istrian peninsula: all-in-one resort luxury. The establishment has beautiful rooms, a golf course, the sea and a spa centre – when you check in, there is little reason to leave. It is located outside Savudrija, where the Adriatic's oldest working lighthouse stands on Croatia's westernmost point, a beacon to the rest of Europe.

This is one of the few five-star venues on the entire peninsula. (There are only two others: one in Rovinj and one in Umag.) It is open all year round with a bevy of off-season specials like stay four nights and get the last night free. The hotel has 186 rooms and suites. Rooms are sleek with chic, contemporary furniture and flatscreen TVs, lined by wood panelling. Big beds look out on to seaside terraces, where patio tables and chairs await tea-time.

Outside, there is an 18-hole championship golf course. It was the first in Istria, and remains one of the precious few in the entire country. Right on the Adriatic, the complex has a driving-range, chipping and putting greens, a golf academy and a 19th-hole bar with views of the Alps.

The spa centre naturally offers a host of saunas and beauty treatments. The gym has a weights room and a cardio area. There are four tennis courts and three swimming pools, two outdoor and one in. The staff can also arrange sailing excursions.

For those looking to relax while on holiday instead of playing a round, pumping iron or fighting the waves, the resort has two restaurants: Dijana and Slice. Expect a combination of seafood and Istrian specialities such as pastas, wild asparagus, truffles, and local sausage and prosciutto. In all, there are four bars on the premises including the Beach Bar, Golf Bar and Pool Bar.

Island, or Red Island, houses this four-star hotel complex of 326 rooms (plus more at the nearby Park Hotel under renovation), four restaurants, three bars and three pools. A beach is within 50 metres, while activities include yachting, windsurfing and football on a full pitch. As for the spa, there's relaxation and recharge massages, whirlpools indoor and out, Turkish and Finnish saunas and Kneipp baths. All is set amid greenery, the interior imbued with relaxing scents and tones.

Hotel Maestral

Terre, Novigrad (052 757 557, fax 052 757 314, www.laguna-novigrad.hr). Closed Nov-Mar. **KKK**.

This four-star is a 15-minute walk to town and has all the amenities: indoor and outdoor pools; bars inside and out; Wi-Fi; spa and fitness room; massage rooms – all a 150-metre hop to the sea. Half the rooms, big and simple, are on the waterside and have balconies. If a worry-free, semi-luxurious holiday is what you're after, this will do just fine.

Hotel Monte Mulini

A Smareglia, Rovinj (052 636 000, fax 052 636 001, www.maistra.hr). **KKKK**.

At Rovinj's big hitter, the facilities match the fabulous setting. The five-star makeover of Monte Mulini gave a big shot in the arm to the area's tourism – and with good reason. With two gourmet restaurants under executive chef Tomislav Gretić and 99 rooms (including 14 suites) reconfigured and refurbished by top designers, Istria's posh resort has gotten itself a posh resort hotel. All rooms, fitted with bespoke furniture, have balconies; the hotel brushes up to a rocky beach with natural shade from nearby greenery, amid the Golden Cape. Sports facilities include four clay tennis courts, a basketball court, a bowling alley and gym. There are pools indoor and out, plus a two-level spa with massage (including stone and wood) and beauty treatments (24-carat gold body and face, and a caviar facial). Mediterranean fusion dishes feature at the sea-view

Hotel Nautica, Novigrad p173

Hotel Cittar, Novigrad p170

terrace restaurant; French delicacies at the Corsican Wine Vault, with tastings and a choice of 550 labels.

Hotel Nautica

Sv Antona 15, Novigrad (052 600 400, fax 052 600 450, www.nautica hotels.com). **KKK**.

A four-star hotel opened in 2006, the Nautica is uncompromisingly contemporary. The spacious, sumptuous complex has an ongoing nautical flavour. The dark-wood, leather and brass furniture is styled after on-board outfittings, extending to the ship's wheel headboards. With a restaurant – Navigare is excellent in its own right – a large lounge bar, indoor pool and spa, this is a fine addition to Istria's rapidly improving hotel stock. For those on sailing holidays, the ship-to-shore facilities could not be better. Plans to become a five-star, involving the inclusion of an outdoor pool, are in place.

Hotel Palazzo

NEW *Obala maršala Tita 24, Poreč (052 858 800, fax 052 858 801).* **KKK**.

Opened in the summer of 2009, the four-star Palazzo is a much-needed option in the centre of Old Town Poreč. Right on the water off the main seaside promenade, it sits on a little square of land jutting off the south-west tip of the peninsula containing the ancient city. Once the Hotel Riviera, it was completely renovated and now offers 70 rooms and four apartments. The bedrooms are of the classic four-star ilk with high ceilings and well-appointed with big beds, wood floors and tasteful, dark wooden furniture. The back of the hotel opens out onto a marina. There's an à la carte restaurant, plus booking of excursions and yacht rental.

Hotel Pineta

Vrsar (052 441 150, fax 052 637 550, www.maistra.hr). Closed Nov-Apr. **KK**.

This three-star hotel is sited on a slight hill, across from Vrsar, at the edge of a pine forest, hence the name. Billed as the town's most luxurious hotel, the Pineta is functional, its semi-circular format funky, and you have views over Vrsar Bay. There is air-conditioning throughout and an indoor pool, spa, gym and a conference room. Pineta offers 99 rooms and four suites.

Hotel Poreč

Rade Končara 1, Poreč (tel/fax 052 451 811, www.hotelporec.com). **KK**.

This blocky building with 54 rooms is near the bus station and a small park by the marina. It was renovated in 2004. Of all the hotels in town, this is furthest from the holidaymaker bustle. On site is a beauty salon and casino. They can organise diving, jet skis, water-skiing, tennis and golf lessons. The comfortable air conditioned rooms all have balconies, though the views are bland.

Hotel Villa Angelo d'Oro

Via Švalba 38-42, Rovinj (052 840 502, fax 052 840 111, www.rovinj.at). Closed Sept-mid Mar. **KKK**.

This four-star is set in a wonderfully restored old building on the site of a 17th-century bishop's palace. The location, along a narrow, winding stone-paved street halfway up the hill that defines Rovinj's Old Town, is quiet and central. The lobby, museum-quality stairway and individually styled rooms all ooze antique opulence. The garden café, hidden from the street by ancient stone walls, and the sheltered rooftop loggia with its sea views, provide stunning sanctuary. The wellness area includes a sauna, jacuzzi and solarium. It has a superb seafood restaurant worth visiting even if you're not staying, and a wine cellar for tastings. Only 24 rooms, so book early.

Kempinski Hotel Adriatic

NEW *Alberi 300A, Savudrija (052 707 000, fax 052 707 011, www.kempinski-adriatic.com).* **KKKK**.

See box p168.

ESSENTIALS

Koversada FKK

Petalon 1, Vrsar (052 441 171, fax 052 444 255, www.maistra.hr). Closed Nov-Apr. **KK**.

If you'd rather holiday *au naturel* then head for one of the world's largest nudist colonies, housing up to 7,000 guests in lodging that includes apartments (119 four-star, two-person), camping, villas and bungalows, all right on the beach. Koversada's claim to fame is having been the only such spot in Communist Europe, open since 1961.

San Rocco

Srednja ulica 2, Brtonigla (052 725 000, fax 052 725 026, www.san-rocco.hr). **KKK**.

For lodging, you'd be hard pressed to do better: the four-star San Rocco won the Best Small Hotel award in Croatia for 2007 and 2008. Ten beautifully furnished rooms are ranged around two pools, a wine shop, wine cellar and, best of all, a restaurant, which also matches any in the area bite for bite. There's a wellness centre with spa and massage treatments. The rooms are manor-style rustic with exposed wooden ceiling beams and spacious floor plans. They have internet and hydro-massage tubs. Some have sea views, others vistas of picturesque Brtonigla.

Sol Coral

Katoro (052 701 000, fax 052 701 999, www.istraturist.com). **KK**.

The five-star jewel in the crown of Istraturist's hotels in and around Umag, the newly opened Sol Coral appeals to the active business visitor of both sexes. Exotic Thai treatments and other Oriental preparations, saunas and two seawater pools are complemented by indoor and outdoor tennis courts, a riding centre, a shooting range and any number of sundry sports courts. Congress halls and meeting rooms, four in number, are all equipped with modern facilities. The complex enjoys a beach-side location and all 200-plus rooms have bathtubs.

Sol Umag

Jadranska (052 714 000, fax 052 714 999, www.istraturist.com). **KKK**.

Set on the beach just outside Umag, this four-star offers some of the best spa treatments in Istria. A Roman bath, a 'biosauna', a whirlpool scented with citrus aromas, a number of outstanding features make the SPA Oasis a major attraction at the peninsula's north-west corner. Treatments include facials with oyster extract or caviar, ocean mineral peeling and one involving 'Cleopatra mud'. Throw in three swimming pools, tennis courts (and tuition) mini golf and beach volleyball, facilitating a free activities clubs for all ages, and you have an impressive selection indeed. All 200-plus rooms have balconies and bathtubs.

Torci 18

Torci 34, Novigrad (052 757 799, fax 052 757 174, www.torci18.hr). Closed Oct-Apr. **K**.

Djurdja and Lino Beletić run this sturdy three-star pension and restaurant in the centre of town with a dozen clean, comfortable rooms, some overlooking a courtyard. Their homely yet well-appointed eaterie is also a worthy destination in itself, with dishes such as steak, scampi and lobster; a fine spread of local specialities at knockdown prices to guests and non-guests alike.

Valamar Club Tamaris

Lanterna, Tar (052 408 000/ reservations 052 465 000, fax 052 441 440, www.valamar.com). Closed Nov-Mar. **KK**.

Set by the fine beaches of the Lanterna peninsula just outside Poreč, the four-star Tamaris provides the ideal active family retreat. Three outdoor pools, free babysitting for under-fours (the in-room service is paid for), free cycle hire, sports courts, tennis, children's entertainment all summer long, mini-disco and a mini-cinema are all on-site, with sailing and diving schools nearby. All rooms, more than 300 of them, have

Agrotourism Tikel, Karojba

balconies, but the building is a toddler-friendly three storeys high, with a lift. Look out for the attractive half- and full-board rates.

Valamar Diamant Hotel

Brulo (052 408 000/reservations 052 465 100, fax 052 441 440, www.valamar.com). **KKK**.

A beachside four-star for grown-ups and children, the Diamant combines business (conference and congress rooms) with pleasure (gym and spa treatments) a short drive from Poreč – there's free parking too. Kids have separate pools indoor and out, and are provided with entertainment all summer, although the hotel itself is year-round.

Villa Rosetta

Crvena uvala 31, Zambratija (052 725 710, fax 052 725 720, www.villarosetta.hr). **KK**.

Just 50 metres from the sea, Rosetta is best known for its restaurant and Mediterranean cuisine. It also has 23 sea-view rooms and an apartment, hence the villa part. The rooms have parquet floors and a balcony overlooking a private beach with a cocktail bar. There is also a spa, dry and steam saunas, and massage treatments. It's on the Savudrija Riviera, four kilometres (2.5 miles) from Umag.

Villa Valdibora

Chiurca Silvana 8, Rovinj (052 845 040, fax 052 845 050, www.valdibora.com). **KKK**.

This 18th-century, recently renovated townhouse of six studio apartments and three doubles offers tasteful lodging in the Old Town near the sea. Services include laundry, laptop rental and bike hire. Staff can advise on other activities close to hand: tennis, minigolf and kayaking, all paid extras. There are boat trips too. There is a children's pool and playground close by.

Interior

Agrotourism Tikel

Špinovci 88, Karojba (052 683 404). **K**.

Run by Mario Tikel and his two sons, this classic agrotourism spot is set at the end of a long winding road off the main thoroughfare from Motovun, which is about five kilometres (three miles) due north. At the end of the country drive, Tikel sits on a little hill surrounded by farmland – theirs – and has a perfect view of Motovun in the distance. In the autumn (a great time to visit) you can often see the hilltop town sitting among the clouds, and walk to it on a hiking path. As is mandated by

ESSENTIALS

the tourist board, all food served is grown or raised on the premises. Tikel has five rustic farmhouse rooms. Ask in advance to go on a truffle-hunting expedition with Mario.

Beli Mate

Sv Martin 39, Buzet (052 663 329). **KK.** No credit cards.
Another Domus Bonus lodging (so called because it meets tourist board requirements for size and amenities), Beli Mate is a rural house just north of Buzet. Set beneath the Ćićarija mountains, it has grand views in all directions. The price is for the whole house including a big master bedroom filled with antique furniture, a fireplace and a shag rug. Outside there's a terrace and veranda for tea, a lawn with pink and purple flowers, and a views of the vineyards above Buzet.

Bella Vista

Gradiziol 1, Motovun (091 523 0321 mobile, www.apartmani-motovun.com). **KK.** No credit cards.
Right in the middle of Motovun's Old Town set in the 19th-century Bazziaco Villa, the pretty Bella Vista contains a handful of Domus Bonus units. The apartments have modern furnishings

– big double beds, flat-screen TVs, air-conditioning – with exposed stone decor. Each has a different design, and kitchenettes. Regardless of which you choose, the kicker is the panoramic view across the Motovun Forest and the Mirna river.

Casa Roma Villa

Sv Kirin (+44 20 7585 0568, www.istriadelux.com). **KKKK.** No credit cards.
On a hillside between Motovun (about ten kilometres/six miles west) and Buzet (due north), around a 20-minute drive from either, Casa Roma is an example, albeit a particularly luxurious one, of the sort of villas that are popping up around Istria. The views, over Butoniga Lake, vineyards and the valley to Motovun, are only part of its allure. Opened in 2008 by two English families, the villa is something of a modern-meets-traditional set-up with a heavy nod to the former. It sleeps eight; it has a stainless-steel kitchen; each bedroom has a bath; and it has a 25-metre, palm-framed, infinity lap pool. The interior is expansive with floor-to-ceiling windows and wooden beams against white plaster and stone – a veritable palatial getaway.

Hotel Kaštel, Motovun p177

Hotel Fontana

Trg Fontana 1, Buzet (052 662 615, fax 052 662 596). **KK**.

Renovated in 2009 to three stars, the Fontana is nothing fancy, but it is a clean, well run, reasonably priced hotel in the centre of Buzet. It is also the only hotel in town, used as a headquarters for events such as the paragliding championships that take place in the mountains just north of town. The 50 or so rooms are spread across three floors and the restaurant serves Istrian specialities. Plans are afoot for a spa.

Hotel Kaštel

Trg Andrea Antico 7, Motovun (052 681 607, fax 052 681 652, www.hotel-kastel-motovun.hr). **KK**.

The only hotel in town opened a spa in 2008. At that point the attractive Kaštel moved up from being a homely three-star to one of the best mid-priced, stay-and-relax deals in Istria. The spa centre, made of Istrian stone, offers covered hydromassage pool, chromotherapy and dry and steam saunas, plus views of the verdant Motovun landscape. The hotel consists of 34 well-appointed rooms (some with balconies) behind a red façade, and can provide half-board rates; the restaurant is a destination in its own right, with quality Istrian cuisine served in the shade of age-old chestnut trees.

Hotel Lovac

Šime Kurelića, Pazin (052 624 324, fax 052 624 219). **KK**.

Lovac ('hunter') has 25 rooms in a hotel that was first opened in 1972 as a hunting lodge. It teeters on the edge of Pazin's gorge and has some of the best views (16 rooms face the gorge) in town – sitting directly across from the castle built in 983. The idea is to make this a four-star; the renovation of the bottom-level restaurant shows what the owners have in mind. At the moment the rooms are run-of-the-mill, smallish but passable. Locals come for its upper restaurant, which serves inexpensive,

Villa stays

Istria lends itself to villa life. For much of its area, the peninsula is wide open, with picturesque villages sitting atop rolling hills offering views across vineyards, olive groves, Roman ruins and the sea. By renting a villa, you can experience the character of this region for yourself, on your own terms. Istrians, and foreigners, now recognise this and have begun to build modern-day properties to match Istria's ever-evolving tourism offers: high-end gastronomy, outdoor activities and sightseeing.

According to Caroline Hopkins, founder of **Istrian Property Management**, which handles 30 sites, focusing on larger villas with pools, the touring opportunities and day trips through the peninsula provide a framework for enjoying a luxurious week-long stay. And while villas are dearer than the hotel alternative, they are usually better priced than you think, especially when the cost is shared between a group of friends. The properties are all-inclusive operations, with an agent to see to your needs.

'Soft tourism what is taking place here: each village or town has something to offer, whether it's a 15th-century fresco, a dinosaur remnant, a village festival, a vampire myth or a Venetian landmark,' says Hopkins. 'As well, wine routes have sprung up and truffle-hunting trips are on offer. Villas are great bases to explore Istria's pleasures in the morning and then return to spend an afternoon by the pool.'

hearty meals – home-made bread, prosciutto, cheese and good house wine – and for the terrace which looks down into the crevasse between diners and the castle.

Istria Property Management

Trg slobode 4, Višnjan (098 957 5345 mobile, www.istriaproperty management.com).
See box p177.

Laura

Antuna Kalca 10A, Pazin (052 621 312). **KK**. No credit cards.
A charming house with four double rooms and four apartments, this is a great budget-minded option in the centre of Pazin. The balconies have a view of the castle and the gorge. The apartments are no-frills but have been newly renovated with kitchenettes. Parking is included; breakfast is 28kn.

Motovun House

Barbacan 4, Motovun (091 200 2582 mobile, www.motovunhouse.com). **K**. No credit cards.
Something of a misnomer, Motovun House is actually two houses in one. The primary locale, the so-called red house, is on Barbacan, just down from the main part of Old Town. This sleeps nine and has three spacious bedrooms with three baths, a big kitchen with dining table and a terrace with fireplace grill. All the rooms have been beautifully renovated. If you don't have nine people, a minimum of four is necessary for a minimum of a week's stay. The second property is located down the street at Borgo 21: the yellow house. Smaller in scale (this one sleeps six), it has also been refurbished and can be rented by a couple, but naturally discounts apply if you are coming with a full complement.

Pintur

M Gorjana 9, Grožnjan (052 731 055). Closed Jan-Mar. **KK**. No credit cards.

This modest little guesthouse, across the street from the landmark Bastia restaurant, has four (three doubles and one single) three-star rooms. It is best known for its restaurant downstairs, which has a cosy indoor dining room and stone terrace outside. Something of a gathering place on the cobbled piazza adjacent to the square where musicians play for the annual jazz festival, this is an ideal spot for a no-frills, clean room and to feel like part of this artistic community.

San Mauro Agrotourism

San Mauro 157, Momjan (052 779 033, fax 052 721 380, www.sinkovic.hr). **K**. No credit cards.
This family-run business on the edge of Momjan is deep in wine country; they produce Chardonnay, Muškat, Malvasia and Teran. Besides their clean and adequate nine apartments (all with their own kitchens but breakfast included), they have olives, chickens, pigs and a delightful restaurant for guests to try their specialities – including 40 types of fruit grappa. Roaming the grounds, and not for eating, are Vietnamese potbellied pigs Jack and Gigi, who make pillows for the cats and temporary pets for children.

Villa Angelica

Matka Laginje, Oprtalj (052 758 700, fax 052 758 610 fax, www.solea.hr). **KKK**. No credit cards.
The 19th-century Villa Angelica, renovated in 2008, sits on the edge of Oprtalj like a jewel. A five-star, six-bedroom villa, it has a swimming pool, a spa (steam bath, Turkish sauna, jacuzzi and gym) with a panoramic view over the valley, a maid service and terraces all over the place. There's a banquet table by the kitchen, and even the option of a private chef and masseuse. It also has a wine cellar for gatherings, and culinary workshops. And, if split 12 ways, the price is surprisingly reasonable, given the quality services on offer.

Casa Roma Villa, Sv Kirin p176

Villa Višnjan

Kovačeva 9, Višnjan (052 449 316/ 091 577 4908 mobile, www.villa-visnjan.com). **KKK**. No credit cards.
This restored stone country house with ten apartments and studios is in the heart of Višnjan Old Town. The apartments are spacious comprising two rooms, kitchens and nooks for reading or taking breakfast coffee. The studios are also roomy. There are wooden floors and ceilings throughout. Rates are for the week with four-day minimums, a drawback if you're looking for a mix-and-match kind of holiday. If not, the pool and terrace out back should suit your pace.

Volta

Matka Laginje 7A, Oprtalj (091 206 0538 mobile). **K**. No credit cards.
Run by the same family that owns the forward-thinking Ipša olive-oil firm down the valley, Volta is a spotless locale with an apartment, two doubles and a single – all simple and well-priced – in cobbled Oprtalj, due north of Motovun. Deemed Domus Bonus for tourists, it has views of the town's loggia. Breakfast is included.

East Coast

Adoral Hotel Apartments

Obala maršala Tita 2A, Rabac (052 535 840, fax 052 872 149, www.adoral.hr). **KK**.
Opened at the end of the 2006 season, the Adoral is just that step ahead of most offerings in the Rabac/Labin area. This four-star property has 12 units: nine apartments and three double rooms. All have balconies with views straight down to the sea a few hundred metres from the main harbour promenade area. The decor is modern but with a warm Mediterranean vibe: straight-back chairs around the dining table; homely wood and cloth chairs around the wooden balcony table with the sea beyond. It has Wi-Fi and serves a fine spread for breakfast.

Hotel Amfora

Rabac (052 872 222, fax 052 873 345, www.hotel-amfora.com). Closed Nov-Apr. **KK**.
Right in the thick of things, Amfora is 30 metres from the seafront and within walking distance of the restaurants, cafés and bars of downtown Rabac.

Renovated in 2003, it features air conditioning, a summer terrace and a small swimming pool. Half the 52 rooms (there are also two suites) look out on to the sea, and the others have a park view. Keep your eye out for room specials in autumn, a neglected season on the east coast.

Istrapartner Agropansion

Bratulići 17, Barban (052 544 400, fax 052 544 401, www.agropansion-partner.com). **K**.

Istrapartner has six decent-sized double rooms outside Barban between Pula and Labin. These are rustic, with exposed stone and wooden ceiling beams, decorated with antiques which give the place a manor feel. Perhaps the best amenity is the restaurant in a stone house across the grassy courtyard. All food is fresh and home-made.

Valamar Bellevue Hotel & Residence

Rabac (052 465 200, fax 052 872 561, www.valamar.com). Closed Nov-Apr. **KK**.

This impressive four-star under the Valamar umbrella is situated on the beach just north of Rabac and connected to town by a little train. In total, the Valamar Bellevue Hotel & Residence comprises 154 rooms spread across five floors with 20 luxury ones in separate villas. There are also two swimming pools (one for kids), a jacuzzi, a diving centre 100 metres away and family entertainment laid on all summer long. The panorama over the Kvarner Bay is a showstopper. Rates are half-board and reasonable. All has been recently renovated.

Villa Annette

Raška 24, Rabac (052 884 222, fax 052 884 225, www.villa annette.hr). **KK**.

A stunningly modern boutique hotel overlooking Rabac Bay, the Villa Annette has fabulous decor with plenty of well-placed artwork; its 12 suites are well-designed, with space and character. Villa Annette also features an infinity pool with views out to the islands of Cres and Lošinj and a great slow-food restaurant. Rates are not exorbitant considering the quality on offer. There are also various suite options worth considering.

Valamar Bellevue Hotel & Residence

Getting Around

Arriving & leaving
By air

Istria's only airport is at **Pula**. Others within easy reach are at the Croatian capital **Zagreb** (www.zagreb-airport.hr), Slovene capital **Ljubljana** (www.lju-airport.si), and, in Italy, **Trieste** (www.aeroporto.fvg.it) and **Venice** (veniceairport.it). Bus and rail transport is limited between the Italian hubs and Istria.

Pula airport

052 530 105, www.airport-pula.hr.
Eight kilometres (five miles) north-east of town, Pula airport is not served by public transport – a taxi (052 223 228) costs around 150kn. Flight-time from the UK is less than three hours. National carrier Croatia Airlines flies from London Gatwick. In season, Ryanair flies from London Stansted; Thomsonfly flies from Birmingham, Gatwick and Manchester.

By boat

Venezia Lines

052 422 896, + 39 041 242 2646, www.venezialines.com.
Routes to and from Venice serve Pula, Poreč, Rovinj and Rabac. Bookings are now taken online.

Jadrolinija

051 666 111, www.jadrolinija.hr.
This national ferry outfit links Istria to the Croatian coast via their base at nearby Rijeka. In season, a frequent service connects Brestova, just north of Labin with Cres. Foot passenger fares are laughably cheap: Brestova-Cres is 17kn. Taking an average-sized car would cost 113kn – but obviously other prices vary.

By rail

Details on connections can be found at www.db.de or www.hznet.hr. In Istria, hub stations are at **Pazin** (Stareh kostanji 1, 052 624 310); **Pula** (Kolodvorska 7, 052 541 733); and, nearby, in **Rijeka** (Trg kralja Tomislava 1, 051 213 333).

By bus

Istria is connected on international lines with stations at: **Pula** (trg 1. istarske brigade 1 (052 500 012, 060 304 090); **Rovinj** (trg na lokvi 6, 052 811 453); **Poreč** (Karla Huguesa 2, 052 432 153); **Novigrad** (Murve 15, 052 757 660); **Umag** (Joakima Rakovca 11, 060 381 381); **Labin-Rabac** (Trg 2. ožujka, 052 855 220); and **Pazin** (Miroslava Bulečića 2, 52 624 437).

The main Croatian bus company is **Autotrans** (www.autotrans.hr); **Pulapromet** (www.pulapromet.hr) is based at Pula.

By road

Istria's highway is called the 'Y' (*Upsilon*) because of its shape. It runs for 140 kilometres (87 miles) with two toll booths: one in the east near Rijeka (Učka Tunnel); the other in the west near Novigrad (Mirna Bridge). Expect more tolls as the new four-lane highway is completed in the coming years. The B8 from Rijeka meets the B9 in Kanfanar near Istria's centre. From here the B9 runs both north towards Umag and south to Pula.

Though the Y has regular exits and road facilities, driving around Istria means much time on minor roads, some little more than gravel paths. For the most part, these are signposted. The speed limits are 50km/hr (31mph) in built-up areas; 80km/hr (50mph) in surrounding areas; and 130km/hr (80mph) on main roads. In case of emergency, call 92. For roadside assistance, dial 987 or contact the Croatian automobile club (www.hak.hr).

Car hire

Renting a car in Croatia can be dear with prices in the 500kn/day range for a family vehicle. Try to get quotes online before you travel to avoid any surprises when you arrive. In all cases below, the rental companies have locations in Pula and/or Rijeka, some in Poreč.
Avis *052 223 739, www.avis.com.hr*.
Budget *052 218 252, www.generalturist.com*
Dollar & Thrifty *051 337 917, www.thrifty.com*
Hertz *052 210 868, www.hertz.hr*

Parking

Parking is usually quite a simple and relatively cheap proposition. It can be harder and more expensive in the busier spots like Rovinj, but most car parks never run higher than 10kn per hour and can be less. Parking can be paid for on your mobile phone – look for signs indicating the proper code for the town or city you are in. Parking is almost always free in villages.

Bringing your own car

To enter Croatia by car you need a valid driver's licence with a photograph, vehicle registration documents and insurance documents (with a Green Card).

Petrol stations

Petrol stations are found in main towns and usually open 7am-7pm.

Getting around

By rail

Rail connections into Istria are very limited. A line runs to Pula, but to link with Rijeka, change for a bus at the little station of Lupoglav. Details on www.hznet.hr.

By bus

Buses are not only the best way to get from village to village in Istria, they are the only public transport. In quite a few cases, particularly where the hilltop villages of the Istrian interior is concerned, the bus stop will be a couple of kilometres from the village itself and passengers need to either climb the hill themselves, or rely on the commonly used method of asking a passing local for a lift. *See p181* **By bus** for main bus firms.

Main towns Pula, Rovinj and Poreč have their own bus services – tickets are sold at newsstands.

By taxi

Taxi stands are at bus stations and and other hubs in main towns. Expect to pay 20kn start-up then 10kn per km.
Pula *Hallo Auto City (052 500 057)*; *Taxi Pula (052 223 228)*.
Rovinj *052 811 100*.
Poreč *052 432 465*.
Novigrad *052 757 224*.
Labin *Jasmin (098 916 1863 mobile)*; *Nikola (098 366 030 mobile)*.

By bike

Cyclists will enjoy local landscapes if not pot-holed roads and hairpin bends. Istria's tourist bureau has done a great job of mapping and listing all necessary resources – see pp45-47 Istria by Bike.

ESSENTIALS

Resources A-Z

Accident & emergency

Take out medical insurance when travelling to Croatia. The country's reciprocal agreement with the UK covers only emergency treatment, and only 80% of that. The standard of care in Croatia is good. Your best bet is to go to the local hospital or emergency unit where a duty doctor can have a look at you. In the bigger towns these centres should be able to help you:

Poreč Health Centre
Maura Gioseffia 2 (052 451 611).

Pula Hospital
Zagrebačka 30 (052 376 500, www.obpula.hr).

Rovinj Ambulance Emergency Ward
Istarska (052 813 004).

Emergency numbers

Call 92 for the police, 93 for the fire brigade and 94 for an ambulance.

Credit card loss

American Express
Croatia office *01 612 4422.*
Emergencies *01 480 7300.*
www.amextravelresources.com.
This office is in Zagreb. If calling on a foreign mobile, first dial +385 1.

Diners Club
Croatia office *01 492 9000.*
Emergencies *0800 11 44.*
www.diners.com.hr.

Mastercard
Emergencies *(US number only)*
+1 636 722 7111.
www.mastercard.com/hr.

Visa
Emergencies *866 654 0125.*
www.visa.com.

Customs

Foreign currency can be taken freely in and out of the country, and local currency up to an amount of 15,000kn. You are permitted 200 cigarettes or cigarillos or 50 cigars or 250g of tobacco, and one litre of spirits, two litres of liqueur or dessert or sparkling wine and two litres of table wine. Valuable professional and technical equipment needs to be declared at the border. It must leave with you again – you should not sell it while you're in Croatia.

Any cultural artefact, art or archaeological find can only be exported with necessary approval. For information see www.carina.hr.

Dental emergencies

Check with the hospitals and medical centres (*see left*) for details.

Disabled

Croatia is not very enlightened in providing facilities for disabled people. That is changing as a result of those left disabled by the war in the 1990s.

Not all hotels have disabled access and facilities – it would be worth making enquiries first.

For more information, ask the local Association of Organisations of Disabled Persons, www.soih.hr.

Electricity

Croatia uses a 220V, 50Hz voltage and continental two-pin plugs.

Embassies & consulates

These national offices are all in Zagreb. Dial 00 385 1 then the last seven digits if you're calling on a foreign mobile phone in Istria.

Australian Embassy
01 48 91 200, www.auembassy.hr. **Open** 8.30am-4.30pm Mon-Fri.

British Embassy
01 60 09 100, ukincroatia.fco.gov.uk. **Open** 8.30am-5pm Mon-Thur; 8.30am-2pm Fri.

Canadian Embassy
01 48 81 200, www.canada international.gc.ca. **Open** 10am-noon, 1-3pm Mon-Thur; 10am-1pm Fri.

Irish Honorary Consul
01 63 10 025, www.european irish.com. **Open** 8am-noon, 2-3pm Mon-Fri.

New Zealand Consulate
01 46 12 060. **Open** 8am-noon, 1.30-3pm Mon-Fri.

US Embassy
01 66 12 200, www.zagreb. usembassy.gov. **Open** 8am-4.30pm Mon-Fri.

Internet

A growing number of hotels have Wi-Fi or high-speed internet in rooms. Internet cafés abound in bigger towns. Venues include: **Novigrad** Internet Centar *Mandrač 20 (052 726 280).* **Open** *Summer* 9am-10pm daily. *Winter* 9am-5pm Mon-Sat. **Poreč** Internet Centar *Cybermac Mire Grahalića 1 (052 427 075, www. cybermac.hr).* **Open** 10am-10pm daily. **Pula** Cyber@Cafe *Flanatička 14 (052 212 682).* **Open** 7am-9pm Mon-Fri; 7am-2pm Sat.

Rovinj A-Mar *Carera 26 (052 841 211, www.a-mar.hr).* **Open** 8am-10pm Mon-Thur, Sun; 8am-11pm Fri, Sat.

Money

The unit of Croatian currency is the kuna (kn). Coins are for 1, 2 and 5kn, notes for 5, 10, 20, 50, 100, 200, 500 and 1,000kn.

Euros are accepted in some hotels, and shops and restaurants in towns – but the currency in everyday use is the kuna.

Currency can be exchanged in banks, post offices, tourist agencies and at some hotels. ATMs and credit card use are widespread.

Opening hours

Public sector offices and most businesses usually work from 8am to 4pm Monday to Friday. Banks and post offices are open from 7am to 7pm, and generally close at weekends. Shops open from 8am to 8pm weekdays and until 2pm or 3pm on Saturdays, although in summer some stay open longer.

During national, or public, holidays you should expect businesses to be closed, or at least their hours shortened. Holidays are: **1 January**: New Year's; **6 January**: Epiphany; **4-5 April 2010**: Easter Sunday and Monday; **1 May**: Labour Day; **3 June 2010**: Corpus Christi; **22 June**: Anti-Fascist Day; **25 June**: Statehood Day; **5 August**: Victory Day and Thanksgiving; **15 August**: Assumption Day; **8 October**: Independence Day; **1 November**: All Saints' Day; **25-26 December**: Christmas.

Pharmacies

Whereas hospitals and clinics are found in larger towns, almost everywhere is equipped with a pharmacy (*ljekarna*), typically staffed with professional and often English-speaking pharmacists. Below is a list of pharmacies in Istria's bigger settlements:

Novigrad Novigrad Pharmacy *Općinska 2 (052 757 039)*. **Open** 8am-1pm, 5-7pm Mon-Fri; 8am-1pm Sat.
Poreč Gradska Ljekarna *Trg slobode 12 (052 432 362)*. **Open** 8am-8pm Mon-Sat.
Pula Pharmacy *Giardini 14 (052 222 551)*. **Open** 24hrs daily.
Rovinj Gradska Ljekarna *M Benussi ulica (052 813 589)*. **Open** 7am-8pm Mon-Fri; 7am-3pm Sat; 9am-noon Sun.

Police

See p183 Emergency numbers.

Post

Every town will have one. For hours of operation refer to Opening hours (p184). Below is a list of post offices (www.posta.hr) to be found in the larger towns:
Novigrad *Mandrać 28 (052 757 067)*.
Poreč *Vukovarska 17 (052 452 925)*.
Pula *Danteov trg 4 (052 625 209)*.
Rovinj *M Benussi 4 (052 811 262)*.

Safety

Croatia has a low rate of street crime. Visiting women may not appreciate the attention they get from local men, especially in coastal areas. If it's in danger of crossing the line between flirtation and harrassment, don't be shy of making your displeasure known.

Smoking

A large proportion of Croats smoke and it is far more acceptable than in the UK or US. Recent experiments with no-smoking laws had the country smoke-free inside all businesses and public buildings until a law reversal. Now a mixture of smoking areas and ventilation requirements has allowed smoking back in restaurants once more, further proving the country's reliance upon and love of cigarettes. Smoking is not permitted in cinemas and on public transport.

Telephones

When calling overseas from Croatia, the prefix 00 is the international access code. The dialling code for Croatia is +385. Croatian town and city codes have a zero in front of them that must be left off when calling from overseas. The code for Istria is 052.

Public phones

Public telephones use cards bought from post offices and kiosks. They come in units ('*impulsa*') from 25 to 500. Units run down fast calling internationally and you need a card of at least 50 *impulsa*, which should cost about 50kn.

It may be more convenient to place a call from a booth set up at most post offices.

Mobile phones

Croatia relies on the mobile. Roaming agreements exist with international companies and if you have a roaming facility on your mobile, the only problem should be the expense.

An alternative is to purchase a local SIM card with a pre-paid subscription; you can usually buy a card with some start-up time included, although you should make sure your mobile phone is unlocked first. If you're in Croatia on holiday, you may need to buy top-up vouchers sold at newsstands at a current value of 50kn, 100kn and 200kn.

ESSENTIALS

Time

Croatia is on Central European Time, GMT +1.

Tipping

Tipping is expected by taxi drivers and waiters in restaurants. Round up bills to the next 10kn-20kn, or by about ten per cent.

You don't tip in cafés, unless you have received special service or have been there for a while.

Tourist information

Istria is more organised in its tourist provision than other parts of the country. One reason is the peninsula's high number of tourist offices. Nearly every community mentioned in this guide will have at least a part-time office. Below are the addresses and phone numbers for the larger ones. For more information, see Istria's tourism website, www.istra.hr.

Buzet

Trg Fontana 7/1 (052 662 343, www.istria-buzet.com). **Open** *Summer* 8am-3pm Mon-Fri; 9am-2pm Sat. *Winter* 8am-3pm Mon-Fri.

Croatian National Tourist Office (UK)

Croatia House, 162-164 Fulham Palace Road, London W6 9ER (020 8563 7979, www.croatia.hr).

Croatian National Tourist Office (USA)

350 Fifth Avenue, Suite 4003, New York 10118 (212 279 8672).

Labin-Rabac

A Negri 20, Labin (052 855 560, www.rabac-labin.com). **Open** 7am-3pm Mon-Fri.
As well there is an info point at Titov trg 10 (052 852 399).

Novigrad

Porporela 1 (052 757 075, www.novigrad-cittanova.hr). **Open** *Summer* 8am-9pm daily. *Winter* 8am-3pm Mon-Fri; 8am-1pm Sat.

Poreč

Zagrebačka 9 (052 451 293, www.to-porec.com). **Open** *Summer* 8am-9pm Mon-Sat; 9am-1pm, 5-9pm Sun. *Winter* 8am-4pm Mon-Sat.

Pula

Forum 3 (052 219 197, www.pula info.hr). **Open** *Summer* 8am-9pm daily. *Winter* 9am-5pm Mon-Sat; 10am-4pm Sun.

Rovinj

Obala Pina Budicina 12 (052 811 566). **Open** *Summer* 8am-9pm daily. *Winter* 8am-3pm Mon-Sat.

Tour operators

There are more than 100 companies who deal with Croatia. The UK Croatian National Tourist Office (*see above*) has a complete register. Bigger ones include:
adriatica.net *(+385 1 24 15 614/ www.adriatica.net).* Zagreb-based company specialising in lighthouse holidays and trips for special events.
Generalturist *(www.generalturist. com).* Eighty years' experience in local tourism – tours, tickets and travel.
Hidden Croatia *(0871 208 0075/ www.hiddencroatia.com).* City breaks and tailor-made holidays.
Sail Croatia *(020 7751 9988/0871 733 8686/www.sailcroatia.net).* Specialists in sailing holidays from beginners upwards.

Visas

Visitors from the European Union, USA, Canada, Australia and New Zealand do not need a visa if they are staying in Croatia for a period of less than 90 days.

Vocabulary

Pronunciation

c – 'ts' as in 'hats'
ć – a light 'ch' as 'future'
č – 'ch' as in 'church'
đ – 'dj' as in 'jury'
j – 'y' as in 'years'
š – 'sh' as in 'shoe'
ž – 'zh' as in 'pleasure'

Basics

yes *da;* no *ne*
hello/good day *dobar dan*
goodbye *do vidjenja*
hello! (familiar) *bok!*
good morning *dobro jutro*
good evening *dobra večer*
good night *laku noć*
please *molim;* thank you *hvala*
great/OK *dobro*

Useful phrases

Do you speak English?
Govorite li engleski?
Sorry, I don't speak Croatian
Izvinite, ne govorim hrvatski
I don't understand/I don't
know *Ne razumijem/ne znam*
What's your name? (polite/fam)
Kako se zovete/zoveš?
My name is... *Zovem se...*
Excuse me/sorry *Oprostite*
How much is it? *Koliko košta?*
Can I book a room? *Mogu li
rezervati sobu?*

Getting around

Where is...? *Gdje je...?*
Where to? *Kamo?*
here *ovdje;* there *tamo*
left *levo;* right *desno*
straight on *pravo*
backwards *natrag*
A ticket to... *Jednu kartu za...*
single *u jednom pravcu*

return *povratnu kartu*
When does the next
bus/ferry/train leave for...?
*Kada polazi sljedeći autobus/
trajekt/vlak za...?*
I'm lost *Izgubio same se
(male)/Izgubila sam se (female)*
How far is it? *Koliko je daleko?*
arrival *polazak*
departure *odlazak*
station *kolodvor;* airport *zračna
luka;* port *luka;* ferry port
trajektna luka

Time

What time is it? *Koliko je sati?*
ten o'clock *deset sati*
day *dan;* week *tjedan*
today *danas;* tomorrow *sutra*
yesterday *jučer*
in the morning *ujutro*
in the evening *uvečer*
early *rano;* late *kasno*

Numbers

1 *jedan;* 2 *dva;* 3 *tri;* 4 *četiri;*
5 *pet;* 6 *šest;* 7 *sedam;* 8 *osam;*
9 *devet;* 10 *deset;* 20 *dvadeset;*
30 *trideset;* 40 *četrdeset;* 50
pedeset; 60 *šezdeset;* 70 *sedam-
deset;* 80 *osamdeset;* 90 *devedeset;*
100 *sto;* 200 *dvjesta;* 1,000 *tisuća*

Days, months

Monday *ponedjelak;* Tuesday
utorak; Wednesday *srijeda;*
Thursday *četvrtak;* Friday
petak; Saturday *subota;*
Sunday *nedjelja.* January *sljecanj;*
February *veljača;* March *ožujak;*
April *travanj;* May *svibanj;* June
lipanj; July *srpanj;* August
kolovoz; September *rujan;*
October *listopad;* November
studeni; December *prosinac*

ESSENTIALS

Menu Glossary

The Croatian menu (*jelovnik*) is usually categorised in a simple way. Cold dishes (*hladna jela*) are a common starter (*predjela*), maybe ham or sheep's cheese. Soups (*juhe*) are generally fish (*riblja*) or beef (*govdja*). There will then be a list of *gotova jela*, dishes ready to serve, often risottos and pastas. *Specijaliteti* or *jela po narudžbi* are the specialities, main courses.

Grilled dishes (*na žaru* or *sa roštilja*) include meat (*meso*), fish (*riba*) and seafood, invariably squid (*lignje*). Other main-dish preparations include *boškarin*, oxen indigenous to Istria and, considered the finest delicacy, *ispod peke*. This involves braising the dish – veal and lamb are the most popular – under a bell-shaped lid (*peka*). This is then covered in hot coals so that the ingredients, juices and vegetables and all, exude flavour. The process can take up to two hours and the custom is to order well before you arrive.

Salads (*salate*) usually offered are green (*zelena*) or mixed (*mješana*), although you may be lucky and find one made with *kupus*, cabbage. The desserts section is usually entitled *kolači* (cakes) or *slatkiši* (sweets). Drinks are *pića*, spirits *žestoka pića*.

Useful phrases

Are these seats taken? *Da li je slobodno?*
I'd like a table for two *Molim stol za dvoje*
The menu, please *Molim vas jelovnik*
Do you have...? *Imate li...?*
I'm a vegetarian *Ja sam vegetarijanac*
I'm diabetic *Ja sam dijabetičar*

large *veliko*
small *malo*
more *više*
less *manje*
expensive *skupo*
cheap *jeftino*
hot (food, drink) *toplo*
cold *hladno*
with/without *sa/bez*
I didn't order this *Nisam ovo naručio*
thank you *hvala*
the bill (please) *Račun (molim)*
bon appetit! *Dobar tek!*
open *otvoreno*
closed *zatvoreno*

Basics (osnovno)

ashtray *pepeljara*
bill *račun*
bread *kruh*
cup *šalica*
fork *vilica*
glass *čaša*
knife *nož*
milk *mlijeko*
napkin *ubrus*
oil *ulje*
pepper *papar*
plate *tanjur*
salt *sol*
spoon *žlica*
sugar *šećer*
teaspoon *žličica*
vinegar *ocat*
water *voda*

Meat (meso)

but **leg**
govedina **beef**
grah sa svinjskom koljenicom **bean soup with pork knuckle**
guska **goose**
gusta juha **thick goulash soup**
janjetina **lamb**
jetra **liver**

kunić/zec rabbit
odrezak escalope (generally veal or pork)
patka duck
piljetina chicken
prsa breast
purica/tuka turkey
srnetina venison
šunka ham
svinjetina pork
teletina veal

Fish/seafood (riba/plodovi mora)

grilled fish *riba sa roštilja/ nu žaru*
shellfish *školjke*
bakalar dried cod
brancin sea bass
brodet fish stew
cipal golden grey mullet
dagnje/mušule/školjke mussels
hobotnica octopus
jastog lobster
kamenice/ostrige oysters
kosul john dory
lignje squid
list sole
losos salmon
lubin sea perch
orada gilthead sea bream
oslić hake
pastrva trout
šaran carp
sipa cuttlefish
škampi scampi
trilja red mullet
tuna tuna
zubatac dentex

Accompaniments (prilozi)

fuži pasta twirls
kruh bread
krumpir potatoes
prženi krumpir chips
riža rice
tjestenina pasta

Salads (salate)

cikla beetroot
krastavac cucumber
mješana saluta mixed salad
rajčica tomato
rokula rocket
zelena salata lettuce, green salad

Vegetables (povrće)

cvjetača cauliflower
gljive mushrooms
grašak peas
kuhani kukuruz sweetcorn
leća lentils
mahune green beans
mrkva carrot
paprika pepper
šparoge asparagus
špinat spinach

Fruit/nuts (voće/orasi)

dinja melon
jabuka apple
jagoda strawberry
kruška pear
malina raspberry
marelica apricot
naranča orange
orah walnut
šljiva plum
trešnja cherry

Drinks (pića)

čaj tea
kava coffee
led ice
mineralna voda mineral water
penjušac sparkling wine
pivo beer
rakija brandy (*loza* grape;
biska mistletoe; *šljivovica* plum;
travarica herb grappa;
orahovača walnut)
sok (*od naranče*) (orange) juice
vino wine (*crno* red; *bijelo* white;
crveno rosé; *gemišt* spritzer)

ESSENTIALS

Index

Sights & Areas

ESSENTIALS

Index

ESSENTIALS